Business Process Benchmarking

Business Process Benchmarking

Finding and Implementing Best Practices

Robert C. Camp

ASQC Quality Press
Milwaukee, Wisconsin

Business Process Benchmarking
Robert C. Camp

Library of Congress Cataloging-in-Publication Data

Camp, Robert C., 1935–
    Business process benchmarking: finding and implementing best
practices / Robert C. Camp.
        p. cm.
    Includes bibliographical references and index.
    ISBN 0-87389-296-8
    1. Benchmarking (Management).   I. Title.
HD62.15.C345   1994
658.5'62 — dc20   94-34028
                                                               CIP

© 1995 by ASQC

Trademark Acknowledgments

AS/400® is a registered trademark of International Business Machines (IBM) Corporation.
Docutech® is a registered trademark of Xerox Corporation.
Memory Jogger™ and *Memory Jogger+*™ are trademarks of GOAL/QPC.
Six Sigma® is a registered trademark of Motorola, Inc.
WesTIP® is a registered trademark of Westinghouse Electric Corporation.
XYBEX® is a registered trademark of Master Chemical Corporation.

10 9 8 7 6 5 4 3 2 1

ISBN 0-87389-296-8

Acquisitions Editor: Susan Westergard
Project Editor: Jeanne W. Bohn
Production Editor: Annette Wall
Marketing Administrator: Mark Olson
Set in Palatino by Linda J. Shepherd.
Cover design by Daryl Poulin.
Printed and bound by BookCrafters, Inc.

ASQC Mission: To facilitate continuous improvement and increase customer satisfaction by identifying, communicating, and promoting the use of quality principles, concepts, and technologies; and thereby be recognized throughout the world as the leading authority on, and champion for, quality.

For a free copy of the ASQC Quality Press Publications Catalog, including ASQC membership information, call 800-248-1946.

Printed in the United States of America

 Printed on acid-free recycled paper

 ASQC
Quality Press
611 East Wisconsin Avenue
Milwaukee, Wisconsin 53202

This book is dedicated to all benchmarking professionals, in all organizations around the world, who have been given the opportunity and the challenge to implement this important quality tool, and who are eagerly doing so because they know it works!

Contents

Figures

Figure
Number   Title

Figure
Number   Title

Figure
Number   Title

Foreword

The final decade of the twentieth century is quickly passing. As we prepare for the next decade and the next century, one fact has become abundantly clear. The organizations that prosper and thrive will be those organizations that have learned to change—change quickly, change effectively, and change for the better. Effective change has always been a requisite for organizational survival, but change now needs to take place at a faster pace than before.

The last 15 years have seen a remarkable awakening of awareness of the need for organizational change. We've been through the era of total quality management (TQM), and we've learned to think in terms of our business processes. We've learned the secrets of process improvement—prioritization of effort, use of the appropriate quality tools, and implementation through improvement teams. We've also learned that TQM, used ineffectively, brings change at a rate far too slow to assure long-term survival and growth.

Now we're faced with business process reengineering (BPR)—the focus being on revolutionary rather than evolutionary change. We're being urged to blast away, reinvent, and question the very existence of our business processes. All of that coupled with the need for always assuring that change will be effective—that the change we make today is the appropriate change, and that the change will be nicely assimilated within our organization.

The most efficient way to promulgate effective change is by learning from the positive experience of others. That's what learning is all about, isn't it? Learning takes place when another's knowledge and experience are communicated to you. Very little learning is serendipitous. Most knowledge is gained incrementally. You learn because another learned first and was willing and able to share that knowledge with you.

And that's what benchmarking is all about. Learning. Growth. Effective change. Benchmarking doesn't substitute for BPR or any other strategy. It's not an either-or proposition. Benchmarking is simply the most efficient way to assure the success of a business change initiative. Simply stated, if you're going to radically redefine your business, why not see if someone else, within your industry or not, has already gone in the direction you're headed? You'll save time, and time is fast becoming our most precious resource.

The best organizations today, our organizational role models, are those that use benchmarking and use it well. Those organizations are consistently among the leaders in their industries, and they are consistently the promulgators of effective change—not the followers struggling to catch up. These organizations have learned how to learn. They've learn that, if benchmarking is to help, it needs to be applied with discipline and rigor. Haphazard approaches to benchmarking can bring change; some of it good. But real learning comes most readily when the process for learning is defined and applied consistently.

That's why Bob Camp's experience is so important to us. Bob has been at the forefront of benchmarking since we first learned to treat it as an effective tool to aid the management change process. Bob knows what works and what doesn't. And he's willing to share that knowledge with us. And all of that is why this is such an important book. Bob gives us the benefit of his experience, both positive and not-so-positive. And he concentrates on the things that are important—important to the success of benchmarking.

Additionally, Bob gives us an important new concept—the concept of step zero. Simply stated, Bob reminds us that benchmarking will be most successful when the right process is chosen for study. That's the business process most important to the organization's success. And Bob tells us how to proceed through step zero so that our benchmarking efforts will be effectively directed.

But the advice doesn't stop there. Bob gives us solid coaching through a benchmarking process model—a model that works and works well. And that's reinforced with a number of powerful case studies—examples of excellent benchmarking from leading-edge organizations. Remember, one of the critical factors for assuring a successful benchmarking effort is to use an appropriate benchmarking process. Who better to teach us that process than Bob Camp? Thanks, Bob, for allowing us to be your benchmarking partner.

Harvey Brelin
Jack Grayson
American Productivity & Quality Center

Preface

Business Process Benchmarking is composed of fifteen chapters in three distinct sections with seven appendixes. Each chapter opens with a quotation from Sun Tzu that encapsulates the essence of the chapter. Many benchmarkers consider this fourth century (B.C.) Chinese author of *The Art of War* to be the patron saint of benchmarking.

Business Process Benchmarking is a companion to my 1989 text *Benchmarking: The Search for Industry Best Practices that Lead to Superior Performance.* Both books serve as references on how to do benchmarking successfully. *Business Process Benchmarking,* however, focuses on managing the benchmarking process. The earlier book thoroughly explains the fundamentals, making it an appropriate guide for benchmarking users. The sections of *Business Process Benchmarking* are described as follows:

Section 1—The Process

This section relates the 10-step process described in *Benchmarking: The Search for Industry Best Practices That Lead to Superior Performance* to management. Much has been learned about the 10-step benchmarking process since 1988–1989.

The first four steps of the process must be approached differently by managers. They are the most important steps of the benchmarking process. Therefore, the approach to what to benchmark, whom to benchmark, the data collection method, and the performance gap analysis has been amended in light of new, important learnings for managers.

All experience indicates that if these first four steps are done thoroughly, then benchmarking teams stand the greatest chance of success in the last six steps. It is not that the remaining six steps of the process are not important. On the contrary; these steps deal with implementation. And that phase of the process can prove extremely difficult. It is possible that the subject of implementation may, in light of many reengineering projects, be deserving of a book all to itself. But implementation can only be accomplished if the first four steps of the benchmarking process are completed with discipline.

Section 2—The Leadership and Management of Benchmarking

It is necessary to conduct the benchmarking team activities based on a proven approach, like the 10-step process. But what is becoming abundantly clear is that the 10-step process is not sufficient. There are other things that must be done in order to heighten the chance of benchmarking success. The management process is everything else that must be done to ensure that benchmarking is effectively pursued.

The strategy for, and management of, the benchmarking process (not the 10-step user process) can best be discussed in what must done before, during, and after the conduct of a benchmarking team's activities. Thus, there can be a distinction between the user process (the successful conduct of the 10-step process) and the management process. It is the later that is covered in Section 2.

This includes the establishment and execution of a strategy for the management of benchmarking. Many lessons learned have been by those who have been conducting benchmarking for some time. Almost all the management successes and mistakes of supporting benchmarking have been tried. So that provides a rich source of learning.

Therefore, this second section of *Business Process Benchmarking* covers new material not documented elsewhere. Four chapters, titled "Benchmarking Leadership and Management Process," "Training," "Managers' Resource Guide," and "The Future of Benchmarking," make up the second section.

Section 3—The Case Studies

There has been a recurring and constant demand for case studies of successful benchmarking activities. While there has been an increase in the quantity of written material, including books, reports, articles, and experiences captured through a wide cross section of media, true case studies—along the lines of those produced by business schools—do not exist in adequate number to help with understanding the complete benchmarking process.

Therefore, Section 3 contains six case studies—all from Malcolm Baldrige National Quality Award recipients. Since success in achieving that award requires a substantive amount of benchmarking, I felt it was important to obtain case studies from these leading-edge, quality companies. The case studies are quite varied, and provide a rich source of how-to examples that add to the benchmarking learning.

Appendixes

The seven appendixes of *Business Process Benchmarking* offer significant, additional information. Since 1989 there have been many new books and reports, as well as several hundred journal articles, written about benchmarking. There are now other media where benchmarking activities have been documented. These include audiotape and videocassette. And there have been new services established, including those that provide knowledge bases and electronic bulletin board matching services of those interested in a benchmarking topic. There is also training courseware available.

All these resources are documented in Appendix A. Here is a vast array of materials to pursue almost any benchmarking-related topic.

Appendixes B–G detail the following:

- Appendix B shows two ways to illustrate the best of the best companies.

- Appendix C lists more benchmarking case histories.

- Appendix D shows how to find information.

- Appendix E illustrates the process classification scheme.

- Appendix F is the 10-step benchmarking process inspection checklist.

- Appendix G describes the roles and responsibilities of benchmarking customers and suppliers.

Organizations need goal-directed, rapid, continuous learning to stay competitive, and that excellence is attained through the credible management of the benchmarking process. I commend *Business Process Benchmarking* to your reading and to your pursuit of excellence through benchmarking.

Robert C. Camp

Acknowledgments

The author wishes to acknowledge the many individuals who have participated in the development of this book, particularly the case study contributors.

There is a profound lack of benchmarking case studies to serve as examples of the process. The contributors' dedication and efforts to produce the studies included here are commendable.

There are many benchmarking professionals who have developed during the past few years. Their contacts, networking, and sharing have all added to the art and science of benchmarking. Some of their ideas are included in this book.

Xerox Corporation must be acknowledged for permitting the publication of *Business Process Benchmarking*, in addition to my 1989 book *Benchmarking: The Search for Industry Best Practices That Lead to Superior Performance.*

I also wish to acknowledge Jane F. Crouse for her excellent editorial services in the preparation of the manuscript.

Section 1:
The Process

CHAPTER 1

Benchmarking Update

He who exercises not forethought but makes light of his opponents is sure to be captured by them.

- This Book Is an Updated Companion
- Focus on the Business Process
- Benchmarking Tied to Mission and Objectives
- Managing the Benchmarking Process
- Benchmarking Training
- Benchmarking Code of Conduct
- Beginner to Advanced Benchmarking Skills
- The Future of Benchmarking
- The Concept of Step Zero
- The Purpose of Benchmarking Remains the Same
- Benchmarking Scope
- Benchmarks and Benchmarking
- The Benchmarking Process
- Summary

This Book Is an Updated Companion

Since the publication of *Benchmarking: The Search for Industry Best Practices That Lead to Superior Performance* in 1989, many events have affected benchmarking. The simple fact is that benchmarking has been driven substantially by the Malcolm Baldrige National Quality Award, in which the need for benchmarking is a stated requirement in the application criteria. While the benchmarking requirement is specifically called for in Section 2.2 of the Baldrige award, the need for benchmarking is evident throughout the award criteria. In fact, benchmarking is mentioned over 200 times in the 1994 criteria. Directly or indirectly, benchmarking affects up to 50 percent of the award's scoring, and, therefore, is seen as a critical quality tool. Several large firms that applied for the Baldrige award, expecting to be successful and were not, received feedback indicating that their applications showed little evidence of benchmarking. This message has been telegraphed to others wanting to pursue this achievement. The result has been a substantial increase in interest about benchmarking. But the basic reason for exploring and pursuing benchmarking has always been the drive to be competitive. In a wide variety of firms, benchmarking has proven to be the instrumental process in their turning unproductive operations into efficient, profitable ones. This includes the recent emphasis on process reengineering, which is one of the initiatives that has influenced and added impetus to the need for benchmarking. It provides another incentive to update benchmarking learnings since 1989.

In typical internal assessments conducted against the Baldrige award, criteria, companies are often concerned about several categories including, outstanding efforts and results; effective integration and sustained results; and national and world-class leadership. It is obvious that without effective benchmarking of both products and processes, as well as the resulting performance goals, units or organizations would not know whether they had achieved those levels of performance

The pace of learning about effective benchmarking approaches has not slacked; in fact, it has increased. In this regard the management of the benchmarking process and the effective approaches to training only recently have become well enough understood that they can now be documented. Additionally, there are specific steps in the benchmarking process that now deserve an updated approach and increased emphasis. In particular, the first three steps of the process—what to benchmark, whom to benchmark, and the access of information sources and the actual data collection—must be reexamined. Steps 4 and 5 (analyze the performance gap and project future performance levels) also deserve clarification based on recent experience.

Under these circumstances this book has been written as a companion to *Benchmarking: The Search for Industry Best Practices That Lead to Superior Performance,* the text that explains the fundamentals of doing a benchmarking project. This book includes six case studies from Malcolm Baldrige National Quality Award recipients. Section 2, devoted to the management of benchmarking, will be of interest to those who have implemented benchmarking activities and now need to manage them effectively. The appendix includes a comprehensive bibliography and other important references. The topics that receive emphasis in this companion book are briefly described in the next sections.

Focus on the Business Process

Until recently, benchmarking has been pursued to address concerns that may have resulted from customer feedback, the cost base, a desire to reduce error rates, high asset levels, the need to improve cycle times, or the like. In benchmarking circles this approach has been referred to as *problem-based benchmarking.* It means reacting to some problem and finding effective solutions through benchmarking. Generally, this was the right approach for the earliest applications of benchmarking. A business had problems and benchmarking was used to find innovative solutions to those problems. This was the primary basis for learning benchmarking. But there has been a lingering concern about whether this was the right approach, one that made best use of benchmarking resources and had the highest return.

During the past several years, through some extensive benchmarking efforts, leading-edge firms have come to realize that there is a better way to focus benchmarking activities for greater payback. Firms that have a defined mission, set of objectives, and, in particular, focused priorities have found that they need a vehicle to ensure that there will be continuous improvement toward these goals. The most effective vehicle is the concentration on, and improvement of, the business processes that contribute to the goals; that is, the basic processes on which businesses run. These processes may include order taking, order processing, product servicing, billing, and collection. It is the concentration on the improvement of the business processes that will deliver the outputs that will achieve the results—the firm's objectives, priorities, and mission. This is a new, important, and revolutionary perspective for benchmarking. Now benchmarking has a specific, defined role that directly supports and markedly contributes to the goals of the firm. For if best practices are found and implemented in the basic business processes, then there is a direct contribution to the firm's priorities and its results from benchmarking.

Firms that have realized the value of focusing on business processes recognize there can be a high-level awareness of the need for change by driving the key performance measures established through benchmarking. But it is the insightful firms that recognize that results will only be obtained by changing the processes. That is, it is only by improving key business processes by incorporating best practices in them that will achieve results. Thus, process-based benchmarking is results-based benchmarking.

In this text the terms *business processes* and *work processes* are used somewhat interchangeably; however, each has an explicit meaning. Work processes are those that are entirely within the control of a single function and can be changed as such. Business processes are those cross-functional processes critical to the organization's success. Benchmarking the work or subprocesses without equal emphasis on improving the business processes will only lead to suboptimization and failure to achieve the major improvements envisioned by the culmination of reengineering and benchmarking.

It is the focus of benchmarking on the business process that has come to be accepted as the correct approach for benchmarking. Thus, it is process benchmarking, not problem-based benchmarking, that is needed. This text takes that process approach.

Benchmarking Tied to Mission and Objectives

With the advent of a mature TQM or continuous quality improvement (CQI) approach by many firms, they realize that all their goals, from the top of the firm to the bottom, must be congruent. Therefore, firms that have embarked on a TQM journey have well-developed mission statements, priorities, and objectives. More importantly, these firms can show a direct relationship between the company's goals to every employees' objectives.

Gaining congruence between organizational goals and the processes that deliver them is known in TQM circles as policy deployment. This is where the key organizational goals are articulated and the business processes that drive them are identified and prioritized. The needed improvement strategies based on the now-found benchmark best practices are implemented. Under these circumstances benchmarking ties directly to the improved results desired by the organization's leadership.

The implication for benchmarking is that it also must show direct support for the company's objectives, priorities, and mission. For if direct support cannot be shown, then the benchmarking activity is wasted effort. So an early part of the planning for benchmarking must include a concrete tie to the firm's goals.

But that is only half the effort. Since most organizations have limited resources, and in particular limited resources for benchmarking, the second half of the tie to company goals is to prioritize the efforts to show that benchmarking is focused on the vital few processes that will have the greatest leverage on those company goals. In recent years much has been learned about this increased requirement for benchmarking. For there are consensus ways of prioritizing and analytical ways of prioritizing benchmarking activities.

When the focus of benchmarking activities concentrated on the business processes is prioritized to those vital few processes and combined with the implementation of the best benchmarking practices, then a direct relationship supporting the firm's goals is shown. This is a powerful if not compelling basis for benchmarking activities, and it is the approach that this text takes.

Managing the Benchmarking Process

The overall benchmarking task can be broken down into two major processes. There is the user process and the management process. The user process is the 10- or n-step process that is used to complete a benchmarking investigation. It was the primary focus of *Benchmarking: The Search for Industry Best Practices That Lead to Superior Performance,* and there are several similar processes developed and adapted by other organizations. Alcoa has a nine-step process, AT&T a 12-step process, IBM a five-phase process, and others have similar adaptations (see Figure 1.1).

	4-step	6-step	7-step	8-step	10-step
Planning the study	Prepare to benchmark	Plan	Determine functions or process to benchmark Identify key performance variables Identify best-in-class companies	Define business issue Define what to benchmark Define benchmark measures Determine who to benchmark	Identify process Identify partner
Collecting process data	Research process	Research Observe	Measure performance	Acquire data	Collect data
Analyzing data for results	Document best practices	Analyze	Compare performance and estimate gaps	Compare performance Identify actions to close the gap	Determine gap Project future performance
Adapting for improvement	Report and implement	Adapt Improve	Specify improvement programs and actions Implement and monitor results	Implement improvements and monitor results	Gain support Set goals Develop plans Implement plans Recalibrate benchmarks
Number of companies	6	7	8	4	8
Percentage of companies	14%	17%	19%	10%	19%

Source: Adapted from *Comparing Process Models for Benchmarking*, American Productivity and Quality Center.

Figure 1.1. Benchmarking process models.

The management process is everything else that has to be done to ensure that benchmarking is effectively pursued. There are before, during, and after activities that enhance the user process and, in fact, ensure its success, whereas the user process by itself may be seen to be necessary but not sufficient. There are specific activities for establishing a benchmarking program prior to the pursuit of the user process; there are supporting activities that take place during the exercise of the n steps; and there are sustaining activities that are concurrent with and follow the completion of the user process. These are shown in Figure 1.2. These activities add to the overall effectiveness of benchmarking.

The user process is the process followed by the benchmarking team to complete its project. The management process includes those actions that management does to ensure that the team's operation is successful and that benchmarking has some permanence. It includes creating the environment so that new ideas are pursued to improve business processes; providing training and support; prioritizing the direction of, and encouraging the implementation of, the benchmarking findings.

Benchmarking processes and phases

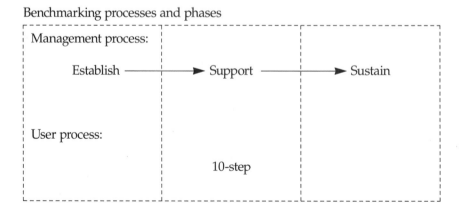

Figure 1.2. The benchmarking task consists of two major processes.

Benchmarking Training

In a similar fashion the subject of training was not addressed in *Benchmarking*. Since 1989 much has been learned about what types of training are desirable and what method of delivery seems to be the most effective. These are especially important training concerns particularly with adult learners. The types of training include awareness training for managers or executive briefings, cross-functional skills training, and benchmarking team training. The audience, requirements, and learning objectives for each are covered in this text.

These training alternatives have been designed, experimented with, and refined through many live training sessions. Their structure has been enhanced by some of the most creative instructional designers. The end result is that there are proven methods for effective benchmarking training that have been shown to meet audience requirements through evaluations that consistently achieve a 90 percent to 95 percent satisfaction score. The benefit to those embarking on benchmarking is that expensive benchmarking training development efforts are not needed since many of these programs are available in the form of excellent training courses and software. Therefore, resources can be spent on adapting the materials to a specific organization or industry to make them more meaningful and on the basics of benchmarking and the experiences needed to train adults.

Benchmarking Code of Conduct

While many of the essentials of benchmarking were covered in the 1989 text and incorporated in its Quick Reference Guides, there was no comprehensive treatment of the code of conduct that is fast taking shape for the benchmarking community. Up until now the code of conduct was a piecemeal affair primarily focused on information exchange and site visit steps; however, more is needed. Participants in a benchmarking study know that they can be persuasive to the effective conduct of benchmarking by doing it right the first time and by incenting others to participate.

Such things as developing guidelines for information sharing, agreements, and visit protocol are becoming better understood by benchmarking professionals. These are the requirements by which benchmarking exchanges must be conducted. So it is important that these prerequisites be completely understood to form the basis for effective benchmarking. While this material may exist piecemeal elsewhere, it is important to bring it together in one place for the serious benchmarker.

Beginner to Advanced Benchmarking Skills

The gap between the beginner and advanced benchmarker's skills is huge. It is evident that not all benchmarking can be based on all companies rediscovering the same information with the same number of benchmarking trips to others. There has to be a way of closing this skills gap and sharing the information in an efficient way. There are several organizations that have stepped into this gap, primarily being led by not-for-profit associations or institutions, and there is precedent for this work. One of the armed services has a best practices program and there are overseas best manufacturing plants as well as government organizations set up to perform interindustry analyses. One government has set up a best practices demonstration program.

These organizations should be the first place where an interested benchmarker can go and learn about this topic, its code of conduct, and the requirements for excellent benchmarking. These organizations will provide training, assistance with information searches, networking, and common interest group facilitation. The array of product and services can only enhance the ability to conduct benchmarking effectively and efficiently to the benefit of organizations large and small.

Additionally, professional associations need to determine what role they will play in this expanding effort. These are the organizations that represent a function or industry and, therefore, the business processes that are the focus of the benchmarking activities. How they organize themselves to affiliate with the central repositories of benchmarking information, or how they become the centers of excellence that a clearinghouse will send benchmarkers to, will require some careful consideration. If an individual association views itself as a clearinghouse for its functional expertise, then how does it coordinate its efforts with the clearinghouse of clearinghouses?

The Future of Benchmarking

If benchmarking and process improvement are the fundamentals of continuous improvement and competitiveness, then what does the future hold for benchmarking? What are some of the requirements that are going to be needed to sustain this business improvement topic over an extended period of time? While there may not be a clear endpoint vision, there do seem to be milestone markers along the way. To the extent that these can be increasingly agreed to by benchmarking professionals then the art and science of benchmarking will prosper.

Some of the requirements include: a consistent message in the TQM/quality arena of what benchmarking is and is not and how it relates to quality initiatives (a lexicon); a definition of what constitutes excellence in benchmarking and what the relevant data and information are that ensure completeness (a template); a basis to share information over time and continuing networking capability (consortia); a taxonomy by which organizations can agree on what is being focused on for benchmarking purposes and is the basis for information sharing (a classification scheme); and a larger contribution to the initiatives for business process management, continuous process improvement, and reengineering.

The Concept of Step Zero

In retrospect, the Xerox 10-step process most likely should have contained more steps. The reason it did not is because the overall quality initiative for Xerox was composed of three processes, one of which was the benchmarking process. The three processes were seen as complete for internal use.

But when the benchmarking process was taken by itself something was missing. A specific step to commission the team was needed before commencing the 10-step process. This fact was discovered when the benchmarking process was itself benchmarked; namely, when the Xerox process was compared to others' adapted, benchmarking processes.

The step to commission the teams within Xerox was accomplished in another process, the quality improvement process. It will be explained in chapter 2.

The Purpose of Benchmarking Remains the Same

The purpose of benchmarking is still the same—to break the paradigm of not being able to learn from others. The purpose of benchmarking is to

• Analyze the operation. Benchmarking firms must assess the strengths and weaknesses of their current work processes, analyze critical cost components, consider customer complaints, spot areas for improvement and cycle time reduction, and find ways to reduce errors and defects or to increase asset turns.

• Know the competition and industry leaders. Benchmarking firms must find out who is the best of the best.

• Incorporate the best of the best. Benchmarking firms must learn from leaders, uncover where they are and where they are going, learn the leaders' superior practices and why they work, and emulate the best practices.

• Gain superiority. Benchmarking firms must try to become the new benchmark.

Benchmarking is an integral part of the planning and ongoing review process to ensure a focus on the external environment and to strengthen the use of factual information in developing plans. Benchmarking is used to improve performance by understanding the methods and practices required to achieve world-class performance levels. Benchmarking's primary objective is to understand those practices that will provide a competitive advantage; target setting is secondary.

Benchmarking Scope

While definitions were covered in *Benchmarking: The Search for Industry Best Practices That Lead to Superior Performance,* there is still some confusion over their interpretation. This confusion goes beyond just the definitions. Therefore, it is worthwhile to reexamine the formal and operational definitions, the four types of benchmarking, what the focus alternatives for benchmarking are, and where it is applied. In addition, the difference between benchmarking and benchmarks is covered, and lastly, a brief overview of the 10-step process is given which is covered in more detail in *Benchmarking: The Search for Industry Best Practices that Lead to Superior Performance.*

Definitions: Formal/Operational

Benchmarking is the search for and implementation of best practices. The adoption or adaptation of the best practices allows an organization to raise the performance of its products, services, and business processes to leadership levels. Benchmarking performance measurements are useful means to identify organizations whose performance is significantly better and who, therefore, may have best practices. The real benefit of benchmarking, however, comes from understanding the practices that permit the performance and the reasoned transfer to the organization.

Therefore benchmarking should be conducted on the following:

• **Products and services** This would establish those features and functions desired by customers that are used in product planning, design, and development normally expressed as product goals and technology design practices.

• **Business processes** These would become the basis for business process improvement and reengineering. These should be an integral part of an overall continuous quality improvement initiative that supports achievement of organizational goals and objectives.

• **Performance measures** The result of benchmarking products, services, and processes is to establish and validate objectives for the vital few performance measures that guide the organization. Therefore, all planning and operational reviews should require presentation of benchmarks and should discuss progress toward the benchmarks as a standard agenda item.

Types of Benchmarking

Internal This is a comparison among similar operations within one's own organization.

Competitive This is a comparison to the best of the direct competitors.

Functional This is a comparison of methods to companies with similar processes in the same function outside one's industry.

Generic process This is a comparison of work processes to others who have innovative, exemplar work processes.

Focus Level: Strategic and Operational

In a *strategic* focus, benchmarking is concentrated on strategic competitive strengths and weaknesses. It is used to understand

and develop competitive product and service strategies; to establish goals for product performance, service, customer support levels, asset usage, and financial ratios; and to develop key practices that will achieve the strategic goals.

Strategically focused benchmarking takes a broad company perspective, often called *scanning*, to detect trends. It is typified by technology direction, industry trends, investment selection, and basic competitive product and service offerings.

In an *operational* focus, benchmarking is used to understand specific customer requirements; to understand the best practices to achieve customer satisfaction by improving internal work processes; and to determine operational performance levels required to become the vendor of choice in the eyes of the customer. Operationally focused benchmarking concentrates on the work processes through which continuous improvement is delivered by incorporating best practices in the work steps.

Approach: Problem Based Versus Process Based

In a *problem-based approach*, if there is no specific plan for benchmarking then the activity is characterized as uncontrolled. Thus, it is often pursued on a problem-by-problem basis, as troubles occur.

In a *process-based approach* to benchmarking, as organizations mature in their pursuit of quality and continuous improvement they often realize that the benchmarking activity must be managed. The approach that has proven to be most successful in bringing some discipline to managing benchmarking and, therefore, its improvement, is to apply benchmarking activities to the vital few business processes.

Benchmarks and Benchmarking

The difference between benchmarks and benchmarking must be clarified. The following is a way to describe the difference.

Benchmarking: A Process or Activity

There are several generic definitions of benchmarking that provide varying insight.

Xerox definition The continuous process of measuring our products, services, and practices against our toughest competitors or those companies known as leaders.

Quality definition A standard process used to evaluate success in meeting customer requirements.

Dictionary definition A standard against which something can be measured. A survey mark of previously determined position used as a reference point.

Generic definition A basis of establishing rational performance goals through the search for industry best practices that will lead to superior performance.

The 10-step process A structured way of looking outside to identify, analyze, and adopt the best in the industry or function.

Benchmarks: An Industry Standard

Benchmarks may be descriptive, as in the description of a best industry practice. They may be converted to a performance measurement that shows the effect of incorporating or adopting the practice.

Descriptive benchmarks or practices Any work process is made up of inputs, a repeatable set of steps based on a set of practices or methods, and outputs. If the practices are the best in the industry, they will deliver the outputs that will completely satisfy customers.

Quantitative benchmarks or performance measurements Benchmark measurements are the conversion of benchmark practices to operational measures. There can be benchmarks for all goals or objectives, such as the following: customer satisfaction; employee motivation and satisfaction; quality and cycle time; and business results.

The Benchmarking Process

The formal 10-step benchmarking process is shown in Figure 1.3. The five phases of the process and a description of each phase are illustrated in Figure 1.4. The 10-step process is summarized as follows:

• **Decide what to benchmark.** Identify the largest opportunity to improve performance in the organization. This requires identifying the key work processes, prioritizing them to the vital few, and flowcharting them for analysis and comparison of practices.

• **Identify whom to benchmark.** Determine which other companies employ superior work practices that can be adopted or adapted.

• **Plan and conduct the investigation.** Determine what data are needed and how to conduct the benchmarking investigation. Observe the superior practices firsthand. Document the best practices found.

• **Determine the current performance gap.** After completing the benchmarking investigation and observation, decide how much better the best practices are than the current work methods.

• **Project future performance levels.** Decide how much the performance gap will narrow or widen in the near future and what repercussions this has for the organization.

• **Communicate benchmarking findings and gain acceptance.** Communicate the findings to all those who have a need to know in order to gain acceptance and commitment.

Benchmarking process phases

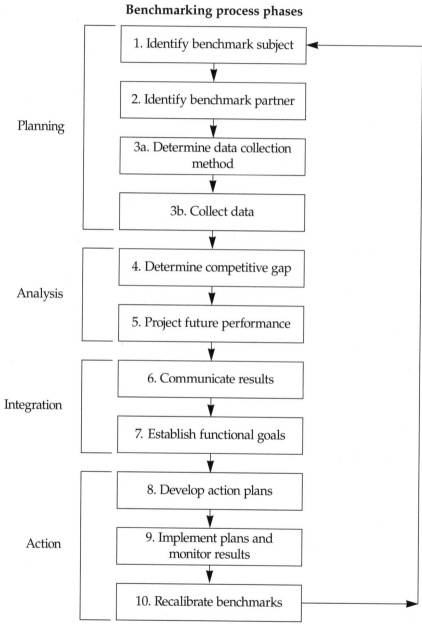

Used by permission of Quality Resources, a division of The Kraus Organization Limited, White Plains, New York.

Figure 1.3. The formal, 10-step benchmarking process.

- **Planning:** Identify what to benchmark, identify whom to benchmark, and gather data.
- **Analysis:** Examine the performance gap and project future performance.
- **Integration:** Communicate the findings and develop new goals.
- **Action:** Take actions, monitor progress, and recalibrate measures as needed.
- **Maturity:** Achieve the desired state.

Phase 1: Planning
A plan for benchmarking is prepared.
- Decide: What to benchmark
- Identify: Whom to benchmark
- Plan: The investigation and conduct it
  —Gather necessary information and data
  —Observe the best practices

Phase 2: Analysis
The gap is examined and the performance is assessed against best practices.
- Determine: The current performance gap
- Project: Future performance levels

Phase 3: Integration
The goals are redefined and incorporated into the planning process.
- Communicate: Benchmarking findings and gain acceptance
- Revise: Performance goals

Phase 4: Action
Best practices are implemented and periodically recalibrated as needed.
- Develop: Action plans
- Implement: Actions and monitor progress
- Recalibrate: The benchmarks

Phase 5: Maturity
Leadership may be achieved.
- Determine: When leadership position is attained
- Assess: Benchmarking as an ongoing process

Figure 1.4. The five phases of the benchmarking process.

• **Revise performance goals.** Convert findings into operational statements that describe what is to be improved based on implementation of the best practices in the business process.

• **Develop action plans.** Create specific implementation plans, measurements, assignments, and timetables for taking action on the best practices.

• **Implement specific actions and monitor progress.** Implement the plan and report progress to key process owners and management.

• **Recalibrate the benchmarks.** Continue to benchmark and update work practices to stay current with ongoing industry changes. Determine where the organization is in its quality pursuit and the implications for benchmarking.

Summary

- Focus on the business process.
- Tie benchmarking to company mission and objectives.
- Manage the benchmarking process.
- Adapt benchmarking training for specific industry or organization.
- Remember the purpose of benchmarking: analyze the operation; know the competition and leaders; incorporate from the best of the best; and gain superiority.
- Recall the four types of benchmarking: internal, competitive, functional, and generic.
- Use process-based benchmarking.

CHAPTER 2

What to Benchmark

*He who knows when he can fight and when he can-
not will be victorious.*

Introduction

There are two old truths that typify the problem of determining what to benchmark. The first is, "Measures are overemphasized and processes are overlooked," and the second is, "*What* without *how* is an empty statement." It is unknown whom to attribute the sayings. They are, however, symptomatic of the trap into which many beginning benchmarking efforts fall.

The initial reaction to benchmarking is to think solely in terms of performance measures. Managers want results. They want to know what is the bench*mark*? The process that was the underlying basis for delivering the output that gave the result, the *benchmark,* is overlooked. Also, concentration on the benchmark, the measure, is really an empty statement until it is traced back to the practice—the best practice—in the process that achieved the performance.

Therefore, benchmarking professionals realize that it is the focus of benchmarking activities on the business processes, and on the improvement of those processes, that yields the greatest payback. In an undirected benchmarking approach, the pursuit, at best, is a random effort of chasing problems. This approach has no overall rationale for benchmarking that is likely to achieve the desired performance results.

Benchmarking professionals have always wanted a better way of directing their efforts. A more planned, productive approach for pursuing benchmarking was desired. Companies like IBM, Ford, Boeing, GTE, McDonald's, Motorola, AT&T, UPS, and Xerox have arrived at that understanding. The focus has been driven by the process-related question format of the Malcolm Baldrige National Quality Award criteria. It has sensitized organizations that there is still a need to get back to the basics of running efficient and effective organizations; that the approach must be to improve business processes; and that this is the main route to planned, disciplined, and successful continuous improvement.

It is this author's finding that organizations have lost touch with their basic business processes. It is difficult to find knowledgeable individuals in the organization who can describe how a critical process works. Processes have inputs, process steps, outputs, feedback, and results. See Figure 2.1, which shows a generalized process schematic that will be used throughout this text to describe not only the approach, but also the use of the process diagram in each step of the 10-step benchmarking process. These steps will be explained shortly. For the moment, however, it is instructive to use this typical process model as the perspective to understand what to benchmark and to direct the benchmarking efforts.

In analyzing what to benchmark, examine the generalized model and overlay specific examples of what could be benchmarked (see Figure 2.2). In this instance the activities that constitute a customer interaction from beginning to end have been arrayed by summary steps. These activities include marketing, producing, delivering, servicing, and invoicing. For each of these activities a specific subprocess has been named along with its inputs, outputs, and results measures. The first of these activities examines the problem resolution process, a major subprocess within marketing. The inputs are identified as "customer inquiries,"

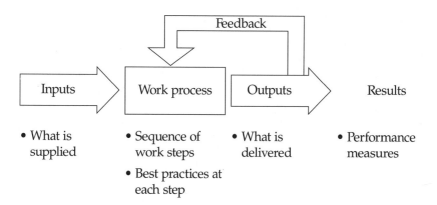

Figure 2.1. Benchmarking processes.

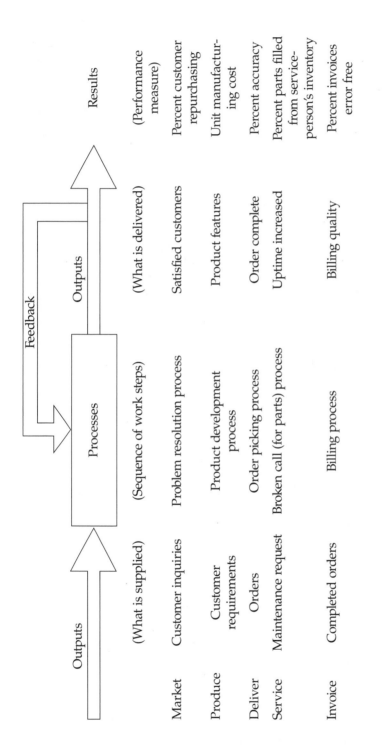

	Outputs		Processes	Feedback	Outputs		Results
			(Sequence of work steps)		(What is delivered)		(Performance measure)
Market	Customer inquiries		Problem resolution process		Satisfied customers		Percent customer repurchasing
Produce	Customer requirements		Product development process		Product features		Unit manufacturing cost
Deliver	Orders		Order picking process		Order complete		Percent accuracy
Service	Maintenance request		Broken call (for parts) process		Uptime increased		Percent parts filled from serviceperson's inventory
Invoice	Completed orders		Billing process		Billing quality		Percent invoices error free

Figure 2.2. What to benchmark.

the outputs are identified as "satisfied customers," and the results measure is identified as "percent customers repurchasing."

There are other examples in which the generalized process model is used to lay out the components of a subprocess. Using this approach may be helpful in bringing clarity to the subject of this chapter, namely what to benchmark. For the team can array several alternatives, detail their components, and then decide which is the most important to benchmark. In addition, the process model makes the very important point that if one wants results then they are delivered by outputs from work processes. It is only the improvement of the steps in the work process that delivers the desired results. *It is only by finding better practices through benchmarking and incorporating them in the work processes that the desired results will be achieved.* This is the essence of why the process model is so important to the benchmarking pursuit.

This text will take the process focus for benchmarking and will increasingly expand on its understanding. While it is easy to state that benchmarking should concentrate on business process improvement, there is more meaning to the specific way to do so. Therefore, the rest of this chapter will completely develop the stepwise procedure for benchmarking through focus on business processes. The use of the process model will be covered in each of the first three steps of benchmarking, namely what, whom, and information resources.

The Concept of Step Zero

As noted briefly in chapter 1, there is a tendency when describing the 10-step or *n*-step benchmarking process to jump right in at the first step and determine what to benchmark. Often this can either be fatal or can create unnecessary backtracking and rework. Therefore, while it does not appear as a specific step in many of the benchmarking models, experienced benchmarking professionals have come to recognize that something must precede the actual execution of the traditionally understood model.

This newly introduced step is often referred to as step zero to emphasize the need for preparation before launching into the main activity. What is step zero? There are many variations on the approach, but the one most subscribed to is to go through the first few steps of a quality process. Most organizations pursuing a quality initiative have trained their people on some quality process for pursuing continuous improvement. It may be known by many names: the quality process, continuous quality improvement, TQM, and others.

This quality process normally has at least some variant of the following four steps: (1) determine the output; (2) identify the customer; (3) determine the customer requirements; and (4) develop the specifications to meet those requirements. Benchmarking professionals find this to be an excellent approach to step zero. First the output of the benchmarking team needs to be defined. It normally can be stated as a benchmarking investigation focused on X business process. What this statement does is clarify and give meaning to the output of the team. Second, the customer for the now-defined output must be determined. Often this is a revealing exercise. For the true customer of a benchmarking study may not be the obvious senior manager.

Getting agreement on who is the customer will ensure that action is taken to implement the benchmarking findings. This is crucial. If no customer can be identified for the benchmarking study, or if that customer does not agree to the need for or the focus of the benchmarking investigation, then the effort is wasted. The customer needs to commission the team; determine its members and what skills they need; arrange for workload adjustment; set boundaries for the investigation; remove any roadblocks that may prevent the team from doing its job; and commit to and assist with implementation.

Third, the team needs to determine the customer's requirements for the study. Generally the team can determine, at least on a preliminary basis, what it believes a set of expectations for its work might be. This can be a list, in some detail, of what the team will do. The team should then develop a set of specifications for how each of the requirements will be met. These are statements of how the team will meet the customer's requirements.

Fourth and finally, the team should communicate to the customer its understanding of the requirements, including how it will work; key milestone dates; progress reporting; and an outline of the specifications it believes will meet the customer's requirements

An example of this quality process definition is given in Figure 2.3. It shows the documentation needed for the quality process of a specific project, namely a sale order process. While admittedly this is at the first level of detail, Figure 2.3 shows the kind of information that needs to be documented. In this case, the output, customer, customer requirements, and the specifications to meet those requirements are the most important parts of the document. It would be the back-up detail behind this initial, high-level statement that would provide the basis of understanding between the team and the commissioning manager or customer. This, in turn, would become the basis of negotiation to arrive at an agreement for the benchmarking project.

The purpose of step zero is to obtain consensus on the key facets of the benchmarking investigation before it is launched. Introducing this step in the traditional benchmarking process has proved invaluable in getting the team started on the right track.

Analyze Company and Departmental Priorities

In order to organize its benchmarking activities, the team should gather all relevant materials that will give it some guidance on the firm's direction. The team will want to ensure that its activities

---

Output
• Define a low-cost, high inventory turns, order fulfillment process

Customer
• Steering committee

Requirements
• Define the benchmark order fulfillment process and industry best practices that support the process

Specifications
• Investigate how end-user customers do business with office products companies
• Benchmark the process by visiting a cross section of firms

Work process
• Source candidate companies for visits
• Document findings
• Define opportunity areas

Next steps
• Decide on implementing strategy
  —Revise existing process
  —Start new
  —Use service bureau contract
• Define detailed implementation plan

Figure 2.3. Process definition.

are in concert with, and specifically contribute to, if not leverage, that direction. Thus, the benchmarking team should gather all materials that are specific statements of mission or vision and goals or objectives. The team should first focus on the organization as a whole and then on the department or division under study.

The team should find the statements, document them if they are not readily available, and display them prominently for all members to see. This way all team members are reminded of what they are ultimately trying to accomplish. These statements may exist in the form of wall charts, plaques, or statements of direction. They are often recreated in pocket reminder cards or on business cards.

The organization may have a vision or mission of having business processes be a key component of value delivered to customers. The organization's intent may be to be easy to do business with or to become the vendor of choice in the eyes of the customer. It may also have a goal to become the most productive organization in its marketplace or industry. These statements will be instrumental in directing the team's efforts. They will be pervasive in pursuit of the team's benchmarking activities to show that the best practices found will directly contribute to achieving these operational statements of intent.

There can be no more compelling basis for conducting benchmarking than to be able to show that the specific direction and key process being studied for improvement directly support the company's mission, goals, and objectives. In fact, part of the team's efforts will be to ensure that it can show just that.

What if the team could not ensure that its activities supported the organization's goals? What if the team was unable to find statements of the firm's direction, goals, and objectives? This could indicate that there would only be a casual need to improve the process or that the team had no specific purpose. The benchmarking effort could be jeopardized, disbanded, or viewed as insignificant. It might be reason enough to stop the team's activities until the firm's goals were clarified.

In addition to these considerations, this facet of the team's efforts will become even more important when it prioritizes its efforts. Team members will want to show that they are directing their activities toward accomplishment of a stated goal. For example, if the stated key goal is customer satisfaction and the team is concentrating on improving the billing process, then it will want to show how there is a direct relationship between improving the organization's invoices and improving customer satisfaction levels. This is most forcefully done using a tree diagram, which is illustrated and discussed later in this chapter.

Another consideration, if not already included in the stated goals, would be that of the customer perspective. If there is some customer satisfaction measurement system, as many organizations have, then that data should also provide insight to the reason for the team's efforts. Many of the measurement systems, in addition to capturing data on satisfaction, also capture data on customer dissatisfiers.

It is the analysis or diagnosis of these dissatisfiers that provide direction of the team's efforts. For example, while there may be an overall goal for the organization to improve its customer satisfaction level, one of the key dissatisfiers may be the technical or repair service customers receive. This may lead the team to concentrate on the service process as the focus of its investigation, with the specific intent to find the best practices to improve customer satisfaction. One of the best practices may be a new form of preventive maintenance, an early equipment repair need, or a diagnostic tool or device. A tree diagram for accomplishing this diagnostic step will be covered in a later section of this chapter.

Thus, it is the combination of organizational goals along with specific input from customers in meeting their requirements that provide the needed direction for the benchmarking team. This prioritization process is the ultimate reality check.

The Business Processes

Identifying and classifying business processes involve the following steps.

1. Create a high-level, overall process view of the organization. This might be how the customer is handled from beginning

to end or how products are delivered from development through to availability at the factory gate.

2. Classify the basic business processes that support the high-level organization description. This might be an increasingly detailed description in a cascading or hierarchic fashion.

3. Determine the critical measurements for the now-defined business processes.

Identify the Business Processes

The first step, create a high-level or helicopter-view flowchart of the organization, can be accomplished in at least two ways. Using one method, the existing, traditional functional organization is described and the normal work flow mapped from beginning to end across a flowchart. Using another method, the functional organization is disregarded entirely and the logical flow of work is described. This includes a logical progression of developing and producing products or services and delivering them to customers.

Figure 2.4 is a representation of such a high-level process view. It shows, in overview form, the major processes and their interrelationship tracking the handling of the customer from order taking through to receipt of payment. Each of these major processes can be further broken down into its elements or subprocesses.

With this high-level view of the organization, the elemental business processes can be identified. This can often be accomplished by a knowledgeable representative from each functional organization; however, if not immediately apparent, then an interview approach will generally help. In that approach the team identifying the processes interviews the functional organizations, concentrating on what they do, not how they do their work.

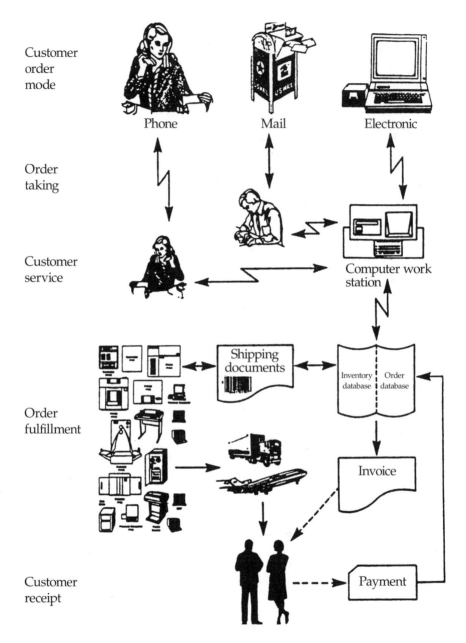

Customer
order
mode

Phone · Mail · Electronic

Order
taking

Customer
service

Computer work
station

Order
fulfillment

Shipping
documents

Inventory
database · Order
database

Invoice

Customer
receipt

Payment

Figure 2.4. Helicopter-view of a business process.

The objective of this approach is to get agreement on a defined set of work processes. What are they? How are they described? How many are there? Can the full set of processes be defined? Experience indicates that this approach of breaking down the processes into increasing detail will result in a defined set of processes at the third or fourth level of detail, with fewer than 200 processes being identified. At the highest level will be the overall business or enterprise process such as product delivery or customer satisfaction. At the next level will be the overall process of managing customer interactions from beginning to end, with six to eight high-level sequential processes being defined. Lastly, below each of the sequential steps, will be the elemental processes, with perhaps eight to 10 processes defined for each step. In addition to the logical progression to managing customer interactions, there will be a set of support processes that are common across all others. These include financial, information systems, and human relations processes.

Why go to this detail to define the set of business processes? From a benchmarking viewpoint the projects undertaken should be prioritized to ensure that they are the vital few contributing to results. If the set of business processes cannot be identified, how can they be prioritized to select the vital few? If the full set is not the basis for prioritization, then the selection of the vital few is simply a matter of judgment and visceral feel, not informed, fact-based selection.

Perhaps more importantly, however, this is the place in the overall benchmarking approach where the management team is engaged. Line managers must be involved; they must agree to the set of business processes; and they are responsible for prioritizing and selecting the vital few to study. The managers' contribution to this step keeps them involved and committed to benchmarking. For if they have participated in the vital few process selection for improvement through benchmarking, then they have some commitment, and "skin" in the final outcome of benchmarking.

Is this approach of classifying business processes possible for organizations, whether they are manufacturing or service industries, public sector companies, educational or governmental institutions, or nonprofit organizations? The experience of those who have led the way may be instructive. Xerox has identified 67 business process for a major business unit involved with sales, service, and business operations (see Figure 2.5a). These have been further categorized into 10 areas for management. It should be noted that the processes in the left column are the logical flow of handling the customer and those in the right column are the support processes common to the others. Xerox has also identified 76 processes at a higher, companywide or enterprise level to cover the full spectrum of operations from product inception, design, engineering, and manufacture as well as customer delivery (see Figure 2.5b). Others have a similar scheme. IBM has its Enterprise processes. The International Benchmarking Clearinghouse service of the American Productivity and Quality Center has a similar SIC code classification of business processes. It is apparent that business processes *can* be categorized.

Whether an organization initially sets out to identify and classify its processes and then starts its process improvement activities through benchmarking, or starts with some internal pilot case study applications of benchmarking, is a matter that deserves consideration. It will quickly be seen that determining the processes and gaining agreement is a time-consuming activity. It may be of equal importance to start benchmarking even without the aid of the process classification. One cannot wait for the other. It has been the experience of this author that both need to be started. They eventually will merge to form the basis for what is found to be most productive, namely focus benchmarking on improving identified, prioritized business processes.

Market management
- Market planning
- Product planning and development
- Pricing
- Market tracking
- Product life cycle management
- Marketing communications

Customer engagement
- Sales territory planning
- Prospecting management
- Enterprise management
- Agreement development
- Agreement management
- Customer support

Order fulfillment
- Order processing
- Scheduling
- Customer preparation
- Staging and preinstallation
- Delivery/removal
- Installation/deinstallation
- Product production

Product maintenance
- Service call management
- Service dispatching
- Product servicing
- Service call closure
- Product maintenance planning
- Equipment performance monitoring
- Technical information provision
- Service territory planning

Billing and collection
- Invoicing
- Bank operations
- Cash application
- Collection
- Third-party leasing administration

Financial management
- Financial planning
- Financial analysis and reporting
- Financial outlooking
- Tax planning and management
- Accounting operations
- Financial auditing
- Disbursements
- Financial asset/cash planning
- Financial asset control

Logistics and inventory management
- Physical asset acquisition
- Inventory management
- Physical asset planning
- Logistics planning
- Logistics operations
- Logistics engineering
- Vendor management

Business management
- Business strategy development
- Business planning
- Business process and operations management
  —Process specification
  —Coordination and integration
  —Inspection
  —Benchmarking
  —Process improvement

Information technology management
- Information strategy planning
- Systems analysis and design
- Systems development
- Production systems support
- Research and development
- Business systems management and coordination

Human resource management
- Workforce requirements planning
- Hiring and assignment
- Benefits and compensation management
- Personnel management
- Workforce preparedness
- Employee communications

Total processes: 67

Used with permission of Xerox Corporation.

Figure 2.5a. Business processes: Sales, service, and business operations.

Market management
- Market selection and analysis
- Customer requirements/segment understanding
- Produce requirement planning
- Market planning
- Marketing support
- Market communication
- Market tracking

Product design and engineering
- Product concept design
- Product detail design
- Product design configuration management
- Product design standards measurement
- Product launch quality assurance

Product operations
- Production line design
- Production line operations
- Product quality assurance

Supplier management
- Supplier identification
- Supplier development
- Procurement
- Supplier administration

Customer engagement
- Coverage planning
- Customer account management
- Prospect management
- Agreement development
- Agreement management
- Order management
- Customer support

Logistics and inventory management
- Physical asset configuration management
- Logistics and physical distribution planning
- Inventory planning
- Logistics operation and material control
- Delivery management

Product maintenance
- Product maintenance planning
- Service call management
- Service dispatching
- Service call closure
- Product performance monitoring
- Technical information provisioning

Business management
- Business strategy development
- Business planning
- Business process management
- Business risk management
- Business development
- Business organization strategy development
- Business communications

Technology management
- Technology identification
- Technology evaluation
- Technology development
- Technology application management
- Technology portfolio management

Information management
- Information strategy planning
- Business solutions development
- Information integration management
- Technical environment management

Financial management
- Financial planning
- Financial analysis and reporting
- Financial outlooking
- Accounting
- Financial asset management
- Tax planning and management
- Financial auditing

Asset management
- Leased and capital asset planning
- Leased and capital asset life cycle management

Legal services
- Research and analysis
- Counseling services
- Dispute management
- Patent and copyright administration

Human resource management
- Workforce requirements planning
- Recruitment and staffing
- Training and development
- Compensation and rewards management
- Benefits management
- Personnel management
- Employee communications
- Industrial relations

Total processes: 76

Used with permission of Xerox Corporation.

Figure 2.5b. Business enterprise processes.

Classify the Business Processes

The next step is to classify the business processes. While this already has been briefly described, the rationale for doing should be explained. There should be, as a natural outgrowth of the process classification, some logical layering or sequence to the approach. This is because organizations are made up of processes, and all work is a process, whether it is bringing a product to market, a retail checkout, the reservation of a traveler at a hotel, the admission of a patient to a hospital, or the preparation of a tax return. If this were not so why would the organization exist? Thus, there should be some sense to the overall classification that logically shows what the organization does.

This high-level road map or work process classification is crucial in other ways. It defines the outputs that are produced and handed off to the next step in the overall process. It defines the sequence of the various steps in the process. It forces the organization to define who produces the outputs. It reveals the boundaries of the elemental processes. It clarifies or forces clarification of the boundaries of the processes, often the most ambiguous and unclear of understandings: the interface handoffs where much of the organization's inefficiencies exist. Last, but not least, this classification forces the organization to define who owns the process and who, therefore, is accountable for its detailed understanding and improvement through benchmarking.

At some point taking the time to classify business processes as a precursor for benchmarking could be challenged as being unnecessary. It is needed on two levels, a very practical one and a managerial one. First, in selecting business processes to benchmark there needs to be a source from which to select. Except for one developed for and tailored to the organization, that source does not exist. SIC codes and descriptions do not help. They are not defined in process terms. They define industries. While there may be alphabetic descriptions of functions or activities produced by professional or trade organizations who see themselves as covering these activities, it becomes extremely difficult to prioritize an alphabetic list. But second, and more importantly, the current emphasis on process improvement and reengineering is bringing this activity to the attention of senior managers. They need the process classification, presented in some logical fashion, to pursue those initiatives and to promote upstream and downstream thinking as a basis for continually finding efficiencies at process interfaces.

From a management perspective why concentrate on business processes? Fundamentally, because the approach corrects two major deficiencies that historically have been significant problems in bringing about continuous improvement or productivity. Classification provides a discipline and it institutionalizes the methodology of the approach. It provides the basis for a plan and the discipline in execution. The approach to pursuing continuous improvement by concentrating on a careful, reasoned selection of business process from a defined set, and sequentially improving them, brings the needed discipline to see the productivity delivered. Therefore, it is not a random or potentially biased approach based on the individual function's candidate process advocacy, but a reasoned, informed selection and a commitment to an overall program to continuously improve all processes. Classification also institutionalizes the approach for continuous improvement because it defines how it is to be done—namely, continuous improvement will be delivered by sequentially improving all processes.

Determine the Results Measure

Given that there is a high-level view of the organization and that the subprocesses have been classified, the final step is straightforward. Determining the measurement definition and selection is now rational. The units of measure and the actual statistic or numerical values are directly related to the process. These should include consideration of overall output measures or results. Additionally, pre-, in-process, and postprocess measures can be considered. Using the process diagram, and understanding it, will clarify the correct performance measures to select. An example of the relationship of results (R) and process (P) measures is shown in Figure 2.6.

What is desired is not comprehensiveness. What is needed is the selection of the vital few performance measures that represent the correct performance of the process. These usually involve the selection of the key company priority performance measures, then a selection of key functional performance measures that would be common across all functions, and lastly a few tailored performance measures unique to the function. These tailored measures are almost always process related. An example might be the organizational goal of n percent customer satisfaction, with some percent of customers very satisfied in the billing organization as the common measure across all functions, and billing quality as the tailored performance measure for the particular function.

In this fashion a structured approach to the selection of key performance measures is used for benchmarking information exchange. This directly supports the business process approach.

Link Business Processes to Goals That Leverage Priorities

Once business processes have been identified and classified, the next logical step is to prioritize them to affect organizational goals and to improve business results. Experience indicates, however, that an intermediate step is worth considering. That intermediate step is to visually display the linkage to organizational goals on the one hand and the business processes on the other. This picture, often worth a thousand words, is helpful not only to

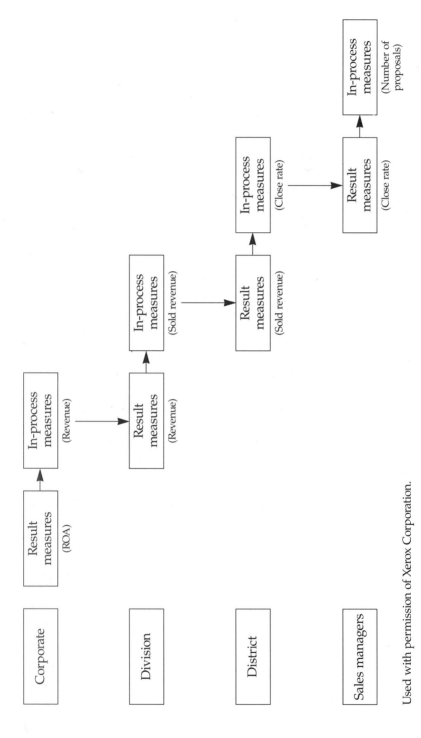

Used with permission of Xerox Corporation.

Figure 2.6. Relationship of R and P measures.

get an understanding of the direct relationship of business processes to goals, but also to once again obtain commitment and buy-in from the management team.

How is this done? The best way is to visualize a tree diagram, on its side, with the organization's goals stated at the root of the tree. From the root is an increasing number of branches that cascade outward in increasing levels of detail and understanding. The performance or goal desired at the root of the tree may be stated in words, such as *customer satisfaction,* and supported by numerical data, such as *92 percent customer satisfaction for the organization and 94 percent customer satisfaction for the industry or the benchmark.*

This tree diagram is represented in Figure 2.7, in which first the performance or results desired (organizational goals) are displayed on the left. An example is customer satisfaction. Next, the items that customers are dissatisfied with and that need improvement are shown. Technical service is an example. Next, who or what is affected by the dissatisfiers is identified. This may include a market segment like low-volume users. Then the process that directly affects those dissatisfiers, and consequently affects the goal of customer satisfaction, is identified. As a further enhancement, the practice that needs improvement could be added, as well as the names of the process owners. This would provide direct linkage from process to goal. On the basis of this diagram, line-of-sight decisions could be made on which process would leverage the goal the most and, therefore, be the priority process to improve through benchmarking.

At the next level is the diagnosis of the gap. This takes branching out to the second level of performance dissatisfiers and the third level of whom or what is affected. In each of these branchings it is not the intent to have the detail encompass all possible combinations. That would be detail beyond reasonable comprehension. Experience has shown that the top three are

Performance (Results)	Performance dissatisfiers	Who and what is affected	Processes	Practices
Customer satisfaction	Technical service	Low volume customers	Frequency of service	Preventive maintenance
Employee motivation and satisfaction	Job satisfaction	Clerical staff	Training received	How people are selected for training
Market share	Coverage	Electronic repro	Contested transactions	Pricing
Return on assets	Return on sales	Revenue growth	Equipment sale	Sales and compensation

Figure 2.7. Tree diagram of business processes linked to organizational goals.

adequate. Thus, for the 2 percent customer satisfaction gap, the diagnosis might show that technical service is the primary contributor to the dissatisfaction (the 2 percent gap), and further diagnosis shows that a certain class of customers or product types are the third level of who or what is affected.

The next level, the fourth, is where the business process is identified that corrects the performance dissatisfaction. In this case it might be the service process, namely the way in which the product is serviced. In this concise way a named business process has been identified that directly affects a stated organizational goal. This line-of-sight relationship is often extremely helpful to prioritize the processes.

Further refinements to the tree diagram would be to add a fifth level. This would identify the process owner to show the accountability not only for the process but also for finding the best practices through benchmarking. Thus, it would be known who should incorporate the best practices into the process to overcome the dissatisfiers and to improve the organizational goal. If at some level of benchmarking completeness the best practices are known or surmised, then they could be added at another level. The liberal use of space on the chart would permit incorporating, at any point, other information that would enhance understanding through the simple mechanism of a box or table.

Is this a new technique? No! It is simply a use of one of the new quality tools as described in *The Memory Jogger Plus+* by GOAL/QPC. It is, in fact, an application of one of the seven management and planning tools, namely the tree diagram. It answers the question: What are the key processes that need to be improved in order to fully address the priority goal selected?

What has been accomplished with this intermediate step in determining what to benchmark? First, as a prelude to prioritizing the vital few business processes, a common display methodology has been used to systematically map the linkage of a set of identified processes to the organization's priorities and, therefore, its business results. It is a visual representation of that relationship for purposes of understanding in the next step, prioritizing the processes. Second, this intermediate step can incorporate all key performance measures, including goals, internal performance measures, benchmarks, and external industry performance measures. This provides easy access to relevant, factual data. The tree diagram serves as a communication device to obtain consensus on the facts during the prioritization. It focuses attention on the key issues and presents a unified performance picture. It defines the gaps based on factual information, both analytical and logical, to serve as a starting point to gain consensus on what should be the next steps.

How does such a tree diagram get assembled? It has proven successful to gather a team of relevant data owners to complete the first three levels. This information is often in the hands of a few key participants who are responsible for goal diagnosis. It is a doable task. The next two levels are completed by process-knowledgeable individuals supplemented by those concerned with future planning and by benchmarking professionals. The process-knowledgeable individuals will know the key processes affected; those in a planning capacity will know the key business issues that need to be addressed; and the benchmarking professionals will know where benchmarking can be performed to find best practices to assist the process owners.

The utility of the tree diagram obviously extends beyond benchmarking. It is a tool that shows how benchmarking directly addresses organizational goals and, therefore, validates the need to find and implement best practices. Is it absolutely necessary to prepare a tree diagram? No, but it is an excellent approach to start the discussion of which process to benchmark and why.

The tree diagram is an executive summary of overall performance, benchmarking information, and fact-based linkages to planned actions and accountable owners. It is an excellent pre-cursor for the next step, prioritizing the key processes.

Prioritize Business Processes to Affect Priorities and to Improve Business Results

For companies with established organizational goals, bench-marking activities should contribute to, if not directly leverage, their achievement. Benchmarking must be conducted on work processes that have a significant impact on the work unit's out-puts and, therefore, on results and the quest for continuous improvement.

Having identified all the potential work processes and having a visual display of how they map to the priorities are helpful, even necessary, but not always sufficient. If it is assumed that an organization typically identifies 80 to 160 key work processes, then it is safe to assume that there are not enough resources to benchmark and improve all processes at once. Organizations rarely have the people or other resources to undertake this mag-nitude of process or continuous improvement. Furthermore, it is doubtful if an organization could digest the level of change implied in benchmarking and incorporating best practices in all its work processes at once. That level of change could bring the organization to its knees since it would mean that everyone is concentrating on change and not on running the business and satisfying customers.

Thus, key business processes must be prioritized to the most critical few, and the remaining processes scheduled for bench-marking and improvement over an extended horizon. Experience indicates that 15 percent to 20 percent of all identified processes could be pursued at any one time. Given that the timeline for assembling a team, documenting the processes, benchmarking them, and incorporating best practices will take months, the organization is facing a multiyear activity. This is just one more reason to concentrate on the vital few processes that contribute the most to the firm's goals.

How are processes prioritized? There are three basic methods: (1) prioritize by management consensus; (2) prioritize by major organization goal, such as which processes satisfy customers the most; or (3) analytically determine which processes are most important in rank order.

Management consensus With the array of data from the process list, process map, and tree diagram supported by relevant facts on where the significant gaps exist, it should be fairly easy to arrive at a management team consensus of the key processes. Other areas that managers might consider important and may want to emphasize, include market share, profitability, competitive pressures, declining leadership products, customer complaints, and the need to improve. Additional management concerns might be insignificant or no change to a process for some years, resistance to looking outside the organization for solutions to problems, or complacency about change in general.

The difficulty with this approach is that, although it utilizes all the relevant quality tools, it is still a judgment call. Also, while the top few processes, say three to six, might gain some consensus, there will most likely be major debates over the remaining.

Satisfaction of a major goal If the organization is driven by one or two major goals, then the processes could be prioritized to affect those goals the most. The logical approach to prioritize the business processes would be to consider customer satisfaction. The management team would pick those processes that were judged to affect customer satisfaction the most. These would be processes that customers come in contact with the most and perhaps have a high level of dissatisfaction.

While this approach is admirable and holds some promise, it depends on the organization's goals and priorities being well entrenched and widely understood. It also will likely result in a few processes being bunched in one functional area, such as in marketing, where the major contacts are made. It may leave other significant processes to later improvement. One way to overcome this problem is to agree to selected demonstration benchmarking projects elsewhere in the company. This would even out the pursuit of improvement through the organization.

One serious consideration for this approach is to ask customers to prioritize the processes. Obviously, this could be conducted through the typical focus group approach. It would indicate where customers felt best or better practices are needed. It would obviously not obtain any feedback on some of the processes that are invisible to customers such as financial or asset management.

Rank order A third way to prioritize the processes is through some analytical approach. It would depend on establishing a set of criteria and numerical weighting for it, and then ranking the processes on the basis of the criteria. The outcome of the ranking would be a numerical score that would prioritize the processes.

This approach has several advantages. First, it depends on managers determining what their criteria were and what weighting they would assign those criteria. This discussion alone could be quite revealing in the sense that managers could no longer make subjective decisions and would, in fact, have to reveal their basis of decisions. It would be completely fact based. Second, the criteria and the results of differences are analyzed for change; what-if questions, to test sensitivity of selections, are applied. This approach illustrates how managers make decisions and what they understand the organization's goals to be.

This approach does exist and is considered a best practice. IBM used it at its Malcolm Baldrige National Quality Award-winning site in Rochester, Minnesota. IBM's use of the approach is detailed in the landmark *Manufacturing Systems'* (April 1991) article "Benchmarking To Become the Best of Breed." The approach is called analytical hierarchic process, or AHP for short. It is a comprehensive process that is relatively easy to use. It is also one of the GOAL/QPC tools, namely the prioritization matrix.

Other considerations in prioritizing work processes involve the following: what processes or steps in the process look redundant; any obsolete work practices that exist; unclear accountability for the process; handoffs at key interfaces that are frequently botched and are sources of errors or delays; and areas where bottlenecks and rework occur.

Who prioritizes work processes? The list would have to include those who come in contact with the process, customers, process owners, knowledgeable professionals, and senior management. This is a particularly important place to involve senior managers to know which processes are, from their view and in light of the data presented, the most important. Gaining senior management's commitment through this approach also ensures that the necessary resources will be available and that the results will be implemented.

Focus of the Investigation

The focus of the investigation further defines the work processes. The focus requires consideration of two key points: adjusting the focus of the benchmarking study from broad to narrow, and determining the boundaries of the process. It is a known fail point in benchmarking circles that tackling too large a project will almost certainly be unproductive. It is akin to trying to solve world hunger with benchmarking. In fact, there appears to be a direct correlation between the focus of the investigation and its success. The more narrow the focus, the higher the success. Experience indicates that the broadly focused benchmarking studies largely become skimming operations and return only superficial understanding. Thus, there is great difficulty in understanding the real practices and their benefits. So at some point the team must address the scope of the investigation to ensure it is adequately focused.

Second only to focus are the boundaries of the investigation. Processes have beginnings and ends. These need to be carefully determined for two reasons: to not allow the process scope to become too large, and to precisely define where one boundary ends and another begins. For example, where does selling end and order taking begin? If the process being benchmarked is order taking, then this could be a nontrivial matter, especially if orders are being taken over the telephone and some selling is done.

Document the Priority Work Process

Now that the business processes have been identified, linked to organizational goals, and prioritized to the vital few, the benchmarking team can get down to the real work of documenting the chosen, high-priority work process. While there are all levels of documentation detail, some basic requirements are important. Once these are satisfied the degree of detail the team selects for the process documentation will be a matter of judgment inasmuch as the team is the process owner.

The basic elements and minimum requirements to documenting a work or business process are the following:

- Picture of the process
- Narrative description of the process
- Description of the process step (what is done)

- Description of the practice at the process step (how it is done)

First, a picture of the process should be developed to give a visual representation to display, to help anyone understand how the process works, and to inspect for key fail points. Those who work the process should be fully conversant with the diagram and be able to describe how it works. The traditional picture of a process is a flowchart but there are alternatives.

An example is shown in Figure 2.8 for the documentation of the benchmarking process. Just like any other process, the benchmarking process must be benchmarked and improved; thus it must be documented. In this instance the parent processes to benchmarking are shown, and the two major subprocesses of benchmarking are documented, namely the management process and the user process. Each subprocess then decomposes into the key steps and each is described.

Second, a detailed narrative of the process should be developed to describe the process and to explain the picture. In some formats the narrative can be placed directly adjacent to the process picture. Third, in the narrative description, two elements should be described: what is done, namely the step in the process; and how it is done, namely the practice at the step in the process.

Since a process is made up of a sequence of work steps, each should be clearly defined. It is often instructive to have the team first concentrate on the documentation of the process by limiting discussion to the picture and narrative. Then, as a second activity, the team should define the practices at each step by describing how the practices or methods in that step are accomplished.

Consider the example of a checkout counter that is universal in all retail businesses, such as department, grocery, or video rental stores (see Figure 2.9). There are several steps in that process including, but not limited to, validating customer credit,

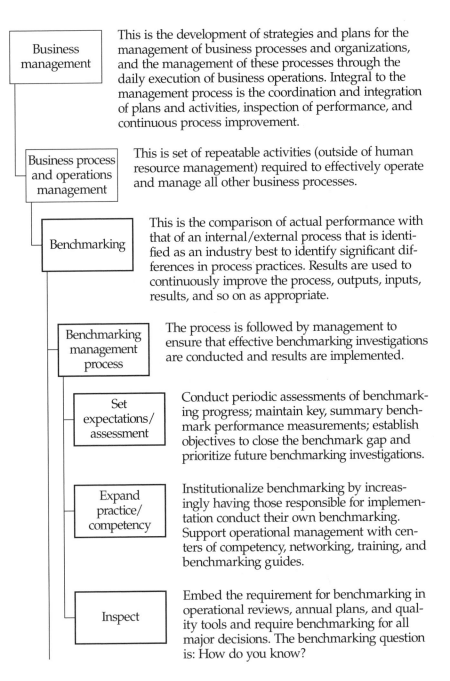

Business management — This is the development of strategies and plans for the management of business processes and organizations, and the management of these processes through the daily execution of business operations. Integral to the management process is the coordination and integration of plans and activities, inspection of performance, and continuous process improvement.

Business process and operations management — This is set of repeatable activities (outside of human resource management) required to effectively operate and manage all other business processes.

Benchmarking — This is the comparison of actual performance with that of an internal/external process that is identified as an industry best to identify significant differences in process practices. Results are used to continuously improve the process, outputs, inputs, results, and so on as appropriate.

Benchmarking management process — The process is followed by management to ensure that effective benchmarking investigations are conducted and results are implemented.

Set expectations/assessment — Conduct periodic assessments of benchmarking progress; maintain key, summary benchmark performance measurements; establish objectives to close the benchmark gap and prioritize future benchmarking investigations.

Expand practice/competency — Institutionalize benchmarking by increasingly having those responsible for implementation conduct their own benchmarking. Support operational management with centers of competency, networking, training, and benchmarking guides.

Inspect — Embed the requirement for benchmarking in operational reviews, annual plans, and quality tools and require benchmarking for all major decisions. The benchmarking question is: How do you know?

Figure 2.8. Documentation of the benchmarking process.

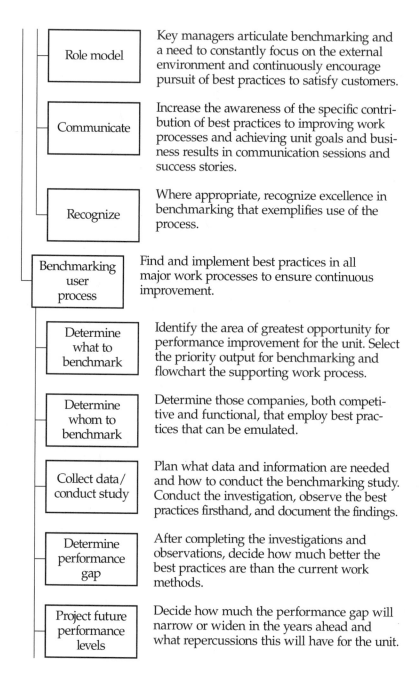

Role model	Key managers articulate benchmarking and a need to constantly focus on the external environment and continuously encourage pursuit of best practices to satisfy customers.
Communicate	Increase the awareness of the specific contribution of best practices to improving work processes and achieving unit goals and business results in communication sessions and success stories.
Recognize	Where appropriate, recognize excellence in benchmarking that exemplifies use of the process.
Benchmarking user process	Find and implement best practices in all major work processes to ensure continuous improvement.
Determine what to benchmark	Identify the area of greatest opportunity for performance improvement for the unit. Select the priority output for benchmarking and flowchart the supporting work process.
Determine whom to benchmark	Determine those companies, both competitive and functional, that employ best practices that can be emulated.
Collect data/ conduct study	Plan what data and information are needed and how to conduct the benchmarking study. Conduct the investigation, observe the best practices firsthand, and document the findings.
Determine performance gap	After completing the investigations and observations, decide how much better the best practices are than the current work methods.
Project future performance levels	Decide how much the performance gap will narrow or widen in the years ahead and what repercussions this will have for the unit.

Figure 2.8. *(continued)*

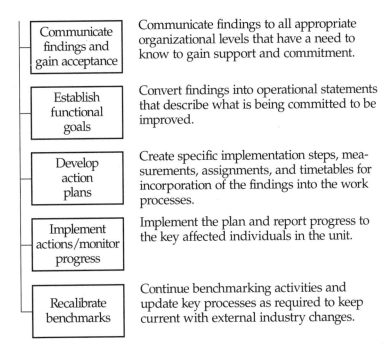

Communicate findings and gain acceptance	Communicate findings to all appropriate organizational levels that have a need to know to gain support and commitment.
Establish functional goals	Convert findings into operational statements that describe what is being committed to be improved.
Develop action plans	Create specific implementation steps, measurements, assignments, and timetables for incorporation of the findings into the work processes.
Implement actions/monitor progress	Implement the plan and report progress to the key affected individuals in the unit.
Recalibrate benchmarks	Continue benchmarking activities and update key processes as required to keep current with external industry changes.

Figure 2.8. *(continued)*

capturing the transaction data, accepting payment, and rendering a receipt. These steps of the process would be flowcharted and documented in the narrative description. On the second pass, at the "capture data" process step, the benchmarking team may document the practice to be "through bar code scanning." So the step is capture transaction data, and the practice or method is using bar code scanning. They are different things: one describes what is done and the other documents the very important practice, or how the step is done. The team will use the process steps to determine how others perform the same steps and to uncover better or best practices to replace the current ones and thereby improve the operation.

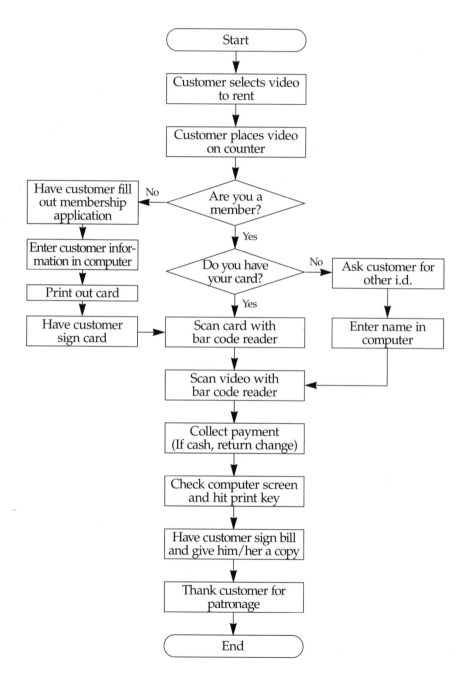

Figure 2.9. The checkout process for a video rental store.

These elements of a process are shown in Figure 2.10. It shows the basic elements of a work process, describes the key elements, and gives a definition of each element. This figure should help you understand the difference between process and practice. A *process* is a sequence of work steps. A *work step* in the process describes what is done. For each step there is a method or how the step is done.

These are the minimum requirements for the documentation of a process. There are, however, other characteristics of process documentation, in the aggregate, that should be considered. These are the full documentation requirements. They include descriptions of the following:

- What business area or function is addressed?

- What is the parent process?

- What subprocess is documented?

Results Those critical performance measures that serve as a report card. Examples: cost per item, output per hour, or percent defects.

Outputs What is produced and delivered to the customer. Examples: finished product or service performed.

Process Steps in the work process, including decision points, handoffs, and practices that are followed to produce an output.

    Steps in the process = What is done
    Practices, at each step = How it is done

Examples: Billing process, curriculum design process, or inventory control process.

Inputs Items provided by suppliers that go into the work process. Examples: data, ingredients, raw materials, and prefabricated assemblies.

Figure 2.10. Elements of a work process.

- What is its description?
- Who is the owner or supplier of the process?
- What are the process inputs? What are the outputs?
- What is the destination process that receives the outputs?
- Who is the customer for the process?
- What are the customer or output requirements?
- What are the supplier specifications for those requirements?
- What are the current measurements for the process?
- What are the measurement specification limits?
- What is the process inspection method and frequency?
- What resources are required to maintain the process in operation?

Obviously these elements involve a great deal of detail for documenting a process. But it is the fullest, most rigorous documentation and is an exercise the team should consider to ensure that all aspects of a process are understood.

What alternatives are there for process documentation? Most likely there are many. It is not the intent here to cover their actual application. The prominent methods are mentioned in the next section. It will be up to the team to consider the alternative methods and select one that is appropriate. A specific documentation method is not recommended, only that the process be documented and that the method meets the minimum requirements noted in this section.

Alternate Process Documentation Methods

Three process documentation methods are discussed: flowcharting, arrow diagramming, and functional analysis systems technique (FAST) diagramming or mapping.

Flowcharting Flowcharting is the traditional standard recognized by many as the usual approach to process documentation. It is composed of standard symbols for representing key items like steps in the process, decision points, information capture, and so forth. It is usually presented in linear fashion or logical next step sequence. Today, there are software applications that will substantially ease the flowchart effort. A narrative can easily follow the stepwise sequence.

Arrow diagramming An arrow or data flow diagram is a variation on the flowchart but with more free form. Arrow diagramming documents the process flows in whatever is seen to be the natural form that they appear. It starts with a key step and builds on that until all the interrelated steps that flow from or to the key step are exhausted. The picture is not neatly sequential; it has overlapping flows. An arrow diagram tends to appeal to some who do not perceive processes to be strictly sequential in operation. It does capture all major interrelationships where those are important. It would be difficult to attach a narrative of the steps directly to the arrow diagram. An example is shown in Figure 2.11.

Mapping FAST mapping is a technique that shows how a process crosses several functions and touches certain levels of the organization. It has functional organizations arrayed across the columns and process steps down the rows. Major components of the organization's levels might have one level where the customer is in direct contact with the organization and one where the process is transparent to the customer but still accomplished. This matrix would then have the traditional flowchart with the key components of the organization as an overlay.

The value of mapping is to directly show which function is handling a step in the process and who is in contact with whom. The map then highlights the responsibilities for process steps

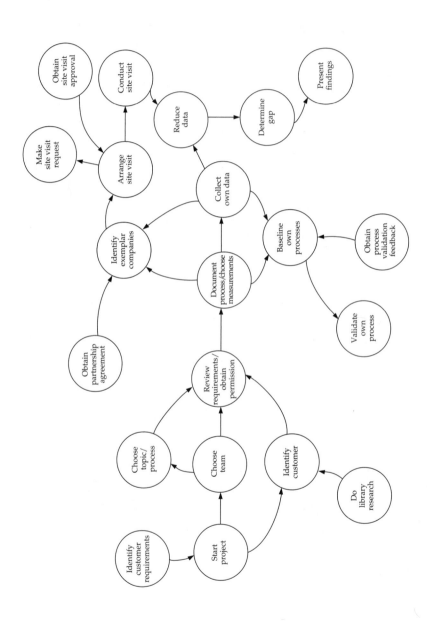

Figure 2.11. Arrow or data flow diagram of simplified benchmarking process.

when, as most processes do, they cross multiple organizations. Mapping also highlights key fail points and critical handoffs among the organization, those being served by the process, and internal customers. An example of a process mapping is shown in Figure 2.12.

Additional meaning can be brought to any one of these diagramming techniques by indicating directly on the flowchart where critical cost base problems occur, where customer complaints are focused, which areas show the greatest potential for improvement and cycle time reduction, and any cross-functional pinch points. The level of detail in documenting a process is governed only by the judgment of those who work the process and their comfort level in being able to describe how they do their work. They know just how far a process needs to be detailed into subprocesses. The key will be to have adequate detail to be able to understand the critical few steps being studied for improvement.

The use of a documented business process is a prerequisite for accomplishing the most credible basis for process-to-process comparisons and, therefore, the potential for uncovering innovative practices. Without this level of preparation, the association of benchmarking as trips to other companies can only be industrial tourism. This rarely finds the best practices.

There are ways to remove some of the perceived drudgery from process documentation. The use of the self-adhesive-yellow-notepad routine is one way. This is where each step is described on one of the ubiquitous sticky-backed papers and then arranged and rearranged on a large wall by team members until there is consensus on all the process steps and their sequence. Once the steps are agreed to, they can be connected with flow arrows to arrive at, at least a preliminary, yet-to-be validated, draft of the process. In this fashion the team can get itself jump-started.

There is a definite side benefit to doing this level of documentation that the team should keep in mind while struggling

Functional process: Train technicians

Curriculum development	Production and graphics	Training center	Audio/visual production
1. Curriculum development • Analyze needs • Analyze tasks • Design blueprint • Write materials • Evaluate results			
	2. Produce drafts • Print laser copies • Photocopy • Distribute		
		3. Pilot test • Teach classes • Assess results	
4. Edit materials • Make pilot revisions			
	5. Produce materials • Typeset print text • Create final artwork • Create mechanicals • Print/bind materials • Edit video • Produce dubs		**6. Produce video** • Final scripts • Cast talent • Dress set • Shoot video
		7. Implement • Teach classes • Add to catalog	

Source: Adapted from benchmarking training material, The Quality Network, Ltd.

Figure 2.12. Process mapping.

through the effort. This is in addition to the direct benefits that may be revealed from examining the process once documented. Such examinations often raise very appropriate questions of "Why are we doing that?" or "Why are we doing that in that way?" or "Why are there more work-arounds than mainline process?" These are important efficiencies to be gained even before benchmarking with others. The benefit beyond those mentioned are directly related to getting others to participate in benchmarking. It has been the experience of many successful benchmarking teams that having a well-documented process is a major incentive for others to participate in the benchmarking exchange. This is because few organizations have documented their processes. When others learn that a documented process detail will be the basis of a benchmarking exchange, they know they stand a major chance of significant insight, understanding, and potential for uncovering innovative practices.

Determine the Key Process Performance Measures

Now that the process is documented, its vital few measurements are determined. These will become the basis of benchmarking data exchange. Certainly the current performance measures should be considered as well as others uncovered during the documentation procedure. A suggested set of performance measurements to consider include the following: customer satisfaction measurements, cycle time measurements, error or defect measurement, and financial measures of cost effectiveness and asset performance.

Ratio data are the performance measures typically shared in benchmarking exchanges. Ratio data allow the participants to judge the efficiency of the process in terms of rates but do not reveal the absolute value of the operation. So asset turns could be freely shared either as a specific statistic or as a range. But dollar value of inventories probably would not be shared because it most likely is of a sensitive nature.

Process-type measures should be considered next. There are two types: outputs or results and key in-process measures. Output measures are what the process should ultimately accomplish. They are the results. The key in-process measures are the vital few that most contribute to the results. Focusing on the principal output or result measure and identifying the key in-process measures will increase the success of recognizing the vital few practice changes that will close the performance gap.

Improve Business Processes by Including Best Practices in the Work Steps

The processes have been identified, classified, prioritized, and documented, and the key performance measures have been determined. The remaining step is to benchmark the steps in the process to uncover best practices and incorporate them. This is the payoff for all the prior work. This step can now be approached with confidence that all the preparation will result in credible results.

The focus of the team will now be to ensure that, through benchmarking, superior work processes will be designed and implemented. This means incorporating best-in-class practices, best-demonstrated practices, or exemplary practices; that is, those that are the model or ideal. The result will be a benchmark process.

At this point the team's investigations shift to concentrate on finding and documenting practices. This is an exercise of comparing the organization's process step to that of benchmarking partners. The focus is not on what is done but on how it is done. The result of this comparison can be visualized as a matrix with the process steps detailed down the rows and the companies whose process is being compared to in the columns across the top from left to right. The subject organization is in the first column. The matrix details descriptions of the practices in use at the other organizations. It is this array of information that the team is heading for in the next steps of the benchmarking process. It will be discussed further in chapter 5.

Performance measures are mentioned at key points of the matrix, but it should be stressed that performance measures are only a report card of progress, an indicator of a what-if scenario; that is, if the best practices were implemented, then what would the performance measures change to? It is only the implementation of the practices that delivers the output that gets those results.

The premises have been the following: superior customer satisfaction is delivered by outputs of work processes; therefore, it is the concentration on the work processes that will yield the greatest returns for continuous improvement; these continuous improvements can be shown to be direct contributions to business priorities and business results from benchmarking; and, therefore, benchmarking has a specifically defined role that supports the goals of the organization.

Thus, the focus is on business processes that directly support the organization's goals by concentrating on the vital few and by incorporating best practices. That is the role of benchmarking. Now that is a significant, if not compelling, basis for benchmarking.

Prepare a Project Description

At this final point in step 1 of the benchmarking process, the team should prepare a brief project description that explains which business process has been selected for the focus of the benchmarking activities. This might involve key statements of the rationale so that those reviewing the results will have a clear understanding of just what was summarized in the previous section.

The project should then be reviewed with the manager commissioning the team's efforts including the process owner and those that work it. This promotes understanding, agreement, and support. The project review may take many forms that the team may want to consider. One successful approach is the use of the storyboard (see Figure 2.13).

Even if a storyboard is not used, the project description should include at least the following:

- Purpose of the project
- Topic and work process selected and why
- Scope of the project
- Vital few output and process measures
- Description of the key practices
- Estimated potential opportunity for improvement
- What and whom will be affected by the results expected

Summary

- Prepare with step zero.
- Document company and department goals and priorities.
- Identify and classify business processes.
- Show process linkage to organizational goals.
- Prioritize business processes to improve results.
- Flowchart and document vital processes.
- Determine key process performance measures.
- Improve processes by focusing on practices.
- Prepare a project description.

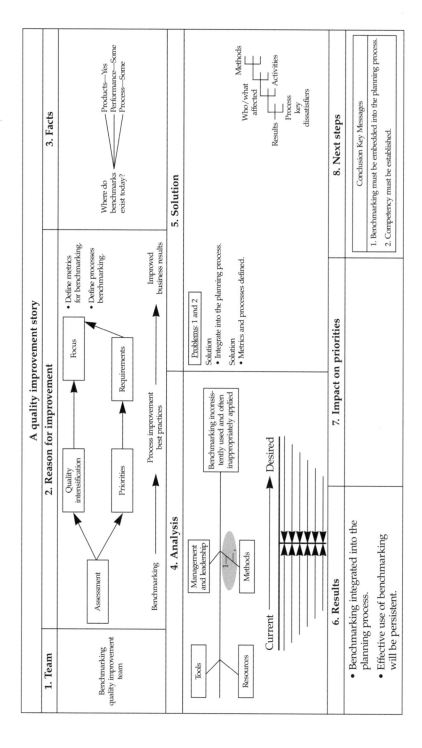

Figure 2.13. A project description using a storyboard.

Whom to Benchmark

If you know the enemy and you know yourself, your victory will not stand in doubt.

- Introduction
- Use the Process Model to Develop a Candidate List
- General Scheme for Where Best Practices Occur
- Develop Candidate Selection Criteria
- Create a Preliminary Candidate List
- Getting Started
- Conduct a Systematic Search by Named Company
- Refine the Initial List
- Prepare a Request to Visit the Best Companies
- Summary

Introduction

Frequently an organization knows what to benchmark more clearly than it knows whom to benchmark. What to benchmark is based on one of two things: known information driven by internal priorities, such as improving processes, shrinking the cost base, or reducing cycle time; or known external pressures, such as from customers or competitors. Whom to benchmark, however, is primarily based on external information and is unknown.

So how is some unknown found? It requires a carefully planned search, and that is how whom to benchmark should be approached. The drawback is that there is no prescriptive way to determine whom to benchmark, but the opportunity is that there is a proven, successful methodology. The overall methodology is to

1. Develop a candidate list using any and all readily available information and some preliminary research.

2. Reduce the list to a target number of companies through secondary research focused on the company and function. A further focus of the investigation is to validate the information from as many sources as possible.

3. Prepare for a contact with the target organization and set up a visit.

The goal of this approach is to identify other organizations that might become benchmarking partners because they have superior or excellent work processes. In turn, those identified work processes that use best practices could be emulated.

While on the surface this would seem to require a major effort, in actual practice it becomes fairly straightforward. Knowledgeable process operators know the leaders in their field or can find them with a minimum of effort. The use of telephone surveys to do some of the initial research or to reduce the list of prospects can help. What follows are the recommended steps to determine whom to benchmark.

Use the Process Model to Develop a Candidate List

One productive way to jump-start the candidate list development is for the benchmarking team to go back to the process model. It is used to provide insight during a brainstorming session (see Figure 3.1). For example, consider the input side. What types of organizations would be placed on the candidate list as input providers? The obvious choice is suppliers. But others might include software providers that have clients who use the software exceptionally well. Thus, the software providers could become candidates.

Consider the output side of the model. Which output providers should become candidates? Again, the obvious choice is customers. But also consider contract providers and possibly third-party operators or service bureau organizations.

The same logic can be extended to the process and results portions of the model to start cataloging potential candidates. In addition to the types of organizations, specific, named companies are added to the list. The process model will not only help to get the team's deliberations started but it will also ensure that all possible sources are considered.

The development of a candidate list should cover a wide cross section of organization types and industries. It is preliminary research focused on information, that will be confirmed later. Then, in-depth data will be collected to confirm the primary choices of benchmarking partners. This targeting process is classical research by desired process, function, or other attribute focused on benchmarking. In this later research the team is looking for confirming evidence that the organization does, in fact, have exemplar practices and should remain on the candidate list.

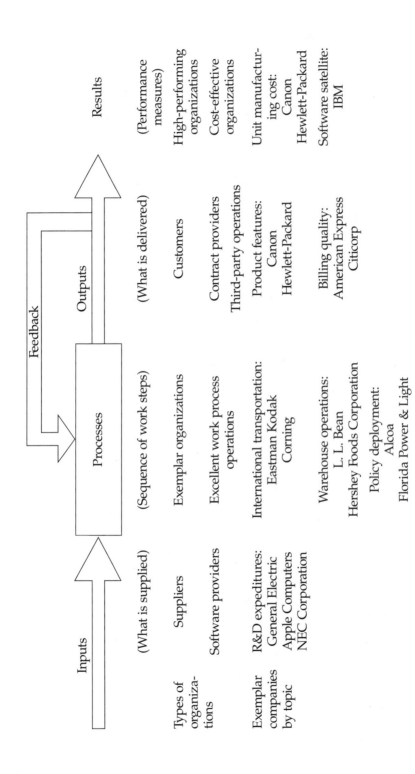

Figure 3.1. Whom to benchmark.

What the team is looking for are statements of pride about the candidate's process. Secondary information to search for includes indicators of potentially excellent processes in organizations that have a focus to satisfy if not delight customers.

There may be some concern for the use of the term *benchmarking partner*. Used in this text, *benchmarking partner* means an organization that agrees to conduct a cooperative benchmarking effort. That is, there will be an equal sharing of information on a mutually agreeable topic. Contrast this definition with that of traditional competitive analysis, which means receiving information about others without reciprocation of similar data. This definition of benchmarking partner even disregards the significant difference between the two types of investigation. With this interpretation there should be little concern for the use of the term *partner*.

General Scheme for Where Best Practices Occur

Before proceeding it is useful to consider the generic sources of best practices. This will focus the team's efforts and provide insight to where best practices are found. Consider the 3×3 matrix shown in Figure 3.2. On the horizontal axis is the subject company's knowledge of best practices. It is divided into three parts: known best practices that have been implemented; known best practices that have not been implemented; and unknown best practices. In similar fashion the vertical scale is divided into the same three parts, but for another company. Now consider the four quadrants.

In quadrant 1 the subject company knows about the best practices and has implemented them. The other company has also done so. Both companies are at parity. Quadrant 2 is composed of two parts. There is a central section of known best practices that have not been implemented by the subject company, and the same is true for the other organization. Again, both companies

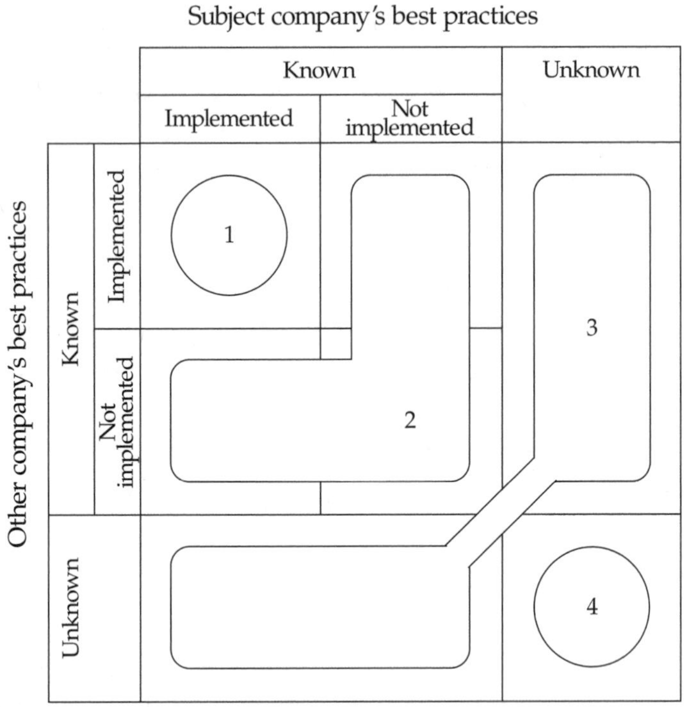

Subject company's best practices

Used with permission of Xerox Corporation.

Figure 3.2. Why benchmark.

are at parity—but only because of inaction. Both groups are missing a potential competitive advantage. The other section of quadrant 2, the arms so to speak, shows the subject company's inaction and the other company's implementation of best practices. Here the other company has a serious competitive advantage. The inaction of the subject company is a serious problem. There are better practices known, but the company, for some reason, has not or will not take action to implement them.

Quadrant 3 shows there are practices known to the other company but unknown to the subject company and vice versa.

Assuming for the moment that the other company is in a dissimilar industry, this is the case for looking outside the industry for better, innovative practices. Finally in quadrant 4, neither company knows about the better practices.

The point of the comparison is that there are a lot of best practices available. Only a disciplined search using benchmarking will locate them. It is this search that whom to benchmark is all about. Although someone may quarrel about the scale of the quadrants, the point is still made: There needs to be a disciplined search or the better practices will never be uncovered. That is why benchmarking exists.

Develop Candidate Selection Criteria

The pool of potential organizations for the candidate list is obviously large. Therefore, a set of criteria should be developed to serve as the basis for selecting companies. Why develop a set of criteria, especially since candidates could later be considered without restriction during generic benchmarking? Here's why. Initially the team will need some filter to quickly reduce the logical set of companies; that is, to speed up the process. At a later date some of the restrictions can be relaxed. This approach of starting small and then growing is more effective than trying to take into account all possibilities at once.

So what might be some of the criteria selected? Obviously that will depend on the specifics of the team's own study, its objectives, and perhaps some companywide standards. Such a list might include, by way of example, the following:

- Fortune 100+ companies
- Recognized industry leaders
- Complex and changing businesses
- Technology-based products and services

- Multiple decentralized field sites for customer contact
- Direct general line sales force
- Worldwide competitors
- Systems competency with operations around the globe
- Technology leaders with unique competencies

With this filter the team can begin to develop the candidate list quickly, because the criteria will immediately exclude a great many potential organizations. Then, if the team feels not enough companies are being sourced, it can consciously relax one or more of the criteria, for good reason, and add candidates.

At this point the process measures developed in step 1, what to benchmark, should be considered. This will aid in the development of the candidate list. The key measures indicate the performance being sought. To the extent that comparable data can be assembled, say from industry-watching organizations, that data will indicate where significant differences exist. Thus, better practices can be found. Even if the data do not specifically exist, it is sometimes possible to make educated assessments of the data from descriptions in articles. As a last resort, it might be appropriate to simply ask the potential benchmarking partner what its performance is. This is especially important if the company is one of the final candidates; the conversation is the initial contact; and what is being referred to is some statement of pride cited in a public domain source.

Create a Preliminary Candidate List

Now that the criteria for selecting the candidate organizations have been established, the actual methodology can begin. There are some general principles to consider in developing such a list. But there also needs to be some rationale for sequentially considering sources of candidates. There are at least three ways to bring some rationale to the search. First, consider candidate companies that fit the four types of benchmarking: internal, competitive, functional, and generic process. That is, revisit the types of benchmarking, consider the definitions, and determine what candidates that method would source.

A second way is to consider a different cast to sources, namely by opportunity area. There are at least four areas that need to be inspected for candidates sources: companies with comparable operations; companies within the same industry; companies where it is known that best practices exist; and dissimilar industries.

A third way to rationalize the search for benchmarking partners is to find sources that have proven successful to other benchmarking professionals. These include the following: lists of companies that are best in class as judged by a periodical's research; companies receiving recognition or awards for some outstanding effort; citations from others such as financial analysts or company watchers; companies that have some indicator of innovativeness such as high patent applications; and companies that receive direct positive feedback from customers and suppliers. This last perception is reality.

A candidate list might look like Figure 3.3. There has been an increase in the number of articles that list what organizations do best. These articles use words such as *excellence, best of the best, best practice companies,* and others to describe for what the organizations are renown. Figure 3.3 shows the top company in seven categories of selling and in nine industries, as determined by independent research. While only the top company in each category is shown, there are second- and third-place companies whose names can probably be obtained. The upshot, however, is that 50 to 60, and possibly more, organizations would be sourced across several industries.

Companies, followed by scores, with a highest possible score of 10.

	Industry	Recruiting top salespeople	Ability to keep top salespeople	Quality of training	Opening new accounts	Holding accounts	Product/technical knowledge	Reputation among customers
	Chemicals	Du Pont 7.77	Du Pont 7.91	Du Pont 7.80	Du Pont 7.09	Du Pont 7.71	Du Pont 8.33	Du Pont 8.12
	Computers and office equipment	IBM 7.79	IBM 7.96	IBM 8.58	IBM 7.56	IBM 8.11	Hewlett-Packard 8.14	IBM 8.29
	Food and beverage	Anheuser-Busch 7.52	Anheuser-Busch 7.61	Anheuser-Busch 7.75	Coca-Cola 7.88	Anheuser-Busch 8.10	Anheuser-Busch 7.91	Coca-Cola 8.10
	Forest products	Scott Paper 6.90	Scott Paper 6.77	Kimberly-Clark 6.89	James River 6.26	Scott Paper 6.93	Scott Paper 7.21	Kimberly-Clark 7.14
	Industrial and farm equipment	Caterpillar 7.00	Caterpillar 7.13	Caterpillar 7.57	Black & Decker 6.92	Caterpillar 7.44	Caterpillar 7.90	Caterpillar 8.29
	Life insurance	Northwestern Mutual 8.19	Northwestern Mutual 8.22	Northwestern Mutual 8.21	Northwestern Mutual 7.35	Northwestern Mutual 7.96	Northwestern Mutual 8.38	Northwestern Mutual 8.70
	Metal products	Ball 6.88	Gillette 6.81	Gillette 6.94	Gillette 6.81	Ball 7.12	Illinois Tool 7.11	Ball 7.72
	Pharmaceuticals	Merck 8.08	Merck 7.84	Johnson & Johnson 7.95	Johnson & Johnson 7.26	Merck 7.63	Eli Lilly 8.29	Johnson & Johnson 8.26
	Scientific and photographic equipment	Xerox 7.59	Eastman Kodak 7.30	Xerox 8.36	Becton Dickinson 7.28	3M Eastman Kodak 7.51	Xerox 3M 8.13	Xerox 8.31

Used with permission of *Sales & Marketing Management* magazine.

Figure 3.3. The best in seven categories of selling.

Getting Started

Getting started should include the exercise of any and all relevant quality tools. The most obvious of these is brainstorming. The team should brainstorm a list of candidate companies based on the following: its own knowledge; input from customers, process owners, and operators; internal experts; and others who may have relevant process or topical knowledge, even if it is peripheral. These initial efforts often provide more candidates, and more innovative ones, than are expected.

The second step is to conduct some quick search of public domain information sources. These are databases of business periodicals and other sources that a trained information search professional would recommend. Most likely, it is a small subset of the full library of available electronic databases. Logical candidates to search for include those in the topical area of focus or those using the named business process. Therefore, business, engineering, scientific, legal, and other relevant databases would be accessed. The objective is to be focused on the topic or process but at a high search level.

Other logical internal organizations should also be contacted. Even though these organizations may not have direct information, they may have peripheral information that could prove helpful. These would include organizations that watch the outside world, such as public relations, market research, or market intelligence companies. While these organizations rarely have company-specific information at the process level, they often have information on companywide activities that may provide some insight into areas of strength or what the organization believes its success is based on. These are the activities and strengths to reference when making contact to interest the candidate in a benchmarking partnership.

Of course, prior benchmarking studies and contact or trip reports should be used. Accessing prior studies ensures that the information is not duplicated and provides ready references to those who conducted the prior study. Here, background information and named contacts, who may be helpful again, have been uncovered. The contact may later prove very useful to get further internal contacts or referrals, even if not in the same unit. The fact that the company has gone through a benchmarking activity will make it familiar with the process and able to provide assurance that benchmarking is something that should be pursued.

Search by Benchmarking Type

One way to help develop the candidate list is to revisit the definitions of the types of benchmarking. These should provide a rich starting point for organizations worthy of emulation.

Internal This is a comparison among similar operations within the subject's own organization. This should always be the starting point. If there is an internal best practices program or best practices library, it will provide ideas on whom to benchmark. There often are similar operations within an organization set up to perform essentially the same function. The list of examples is endless. There may also be one or more operations that is clearly better by some criteria. A select few of these should be on the candidate list.

There is another important reason for considering internal benchmarking. As has been seen, the prerequisite for conducting effective benchmarking is a focus on the work process. The first step is to document the work process as a baseline for any other comparisons, either competitive, functional, or generic. It is the conduct of internal benchmarking that makes a substantive contribution to documenting the process and validating that it is, in fact, correct. So conducting internal benchmarking should be considered not only to source potential better practices but more importantly to assist in the very necessary step of documenting and verifying the correctness of the process description. What is desired is the documentation of the process in an as-is state—as it is operated, in the field or on the line, not as it appears in procedure manuals.

In addition to the very important phase of process validation, the benefits of considering potential internal operational candidates are many. Most importantly, the relevant data and information are easy to obtain; matters of confidentiality are of less concern since data are from another internal unit; and the measurements are almost always similar, or can be easily recast to be similar, and, therefore, assure a high degree of comparability.

There are often some drawbacks to this type of comparison. The most obvious is that the practices may not represent the best and may, in fact, be far from it. But more seriously, there may be internal biases of "not invented here" that limit perspectives. The extreme of this is when internal organizations are reluctant to share because they believe they have an edge over others. It is the overcoming of that attitude that an internal best practices library is established to combat.

Competitive This is a comparison to the best of the direct competitors in the industry. The second place to develop candidates should be other companies in the same industry, namely the better competitors. This is a requirement. Ultimately the organization will want to know where it stands compared to others in the industry. This understanding will become the basis for some level of competitive advantage or superiority in strategic functions of the business. It will be what the organization wants to leverage to its advantage, and when it comes to practices that do not measure up, either improve them or minimize their effect.

There are often concerns of sharing information within the same industry. The U.S. antitrust laws were established to ensure that information would not be shared that would permit price manipulation to the consumers' disadvantage. Benchmarking should completely disassociate itself from this possibility. How is that done? First, the terms *benchmarking* and *search for best practices* should be used in any approach to a potential benchmarking partner in the same industry. The fact that the Malcolm Baldrige National Quality Award calls for benchmarking should be also pointed to when trying to interest others in the process.

These help place the benchmarking activity in a different perspective. The real basis for benchmarking becoming accepted as an information exchange within the industry is because of the focus on the business processes. This exchange can be accomplished, either because of the detailed level of comparison, or, more likely, because of the fact that the business processes are generic, that is, similar even to others not in the industry. So, here again is another reason for taking the business process approach to benchmarking.

In addition to these good reasons, the benchmarking approach has a natural tendency to stay away from legal concerns. Focusing on business processes and exchanging information on best practices do not involve matters of pricing. Best practices for answering the telephone and taking sales orders or for making machine repairs of a common office device are so removed from pricing and other legal matters that this alone becomes a sound basis for the exchange. In addition to this natural division, however, there should be documentation in these exchanges such that if potential legal matters were raised they could be reviewed for correctness.

Every benchmarking investigation should have some stated purpose that is documented. Also, the way the information will be used should be documented. The statement of purpose and the agenda of topics are part of the documentation for a meeting with a partner. The trip report or meeting findings provide the final documentation of the benchmarking study. It is this *audit trail* that is the final basis on which the information exchange can proceed.

Benchmarking within the industry is still difficult and requires careful consideration. The willingness of others to participate is getting better, primarily because of the Malcolm Baldrige National Quality Award requirements and those of similar state and public sector awards. Ultimately, companies are discovering that competitiveness depends on carefully structured cooperation.

Consider the rising matters of environmental safety and health. Why wouldn't companies want to cooperate to make matters significantly better for the industry and therefore reflect positively on the major players? Extrapolating this to other areas where information can be shared is the correct approach.

The drawback to competitive information exchanges is that other parties may not have practices worth emulating. Because of the insular nature of industries, there is a tendency to continue to look only within the industry. While that approach will identify the competitive gap, there may be other organizations that continue to outperform the same or essentially similar processes. That is why benchmarking cannot stop within the industry. It must look outside for innovative ideas; thus, the need for the next two types of benchmarking, namely functional and generic.

Functional This is a comparison of practices at companies with similar processes in the same function but outside the industry. This should be the third place to source candidate benchmarking partners. It is probably one of the most intense searches, since it is in this class of organizations that the most innovative practices are found.

The classic example is the comparison by Xerox of its practices to those of L. L. Bean. This example is still legion in the minds of many. It is representative of the potential for uncovering best practices.

Xerox sought other companies that had the same function, or nearly the same operation, when judged by its critical characteristics. In this case the picking process for assembling customer orders was examined. Why was this judged to be a similar process? There were two main reasons. First, the process characteristics were the same; that is, the products handled varied widely in size, shape, and handling requirements. Second, and ultimately, this comparison led to a realization that the items would have to be picked manually. The process could not be automated, as originally thought.

The striking finding, however, was that Bean's similar picking process was three times faster than that of Xerox. This was why Xerox put L. L. Bean on the list of candidate benchmarking partners.

Functional benchmarking candidates, while perhaps requiring more effort to source than other candidates, have other advantages that make the search worthwhile. There is more willingness to share data, providing the activity is properly introduced and approached with discipline. Site visits are extremely helpful to see practices firsthand and to gain acceptance. Also, the new practices are more readily accepted and implemented since their discovery was nonthreatening; that is, the new practices do not reflect negatively on the organization, because they were unknown prior to benchmarking.

The principle deficiency of functional benchmarking is that breakthrough practices will be missed because the concentration is on the function and not the process. But that is why the team will need to conduct generic process benchmarking to ensure the sourcing is thorough.

Generic This is the comparison of a work process to that of others who are judged to have innovative processes. This is where the concentration is strictly on the process. It may not be found within the function of the organization conducting the benchmarking, or it may be found in a very dissimilar industry.

The approach is to consider that organizations are run on their processes and that many of those processes must have similar requirements, whether they are a billing operation for an industrial or service firm, a hospital for patients, or a hotel for its guests. Given the documentation of the process under study, a careful review of the key steps in the process should start to develop other candidate organizations that could be benchmarking partners. The team will want to think out of the box, or be innovative in its search.

One such innovative approach is the classic story of benchmarking conducted by a DuPont team. A team from the Remington Division was interested in improving a product to fully satisfy customers. The product under consideration was ammunition shells, which are used in the preeminent product made by Remington, shotguns and rifles. In the traditional approach the team had sourced customer requirements, and one was stated as "smoother, shinier shells" for the ammunition.

Now the DuPont team could have satisfied itself with simply considering the traditional internal, competitive, and perhaps functional benchmarking, and it developed some very worthwhile candidates. But the team went beyond and considered generic processes in other industries. It asked: Who is preeminent in making smoother, shinier shells? With concentration on the "smoother and shinier," it is likely that candidates would have been proposed from the jewelry industry, the silverware industry, the makers of ball bearings, and perhaps others that are developed in this manner. But the companies that the team ultimately settled on were those that make lipstick containers. These were judged to be the leaders in what was not only smoother and shinier but also just happened to have the shape of a shell much like what Remington produced. The team was able to source some better practices to implement in its processes to deliver on the customers' stated requirement.

Now while sourcing candidate companies in this category may seem the most difficult, it is the opportunity to find very innovative practices not implemented anywhere near what could be considered in the industry that is the challenge. Therefore, again, concentrate on the process first. If the DuPont team had not considered the process in its broadest terms, it probably would not have sourced companies in the cosmetics industry. This is what results in true competitive advantage, finding practices not considered by others in the industry.

The difficulty in these findings is that, without some creativity and willingness to try to adapt the practice, this type of comparison will be passed off as not readily transferable. That is where the team will have its greatest challenge but likewise perhaps its greatest breakthroughs for improvement. It is the effective implementation of the best practice that is the key to competitive advantage. It is the creativity that comes from adapting some other best practice to fit the industry that should be stressed.

Consider the Process Requirements

By opportunity area Another place to look for candidate companies will be by opportunity area. This perspective provides another way of thinking about where companies with better practices exist. While there is some overlap with the types of benchmarking, this approach should be conducted with the same interest level to source companies. The objective is to go from the most restrictive view of potential candidates to increasingly relaxing the restrictions to consider the broadest view of sourcing candidates.

In companies with comparable operations These are usually of two types: organizations that either produce the same things or provide the same services or those that have the same process. This is the most restrictive view of potential companies. The concentration is on comparable operations. Those that work the process and who have documented it should be those who can come up with this set of candidates.

With companies in the same industry Next consider companies within the same industry. The challenge here is determining what the appropriate definition of the industry is. For example, Xerox could be considered in the copying or document creation industry. It could also be considered in the office products industry. Because of the high number of electronic components in its products, Xerox could be considered to be in the electronics industry. This last categorization provides a different set of companies with which to compare. In fact, there might be some real logic for the last categorization, because most of the products in the electronics industry require repair on customer premises or in the field. This fact may provide some commonality across processes that could be important from a benchmarking viewpoint.

Where best practices are known to occur This perspective helps the team determine who has best practices and add them to the candidate list. On the surface, this may seem a bit optimistic, if not impossible. On careful reflection, the approach is feasible, because everyone is a customer and everyone makes judgments about products and services. Thus, customers are able to describe the differences between good and bad service. This capability has been conditioned by the ubiquitous how-are-we-doing checklists left in hotel rooms. These elicit feedback from a guest on a product or service much like an exit poll elicits voters' opinions on a candidate or issue.

The fundamental point is that customers are constantly faced with good and bad practices and can discern them. This is a natural capability that must be tapped. How is that done? The only way to successfully describe the approach is by way of example. Several will be explained.

The first example describes the need to improve a billing process. This is usually the end result of the purchase of a product or service. There has to be an invoice created to describe the purchase and document the amount of payment. It can occur for a product like a copier, a service like a hospital stay, or it can even be for the collection of taxes. These types of invoices are familiar documents, and most customers have probably formed some opinion of the practices that produce them.

Now the team concentrating on improving the billing process has a challenge. It will have to specify just what it is that must be improved. The team will have great difficulty trying to benchmark "improve the billing process." This is the key to this approach. Bring more clarity and specificity to the true objective for improving the billing process. It could be that the bills should be more readable, that information should be presented in a more logical format, or the true objective could be to have the least number of errors on invoices. This would be confirmed from customer requirements and subsequent feedback. If, after careful deliberation, the team determines that this last objective is its true task, then it knows where to guide its efforts. Thus, the team will seek organizations with the fewest errors on their documents to be on the candidate list.

No doubt everyone receives documents in his or her daily business and personal life. Consider ones that come from monthly billing processes, such as banks, credit card companies, utility bills, and others. Thus, specific banks or credit card companies could be named to the candidate list.

It is this sort of mental logic, of finding the true objective of the investigation and then asking who is the best at delivering it, that allows benchmarking teams to directly determine where best practices occur. In fact, customers are often the best judges of better practices, although consumers are not consciously thought of in those terms.

Consider ordering from a catalog, an activity that many experience quite often. Some companies require a long litany of information before taking an order. Some more advanced and innovative companies, however, those whom customers have ordered from at least once before, ask that the customers give their zip code and telephone number, or the number over their name on the catalog mailing label. Then these innovative retailers are able to simply confirm existing data and do it effectively, quickly, and with little aggravation to their customers. This approach is becoming a benchmark in the industry because of its efficiency.

Here is one last example of customers as the best judges of best practices. Consider the retail checkout process. This varies from restaurants, grocery stores, department chains, and video rental stores. What if the team was challenged to find the most effective checkout process for the operation of a video store? Perhaps it would start to consider the manual preparation of a bill at a small restaurant, then the preprogrammed item on the menu at a fast food franchise, and then the use of a bar code for identifying an item in a grocery store. Thus, the team could determine that the best practice would be attaching bar codes to all the rental videos. Then the checkout process is based on the use of the bar code.

In dissimilar industries Finally, the team will want to consider dissimilar industries as potentially having best practices. This would be the broadest casting of the net for candidate companies. This approach asks if there might be analogous operations in dissimilar industries. For example, a paint company may want to improve its can-filling operation. It can certainly consider the process in other paint companies and perhaps the filling of a chemical container or an oil can. This is not too much of a stretch of imagination. But wouldn't it be logical to consider a food company's can-filling operations? The gallon food container is the same size as the gallon paint can.

These four ways to source candidate companies are helpful by virtue of taking a different perspective from the traditional types of benchmarking. They should be used to test the innovativeness of the team in its search. Finally, there is one more set of considerations.

Other Considerations to Select Candidate Companies

There is a set of considerations that might be characterized as "ask others" or what others have already determined. These should also be part of the team's deliberations.

World-class citations One of the more prominent of these is the increasing popularity of publications, writing in their functional topical area, to determine through commissioned research who is the best in its class. The publications may have already done the work and have a matrix of who is best. Sometimes the article is a result of an industry review. It might cite the excellent companies, for example, in seven categories of selling or nine industry types. There may be articles on world-class benchmarking candidates or best practice companies. These companies may be cited in books, such as *In Search of Excellence* by Thomas J. Peters and Robert H. Waterman, Jr., or *The 100 Best Companies to Work for in America* by Robert Levering and Milton Moskowitz. Refer to Appendix A for more examples.

It is these articles and citations that the team should consider in developing the candidate list. While these lists may require some level of validation, they serve as a ready reference point for the team.

Award-winning companies This category is a natural one in the current quality pursuit by many companies. The most prominent award is the Malcolm Baldrige National Quality Award. There are, however, other industry or organizational awards that can serve as leading indicators of where best practices occur. These are not only quality awards but citations for products, advertising excellence, and for meeting prescribed standards such as at accredited universities and hospitals.

Citation by knowledgeable individuals This is recognition given by people who watch a particular industry or company such as the financial analysts and perhaps financial institutions who periodically give ratings. These expert watchers can be tapped for candidate companies within their sphere of influence.

Indicators of innovativeness Those companies that have some measure of innovativeness, such as exceptionally high patent awards or larger percent than others spent on research and development, should also be used to source candidates. These measures do not directly determine where or why an organization is best, but they should provide positive and forceful reasons for further research into the organization and possible addition to the candidate list.

Customers queries This is the timeless admonition: When all else fails, ask the customer. This perception is reality. What customers believe is a best practice organization may have more to do with how they deal with it in a general way than a defined best practice in a named process. For example, customers may consider an organization superior because of its image toward the environment. This image does not necessarily reveal a best practice but it does hint at an organization that should be researched.

With the extensiveness of the customer satisfaction measurement systems in place this approach is readily accomplished. Of course, it is not just customers that should be contacted but also suppliers.

The objective of this search for benchmarking partner candidates is to eventually create an industry matrix and select the best of the best practices. This will be covered in chapter 5. But the matrix should consist of rows, representing processes or topics of interest, and columns, representing industry types or specifically named companies or organizations. The matrix contents should be the practices of the best or leading-edge companies.

Conduct a Systematic Search by Named Company

At this point the team now has a list of 50 to 80 companies or other comparative organizations in various industries. Now the task is to boil down the list to the vital few organizations deemed necessary for the detailed, process-to-process benchmarking comparisons. How should that be done? It primarily involves a more detailed search by the now-identified company or organization name on the list of publicly available information. It also involves validating the information from as many perspectives as possible to not only ensure that a company stays on the list, but, also, to document the information about the company and its operations. This will help in the forthcoming contacts and visits.

This approach may vary slightly from study to study depending on the focus of the benchmarking investigation, but it should incorporate at least the following: reviewing and creating a list of resources; enlisting the assistance of a trained information search person, usually a research librarian; and then validating the information learned from several sources to see if there is some consensus for the candidate.

Create a List of Resources

The team needs to catalog the resources that it believes will be productive in refining the candidate list of benchmarking partners. Since the team members know the most about their process, they should also know their potential information sources. There may be periodicals focused on the area of interest. There may have been presentations given at professional association meetings or annual conferences. The annual conferences often have proceedings that document the presentations, or they may have been captured on audiocassette.

The team may be aware of the experts in the field or know how to find them. There may be research organizations that concentrate on the selected topic, and they may have already published relevant information in books and papers. While the topic may not be treated exclusively by a research study there may be information in the report by way of references that will be important to the process or benchmarking topic.

It will be the cataloging of these sources, by the team, that will assist the research librarian. The cataloging provides leads to pursue in the formal search. These leads are useful clues to unique databases that will be searched, or to keyword descriptions that might otherwise be overlooked, or to secondary information held by others but not specifically referenced in the public domain.

Enlist a Research Librarian

Armed with the list of candidate companies and potential sources of information as seen by the knowledgeable team members, a careful search using the expertise of a trained research librarian should now be conducted. Most large firms have some literature search capability. It is most often found in a formal library or with an individual who conducts this activity on a part-time basis. If the capability does not exist internally then the team must look outside the company. Local universities or schools of business would be logical candidates for business-related topics. Even a local public library may be able to assist with some search capacity. As a final option there are organizations who will contract to conduct information searches.

The research librarian should be given as much background on the focus of the benchmarking investigation as possible. This would include the report describing the project from step 1 of the process. The more the librarian knows about the subject, the more easily he or she can identify the specific databases and keywords to access.

Some standard things can also be done. It is easy to request a Dunn & Bradstreet report to confirm recent financial activities. An annual report for publicly held organizations can be requested. These reports can be quite revealing because they are often written to showcase company activities. Therefore, they will highlight key accomplishments or have statements of pride in their text. This obviously translates into where best practices may occur and can be used to interest the organization to become a benchmarking partner. Even if a firm is not required to file an annual report it usually will have some year-end summary of activities that accomplishes the same objective. It is revealing to see the extensiveness of information useful to benchmarking in these company documents. As many know, there are significant details to the annual report in the form of the 10-K reports, which must be filed with the Securities and Exchange Commission. These reports provide excellent information as a starting point to become familiar with the operations of, and potential for, best practices from a benchmarking partner.

The research librarian's major effort is a search of information published and available in the public domain. This means a search of the electronic databases that the librarian believes are relevant. Initially the search can be limited to the most recent two or three years. If no information is forthcoming, or if the quantity is less than expected, the time frame can be extended. It takes six months to a year for an article to be written, published, and then referenced in an electronic database. So the most-promising information derived from this source often must be supplemented with a manual search of the most current publications.

There are over 5000 public databases in the United States alone. So the selection of the appropriate ones to search is best left to the experts. They will know the databases to search and their potential coverage of the benchmarking topic. But it is not just the knowledge of the databases that is important. The cataloging terminology is also best left to experts. This is the selection of keywords against which to search the topical area. Knowledgeable use of keywords can be instrumental in quickly and efficiently finding needed references. A example from this author's experience will confirm the need for some assistance.

Before attempting to write *Benchmarking: The Search for Industry Best Practices That Lead to Superior Performance,* this author felt something of value could be gained if the topic of writing a book was researched, that is to say benchmarked. He was convinced that there were books on how to write a book. Having that type of information would be helpful in effectively writing a technical business text. So the author performed his own keyword search using *how to* and *write a book.* To his astonishment little was found and most information was not relevant. He could not believe that with the volume of books published each year some enterprising acquisitions editor had not documented the experience of working with authors, preparing manuscripts for production, and marketing the product. After much anxiousness the author finally contacted a research librarian and was promptly advised that the correct keyword was *authorship.*

While it is highly recommended that these searches be conducted by an expert, it must be noted that the world of information search is changing dramatically. An interested member of the team can personally search databases for relevant information because they are increasingly placed on CD-ROM and made available to public and private libraries. So major business periodicals can be accessed by the team members with a few instructions on accessing procedures. While there may be some hesitancy to do this, it is highly recommended that at least one member become acquainted with the databases. Then that member may spot related information or keywords that would yield an even more detailed and fruitful search.

Whether the search is conducted by a team member directly, by a trained librarian, or by a combination of the two, the results should yield references to articles, documents, reports, magazines, industry journals, and so on. When combined with a company name and cross-referenced with the topic of focus, the search will provide references to the desired information or to those organizations active in the area and possibly having best practices. This last point is not a given. But by virtue of it being in print the area of focus must have had prominence for some reason. Even if the information is tangential in nature, the author or publication can be contacted for further information or referral assistance.

It must be noted that conducting the search at a library is not an obstacle. Most libraries employ guides to their services. The new world of information search will be outlined for the designated team member. The guides usually describe the services in some detail. They can be thought-starters to remind the team of where information not otherwise considered might be found. They often provide tips for working with the librarian and lists of common information sources.

This careful information search, with the tracking down of leads, while at all times being inquisitive and innovative, is the essence of the researcher's job. It is demanding and challenging and most often quite rewarding. Those who enjoy solving a mystery or a crossword puzzle may get the same level of satisfaction out of a well-conducted search.

Validate the Information

Once the information is found and analyzed it should, to the extent possible, be validated. This means checking the information against several other references. It usually means contacting experts in the field. Editors of publications, authors, experts cited in the text, or other industry-knowledgeable individuals or consultants can be contacted. These individuals, when given the completed research, are quite willing to comment on the company cited or the process mentioned. They may also be sources of additional references not uncovered to date. It is often easier for these individuals to participate in the validation, based on their in-depth experience, than it would be for them to develop the list of candidates.

Refine the Initial List

Armed with the information from the search, the team now needs to evaluate and summarize what is known about a candidate company. On the basis of this information the list should be reduced to an accomplishable set of companies to contact. This is usually three to six. It could, however, depending on the scope of the process being considered, be more. For example, one company would be found best only in certain aspects of the process.

The key is finding any information that would directly reveal or would somehow indicate the existence of best practices. These would be statements of pride confirmed by the search or even direct statements published in a recognized periodical covering the benchmarking topic.

The selection criteria should be used at this stage to determine who should make the cut. A matrix of the process steps by named firm can be used to check off what is known, what to validate, and, therefore, who should remain on the list of benchmarking partners.

Exclude Nonrelevant and Inaccessible Candidates

Selling the company on some of the organizations selected for benchmarking partners may raise some skepticism. Thus, it is often wise to exclude those that appear nonrelevant, inaccessible, or not innovative. While this is often the case, especially for beginning benchmarking activities, some care should be used not to discard opportunities.

The nonrelevant or not comparable issue is primarily brought up as a matter of difference in size. How could the candidate company possibly have better practices since it is a fraction of the partner's size? Or its production or transaction volumes are significantly different and therefore judged not to have the economies of scale? These arguments should be considered. It must be pointed out, however, that the focus is on the process, and when the process steps are judged to do essentially the same thing, then they are relevant.

Accessible information is another consideration. The data and information source is confirmed but the other party will not share. This does occur and a judgment of how valuable the information is must be made before trying to access it. The price may be too high in light of finding essentially the same practices or even better practices elsewhere. Information has a value just like everything else.

The real test, however, is to find innovative practices. The team will want to test its judgment on whether there is any likelihood at all of finding innovative practices. If not, the candidate should be dropped. But it is conceivable that before dropping the candidate a contact would be made to validate the information firsthand, especially given the extensiveness of the search to this point.

In these tests for comparability, accessibility, and innovativeness there are often peripheral considerations that would sway the decision one way or the other. The potential benchmarking partner's stance on delivering high levels of customer satisfaction might be one. If there is a history of being customer sensitive, there is often a strong correlation to being innovative. Are the product characteristics similar, even though the products are not? In the Xerox–L. L. Bean example the specific products were not relevant to the picking process, only their characteristics. They were the underlying consideration for the effectiveness of the picking process and the potential for finding best practices, not the products' equivalency.

Given the team's deliberations on this last point, the candidate list should be reduced to a thoroughly researched, well-prepared, manageable few benchmarking partners. Now a plan is needed for contacting them and obtaining their commitment to participate in a structured information exchange.

Prepare a Request to Visit the Best Companies

The actual steps in conducting a site visit have been well documented and should be followed. But there is some preparation as a result of the revised approach incorporated in this new, updated text that must be considered. The basic steps involve identifying the appropriate contact; contacting the counterpart to discuss a benchmarking visit; and preparing a letter identifying the purpose of the information exchange, indicating what level of preparation has been developed, and identifying the information the subject organization is willing to share.

Three events have happened since 1989 that have greatly increased the ease of contacting others for benchmarking. One, the topic has become much more widely known and prominent in organizations' quality pursuits or continuous improvement activities. The terms *benchmarking* and *best practices* are widely understood and accepted. In 1992 there were over 100 articles on the topic, several books, and one had been translated into several languages. So the person contacting a potential benchmarking partner can capitalize on this knowledge and have some assurances that there will be some level of interest.

The second event has been the establishment of several clearinghouses for information, products, and services on the topic of benchmarking. These are excellent places to make informal contacts or to use their formal bulletin board and networking features to locate and eventually make contacts. The clearinghouses also validate the seriousness of potential partners in their benchmarking activities. If organizations are members of a clearinghouse, that has to indicate some serious level of interest. The clearinghouses also subscribe to a code of conduct that includes protocol and legal and ethical standards. These combined with membership are a convenient way to qualify others that want to conduct benchmarking. If they maintain membership they must have some level of expertise beyond that of a newcomer.

But the third and most prominent event to assist with benchmarking contacts is that a significant number of positions have been created in major organizations that are primarily responsible for benchmarking activities. The volume of activities, either outbound from the organization or inbound from potential partners, has become significant enough that centers of competency, benchmarking managers, or simply some designates have the responsibility to coordinate these activities. There are over 250 prominent U.S. organizations that are members of clearinghouses. Many of these company representatives are the principal contact for benchmarking at their firms. So there is, in addition to all the previous ways of making contact, another way that did not previously exist. Even if no titled position exists, it is still appropriate to ask, "Who is the individual responsible for benchmarking?" when contacting another organization.

Following the initial contact, the two parties must negotiate so that they understand the focus of the activities and determine if, when, how, and with whom the information exchange can take place. These are accepted practices in the benchmarking community today. The follow-up to the conversation is a letter outlining the purpose of the visit and a proposed agenda of topics and confirming the results of the conversation.

The need for these preliminary documented arrangements cannot be stressed enough. If at some future time there were inquiries about the nature of the information exchange, then there would be adequate documentation to show that the contact, exchange, and use of data and information were appropriate, legal, and within normally accepted business practices.

It is always appropriate, if not a major opportunity in the negotiations, to mention what level of preparation has been developed. For if a significant business process has been documented, as is recommended, then this is a major attraction and reason why others will agree to benchmarking exchanges. The potential partners know that they stand an excellent chance of discovering some innovative practices, or gaining some important insight into their own process, as a result of the detailed process documentation.

The final item discussed is what information will be exchanged. What are the parties prepared to exchange? There may be some topics that are not candidates for discussion, and that fact alone is acceptable in the benchmarking community today. There may be common interest in the proposed subject, and that is usually the case. But there may be interest in one topic by the contacting organization and another interest in the organization being contacted. These do happen and are part of the reason for negotiation and documentation of the contact.

Summary

- Consider where best practices occur.
- Access primary information sources.
- Develop candidate selection criteria.
- Create a candidate list.

- Conduct a systematic search by selected company and topic.
- Refine and reduce the initial list.
- Exclude nonrelevant, inaccessible, and not innovative organizations.
- Prepare a request for visit.

CHAPTER 4

Data Collection

Subtle and insubstantial the expert leaves no trace;
divinely mysterious, he is inaudible.

- Introduction
- Create a Data Collection Plan
- Research Internal Sources
- Research Public Domain Sources
- Research Outside Experts
- Research Benchmarking Clearinghouses and Centers
- Conduct Original Research
- Breaking Down Barriers to Sharing Information
- Time and Resources to Conduct Benchmarking
- Conduct Benchmarking Site Visits
- Create a Site Visit Summary Report
- Follow a Code of Conduct
- Summary

Introduction

This chapter deals with one of the most extensive steps in the 10-step benchmarking process, namely data and information collection. It is the essence of benchmarking. In any investigation the team must be interested not only in data but also the sources of it. The team is also concerned with what sources there are, why they are useful, and how to access them.

This chapter has two objectives. One is describing the types of data and information sources and the second is how to access them for benchmarking purposes. The most knowledgeable people to access the information are trained resource librarians. They are the search experts. Working with these individuals is covered in chapter 3.

The generic process chart can be used again to catalog information sources. For example, what sources are inputs to a process? These are process-knowledgeable individuals such as experts in the field. Who would be considered from the process? Those with direct information, such as classification schemes, should be consulted. Who would be considered if the output side of the process was examined? These might be organizations responsible for effective performance. Lastly, what results, performance measures, or information sources should be examined? These would be organizations that collect, analyze, and maintain performance statistics.

In this fashion the team has used the process chart to start thinking about information sources. Although this is not a conventional means to come up with these sources, it could provide a way of finding some innovative ones. Then the benchmarking team can turn to other ways to source information.

Create a Data Collection Plan

Some careful thought should be given to the data collection approach. It takes time and money. The team should determine which data sources are likely to be most productive given the limited resources available. Therefore, one approach is to go from the easy to the difficult, which generally means going from the inexpensive to that which requires extensive resources and time. This approach results in the team first considering all internal sources of information, which includes electronic and public databases.

The second set of information sources is external. It can be extensive. The sources include the wide range of experts in the field and those organizations who by their focus have special knowledge of products and services. This later group has secondary information, meaning it is a source to a source. Frequently, it is a supplier to a benchmarking partner.

The third and final category of information sources is the most difficult. It includes custom-tailored original research on the topic, which requires special design, development, execution, and analysis. It can be quite time-consuming and costly.

The team should array the potential sources in each of these three categories. Then it should review each source and decide on its possible value and contribution to the study and any potential drawbacks or problems in using it. These tasks will guide the team's efforts as well as serve as a basis of discussion with the information search professional. Thus, this matrix will enable the team to prioritize its search.

The scheme for approaching the information search, that is, going from easily accessible information to the most difficult, is entirely new. An expanded understanding of the information sources is also summarized.

Research Internal Sources

A thorough canvassing of internal sources is imperative. It is always assumed that when information sources are mentioned they primarily mean external sources. Yet it is astounding what information of a direct, but more likely indirect, nature exists within the organization.

Process owners Using the process focus, it is logical to ask the process owners and those that work it what they already know and what information sources they believe should be tapped. Organizations archive information either formally in company-mandated file retention, or informally, squirreled away in individuals' desks, bookshelves, and file cabinets. The basic principle is that those who are closest to the process are the most knowledgeable, and they should be tapped first.

Functional experts Functional experts are those individuals who have specialized knowledge by virtue of their position in the organization. They may be distribution, process, or industrial engineers or analysts that have the responsibility to continually improve the operation. Because of this responsibility, the functional experts stay in touch with developments in their field through periodicals, conferences, and professional associations. They may participate in the team's benchmarking activities. At a minimum, these experts should be asked for their insight on what information sources to tap. There may be special studies of customer service or industry comparisons of different processes that they may have already participated in or prepared that will give the team new insight.

Networks and historical files With the rise in interest in benchmarking there has been a significant increase in the number of databases to archive historical information. Thus, new information is available to a wide audience that uses electronic networks. Frequently, these networks consist of designated individuals to source information into and out of their organization.

These databases—or more appropriately, these knowledge bases, because they are more populated with information rather than data—have primarily been created to ensure that best practices are documented, shared, and saved for future reference. These knowledge bases can be quite extensive and permit full text searches and cross-referencing by industry, process, and company name. They serve as significant repositories of benchmarking information. They are usually unique and developed within organizations with retrieval software. Provided the benchmarking documents are created electronically, they can be stored quite quickly, usually requiring only a click to an icon representing the software tool.

In addition to the knowledge bases, there are electronic networks and people networks of professional benchmarking individuals. These are both internal and, increasingly, external. The electronic networks permit broadcast messages to a distribution list of knowledgeable individuals. If these link many professionals, the capability for sourcing information quickly and on a timely basis is substantial. These networks can be extremely useful to source who has or who is working with a named company that the team wants to benchmark.

Often these networks keep electronic file drawers of the network operation. These store copies of the network agendas, meeting minutes, benchmarking study status reports, success stories, and other materials that would prove useful in an information exchange. These could include the following: a bibliography of all that has been written on the topic of benchmarking; references to all materials available internally for conducting benchmarking or awareness and team training; an alerting service of items of interest to benchmarking professionals; and a table of contents of the key periodicals published about benchmarking and used to scan for articles of interest.

Internal networks of designated individuals who represent their organizations for benchmarking purposes are another significant information source. Generally there are two types of internal networks: informational and operational. Many large firms have a semiannual internal benchmarking seminar. This takes the form of a structured day intended to keep interested parties informed about the type of benchmarking underway, to showcase success stories, to cover topics of interest to the benchmarking community, and to keep participants at the forefront of benchmarking techniques. These meetings often include invited guest speakers to cover new ideas or experiences. The purpose is primarily information exchange.

There is also an operational network to update ongoing benchmarking investigations, to coordinate company visits, and to share contacts so companies will not inadvertently be visited by the same firm several times, perhaps even for the same topic. The operational network provides assistance and strives for success of benchmarking team studies. There have been countless instances where the existence of such a network has prevented overlap, has uncovered a potentially sensitive issue with a study, or has allowed two functional organizations to pursue a mutually worthwhile benchmarking investigation. The network also operates in a mutually supportive fashion in that ideas and suggestions can be solicited from the members on how to tackle a particularly difficult benchmarking situation.

Research Public Domain Sources

Public domain information sources are researched through an internal library capability or by contracting a service bureau.

Libraries Access to public data and information has been significantly enhanced with the substantial conversion of the old card catalogs to electronic databases. There are over 5000 electronic databases in the United States alone. Even though the rest of the world lags in this capability, it still should not be too long before most information searches anywhere in the world will be conducted electronically. These databases will become increasingly important simply because of their extensiveness. Benchmarking information may take the form of traditional articles, journal references, and books, but it may also be in other mediums including videotape, audiocassette, software, and CD-ROM. It is only feasible to maintain access to these nontraditional sources through library services and electronic means because their appearance is so random.

Service bureaus If a library is not available with the capabilities desired, then there are external service bureaus that will contract for searches on a particular topic. These agencies are often services of some of the large database owners. In addition, there are firms that specifically market a benchmarking or search capability. These often have special capabilities, like access to government publications and an understanding of government organizations. They can provide a turnkey search capability for benchmarking teams.

Research Outside Experts

There are several external organizations and individuals that provide excellent data and information. These include consultants, industry watchdogs, financial analysts, professional associations, and software providers. But one that has gained some prominence in recent years is the article in functional publications that cites companies with best practices.

Articles As noted in chapter 3, with the prominence of benchmarking there has been a significant increase in the number of articles in which benchmarking is described and examples of its application are given. More importantly, the publications also list companies and organizations that have been cited as being the best at what they do. A compilation of the known articles is included in Appendix B.

For example, articles in *Business Week* (November 30, 1992) cite 55 companies in 14 categories under "America's World-Class Champs." *Industry Week* (July 15, 1991) cites 56 companies in 16 categories listed as world-class benchmarking candidates worth researching and emulating. The *World Executives Digest* (May 1991) lists 44 companies in 15 categories as "who should you copy." These are some world-class benchmarking candidates. *Electronic Business* (October 1991) lists 15 companies in six major categories as the "best of the benchmarks." *Transportation* and *Distribution Magazine* (October 1992) lists 63 companies in 16 categories as "benchmarking stars." These are companies that are considered best in class by category. In a landmark article, *Financial World* (September 17, 1991) lists 20 companies that are cited as "best practice companies" with a description of why they are expected to be standard setters for the 1990s. This shows innovative thinking in establishing world-class operating standards.

In the June 1989 issue of *Sales & Marketing Management*, an even more detailed article describing the "best in seven categories of selling" appeared. This was unique in that the seven categories were arrayed against nine industries and cited 21 companies. *Distribution Magazine* (March 1992) published 29 companies cited as "the best" in six distribution or logistics activities.

Obviously, these article are going from the citation of companies that are seen as the best in a major functional area, to those that are best in the functional operations, or more accurately, the business processes. These articles will continue to appear and will be expanded to include foreign publications. Already there is a study about "Britain's Best Factories," (*Management Today* (UK), November 1992). Also, a number of foreign countries conduct what is known as *interfirm comparisons*. While these lists should not be the only search the team conducts, they are good starting points, and they do provide some idea of who may have best practices. Using these articles is another way to get the team jump-started in its deliberations.

Consultants Consultants continue to provide a source of information very important to benchmarking. But their role has changed, and the pool of potential consulting organizations is also different than several years ago.

In the past it was common to turn benchmarking studies over to consultants for them to conduct from beginning to end. It was a turnkey assignment. Part of the reason for this was to maintain the participants' confidentiality. But that has changed in recent years. With the focus on business processes, and the benchmarking study conducted by the process owners and operators, consultants are still used, but in a support capacity. This is more than just a useful role. Consultants have been helpful in developing lists of candidate companies, in preparing to visit them, and in making contacts as a result of prior client relationships. Of course, consulting firms have the ability to quickly deploy resources to a project such that the overall time line is reduced.

The profile of consulting firms has changed as well. The earliest firms used for benchmarking were those from the tax, audit, and management consulting field. These firms have prospered and a number of them have undertaken specifically focused benchmarking consulting lines of business. Many of these are well run and a number are prominent in adding to the body of knowledge on benchmarking and its improvement.

Today, however, there are several small firms that promote themselves as experts in benchmarking. These provide another avenue to conduct benchmarking studies with specialists. What their capabilities are can only be vouched for by their clients. But the significant addition to this profile is the number of individuals who can assist with benchmarking. Because many individuals have been affected by corporate right sizing, there is now a pool of well-qualified benchmarking experts available. These individuals have the background and experience to share with others that are just starting or that need assistance. These professionals are an exceptional resource, and they are indicative of the need for a network to catalog their talent and provide ready access to them.

Watchdogs

As noted in chapter 3, there are a number of watchdog groups that serve as excellent information sources. These include the following organizations.

Analysts Their reports include the latest financial analyses of companies and brief abstracts on a particular industry. Often analysts have special knowledge of the firms they follow. It is common practice to give these company watchers tailored briefings on company operations. These may include new product capabilities, new market assessments, and company strengths. This unique knowledge can be tapped to confirm exemplar operations while not violating any information trusts.

Professional associations The capabilities of professional associations continue to provide excellent assistance to benchmarking activities. Their interest in supporting these activities appears to have intensified. Associations are being asked by their membership to conduct seminars on benchmarking. A number of research topics undertaken by associations are focused on uncovering best practices. Their role as channels to specific functional information and as representatives of their area of expertise in clearinghouses is also expected to increase.

A growing number of annual conferences, seminars, and workshops sponsored by professional organizations now include tracks on benchmarking. This simply is a reflection of the association reacting to its members to fulfill their requirements. Many of these workshops are quite well done, because they concentrate on delivering case histories of benchmarking studies that are functionally related to the association's purpose.

In addition, selected associations are undertaking commissioned research to uncover and publish best practices in the association's area of expertise. This research often cites companies that are deemed to be the best in class. Associations, by virtue of their commitment to a business function, topic, or area of expertise, have the insight to determine the key processes that make up their activity. On that basis they are increasingly becoming the contact point for a *center of excellence* that will be cited by benchmarking clearinghouses. Appropriately, many association presentations and applications show up in conference proceedings.

On the basis of a process classification scheme, a clearinghouse will be able to do the following: determine which association is principally responsible for the process being benchmarked; assure that the association will be able to decompose the process into its elemental processes; determine where in the association there are experts in those elemental processes; and cite companies that are deemed to have best practices.

In an allied way there are conferences, forums, and external seminars organized by professional meeting firms, consultants, and educational institutions. While these do not have the same charter as professional associations, in that they organize seminars on a topical area of interest and they have no long-term commitment to the topic, they do provide a forum for others to learn and they have conducted many seminars on benchmarking. These typically consist of a cross section of presenters giving their view on the topic or covering some application. They often include a consultant who conducted the benchmarking and also a representative from the firm to validate and testify to the worth of the work.

Software providers Software providers are a unique information source. With the heavy computerization of one's personal and business life there is practically a software application for almost everything, including benchmarking. Once the team understands its identified process, it should conduct a concerted search for software that supports the process. The software providers should be asked for information and demonstrations of their applications. But more importantly they should be asked for client references; that is, those who use the software effectively. In this fashion the software becomes a conduit for locating leading-edge firms that have best practices for the subject process.

Research Benchmarking Clearinghouses and Centers

The newest information source for benchmarking assistance is the clearinghouses or benchmarking centers. These central repositories for information, products, and services on benchmarking have emerged since only 1992. There are several clearinghouses; most are associated with not-for-profit organizations. Others are topic or data specific. Many people incorrectly assume that because these agencies have *clearinghouse* in the title they are only databases of benchmarking examples, best practices, and excellent companies. A correct understanding of their capabilities would have probably called these agencies *benchmarking centers,* because they offer a wide variety of products and services for all benchmarking professionals—from beginners through experts, from large companies to small, and for industries and not-for-profit organizations.

One evaluation of clearinghouse services is shown in Figure 4.1. Here services are compared to those of potential near-term and long-term users and by several categories of use. This evaluation helps to determine the center's core services and to justify membership or affiliation with the group. Actually, this tool can be used to evaluate any outside service.

	Near term (One–two years)	Long term (Two–five years)
Will get	User's guide	
Minor use		Contact list Electronic network Member meetings Publications
Expected use	Common interest groups Networking Code of conduct Screening Conferences Assessment	Database Contact service Resource partnerships
Other benefits	Reduced costs Public relations Conspicuousness	
Currently available	Training Referral Information searches Consulting Speakers	

Figure 4.1. Evaluation of clearinghouse or center's products and services.

There is precedent for these organizations. The lists of best manufacturing plants and interindustry comparisons were already mentioned. There are also special topic information repositories, such as the Saratoga Institute, the Strategic Planning Institute, and the Benchmarking Exchange. But the closest analogy is the U.S. Navy's Best Manufacturing Practices program.

A number of the products and services available through clearinghouses will be highlighted and commented on since it is nearly impossible to provide a compendium of all. It is up to the team to decide whether a clearinghouse or center will be of value to the team's specific benchmarking needs. The following products and services are covered: information, networking, benchmarking, partnerships, outreach, and research.

Information These services normally cover information search; advisory and referral; data, or more accurately knowledge bases; library resources; and process classification schemes. While the objective is to have the center become a repository and to have a knowledge base of best practices, that will only come with time as participants conduct benchmarking and donate best practice abstracts under a controlled access security system. In the meantime the center can document the extensive case histories already in the public domain. Over time a best practices library will emerge where individuals can, on the basis of a process nomenclature or classification, search for anything written about who has and what are the known best practices for a process.

A major capability for the center is to have this process classification scheme for member use. The SIC code of business processes is a starting point for the following tasks.

- Determine what participants want to benchmark.
- Clarify process definitions and boundaries.
- Become the basis for coding all information.
- Have the ability to access information quickly.
- Become the hierarchical scheme to breakdown processes such that they may be compared across dissimilar industries and organizations.

Information searching, advisory, and referral services are especially important to those organizations that do not have ready access to these through their own libraries or benchmarking team activities.

Networking Networking can take many forms: electronic; bulletin board contact; common interest groups or consortia; meetings;

speakers' lists; and benchmarking professionals who provide training, have materials, consult, and are knowledgeable of the code of conduct for the ethical and legal conduct of benchmarking. Of these networking choices, the ability to contact others electronically, which at the early stages of use would be limited to other clearinghouse members, will increasingly become one way to conduct more efficient benchmarking studies rather than putting teams on airplanes. Thus, electronic benchmarking should provide substantial benefits as it becomes more widespread and based on an agreed-to process approach and classification scheme.

Second only to the electronic conduct of benchmarking exchanges are specifically designed consortia, round table, or common interest groups. These are organized to conduct benchmarking for the benefit of the participants and to eventually populate the knowledge base. While the main participants, again, are the center's members, it is conceivable that others, having practices worth emulating, will be invited to participate. This activity, sponsored and facilitated by the center, makes participation easy for some organizations because they will operate under an agreed code of conduct and rules of confidentiality.

A significant capability is the center's code of conduct. Developed and approved by members, the code should cover protocol and ethical and legal matters. This provides a set of rules for member benchmarking and becomes a known standard for how to treat one another. The code also provides a mechanism for qualifying the experience level of others who want to benchmark. All that the contacted organization has to do is inquire whether the other party subscribes to the code.

Benchmarking The center can provide a wide range of assistance in the actual conduct of benchmarking investigations. Among these would be the following: screening; contacts; facilitation; and consulting and reference manuals on several aspects of benchmarking. These are developed for members and include the status of benchmarking, the management of benchmarking, the major trends in benchmarking, and an annual report on the center's activities.

The ability of the center to screen candidates to see if they subscribe to the center's approach could be a major capability benefiting firms already inundated by benchmarking requests. These organizations could take the position that they either donate a major portion of their benchmarking findings to the center or participate in common interest groups. Then, those interested should first access and understand that information before requesting face-to-face meetings.

The reports about the current status and future developments in benchmarking will also become a major capability for a center. It would then become the source for benchmarking information for a wide range of participant expertise, especially those new to the topic, small organizations only able to commit moderate resources, and those expanding into other areas beyond manufacturing and service industries.

Partnerships The center should be viewed as a *clearinghouse of clearinghouses.* That is, it should not attempt to duplicate other centers of excellence, but should know of them and maintain contacts with them, so they can provide referrals when appropriate. Central to this effort is a directory of the other organizations and their capabilities. The other organizations, associations, or centers of excellence could expect contacts from the center. This mechanism, while still in early development, is the starting point to a national clearinghouse of experts on any topic or best practice for a given process.

Outreach Outreach covers all that the center does to promote, provide a forum for, and develop an understanding of benchmarking. These activities include conferences, publications, and training. These forums are organized activities where individuals interested in benchmarking gather, learn, and network. This is the center equivalent of a firm's internal network meetings.

Publications are another resource, especially if the center is to become the central source. It should then be able to document the relevant benchmarking materials. These are extensive and include books, articles, proceedings, videotapes, audiocassettes, and software, to name only a few.

The center should also provide training to those who want to learn the steps of the process but cannot afford internal training. Relevant material includes the steps in the process, the management of benchmarking, and advanced benchmarking tools.

Research Lastly, the center is the focal point of benchmarking research. Investigations should be conducted on the members' behalf on how benchmarking will be effectively practiced in the future. Members' ideas need to be cataloged, evaluated, prioritized, and recommended for further investigation. Such a research approach could then have the actual investigation conducted on a collaborative basis from proposals solicited from consultants, academics, or others. They would contribute funding for the privilege of attribution, and later presentation at conferences, and for having their organization associated with benchmarking.

Having a research strategy that would continually source better benchmarking ideas is the lifeblood of a center. The research contribution of the center would be funded by selling the reports and sponsoring workshops on the topic.

Conduct Original Research

The conduct of original research is the last way to source information and the most difficult to perform. It requires the most resources to define the project, conduct the search, analyze the data, and prepare the findings. It also requires the most time to complete. Therefore, it should be approached with care. The telling usefulness of original research is as if a pro forma set of final comparisons, charts, graphs, and cause-and-effect and force field diagrams could be prepared and agreed to before the actual project were launched. This would significantly ensure agreement on the value of the research and assure that the customer's requirements were met.

Breaking Down Barriers to Sharing Information

Major barriers to sharing information exist. Organizations believe that they do not need to be assessed against some excellence standard. They don't believe they should look outside their firms, much less their industry. They also don't believe they can learn from others. Often these firms believe they are the best. These barriers need to be overcome if information on best practices is going to be shared through benchmarking.

One major influence that has removed some barriers to information sharing is the existence and proliferation of quality awards, most notably the Malcolm Baldrige National Quality Award. Organizations now recognize that an internal assessment against the award criteria is an unbiased way to determine where they stand compared to others, and where they are in their quality improvement program. Pursuing the awards, either explicitly or implicitly, requires a willingness to share. That is because benchmarking is used to establish the standard for comparison— the benchmark. The number of these awards at the national, state, city, and regional level is increasing. Furthermore, they are created to encourage various segments of the economy, including the federal government and health care and education institutions, to compete for the awards.

The conduct of benchmarking requires organizations to share. It also requires concentration on the process and, increasingly, has organizations look outside their industry to find best practices. The feedback received from the pursuit of quality awards and the success or failure of achieving them are substantively based on benchmarking.

Organizations often need some motivation to involve individuals to look outside their firms or industries. This is often done by expecting that the investigation will be done and then requiring that the results be reported. This is accomplished from the top, down into the organization, by requiring that benchmarking be included in the business plans. From the bottom of the organization comes the need to improve and the better ideas on how to improve. Many internal idea barrels are currently empty.

When others are asked to participate in a benchmarking study, a significant information-sharing barrier is removed if the partners know that the process has been documented. This presents a level of detail, documentation, and understanding about a process that participants recognize as assurance of gaining some insight to the process and of having a good chance of finding better practices.

It has been said that one can be skeptical, but cynics are not allowed. How is skepticism overcome? The most successful way is to get the process owners and operators involved in the benchmarking. Under the conditions of a well-structured benchmarking visit, it is persuasive to bring selected individuals. This is especially so when visiting noncompeting organizations, because in those situations those owning the process are not threatened. Visitors can start to consider the possibilities and look out of their box.

It is essential that these not be feel-good trips. They must be structured, learning exercises. They will need careful staging, participant preparation, and debriefing to capture observations and gain consensus on what was seen and what could be implemented. Given these conditions this is a most powerful way, and perhaps the only way, that the skeptics will be convinced.

The greatest information-sharing barrier breakdown, however, should be the nagging concern that the organization may not be the best and, in fact, may not even be at parity with others. The fear of not having a competitive advantage or niche should drive the need for breakthrough thinking, development of new and innovative ideas, and the pursuit of the best. While it is true that organizations have talented employees, and they may come up with some innovative practices, it has been the experience of benchmarking that there is also a need to share in order to source additional good ideas. In fact, the combination of innovative practices found through benchmarking and creative implementation by talented process users is the most powerful reason to share information.

Time and Resources to Conduct Benchmarking

Invariably in discussions on benchmarking will come questions on the time line to conduct the investigation and the resources required. These are not easy questions to answer because the scope of the benchmarking study may be large and include several processes. It may also be quite focused. Thus, the resources would be scaled accordingly.

There is a norm for the size of a benchmarking team, however, that has gained some acceptance. For a reasonably well-defined process, say the picking process in a warehouse for assembling customers' orders, the usual team would be made up of three individuals working approximately one-third of their time during 9 to 12 months. Part of the reason for the elapsed time is that while it is possible to do some steps of the benchmarking process in parallel, most of the steps are sequential. That is, what to benchmark must be determined before whom to benchmark, and collecting data follows that. In fact, there is no guarantee that those whom are selected as benchmarking partners will have the availability to host visits on the schedule that the benchmarking team wants. For these reasons the time and resource commitment described is an approximation.

Can the resources be scaled down? Of course! Benchmarking can be conducted by individuals. They can make observations at others' sites over time and develop a list of perceived best practices. This activity can even be done on a part-time basis. Many senior managers conduct some informal benchmarking when they visit with peers in other organizations. But these rarely develop the depth of understanding and detailed knowledge about best practices from a team effort.

Obviously, the resources can also be scaled up. There have been instances of benchmarking teams made up of eight to 18 individuals. But these are generally for several critical processes covering multiple functions.

Conduct Benchmarking Site Visits

Readers are encouraged to read the section on site visits from *Benchmarking: The Search for Industry Best Practice That Lead to Superior Performance.* There is little that is new since 1989, but the conduct of site visits is so important that it should at least be reviewed and summarized. There is new information on handling contacts and that was covered in chapter 3. The key components of a site visit are shown in Figure 4.2.

Many times it is helpful to have two standard documents available for site visits: a who-we-are document and a set of standard questions that the unit would want to know of any benchmarking partner. The who-we-are document covers basics, such as an overview of the company and function, organization charts, descriptions of major functions or responsibilities, maps, and any other company literature deemed appropriate, such as an annual report.

Site visit planning
- Arrange meeting date.
- Send meeting confirmation letter and agenda.
- Confirm meeting attendees and company contacts.
- Prepare process documentation or questionnaire.
- Prioritize questions and answer for own organization.
- Access existing studies, both internal and external.
- Profile all relevant information on company visiting.
- Review code of conduct and guidelines.
- Consider benchmarking in own city as a trial run.

Site visit conduct
- Confirm agenda and facility tour.
- Determine who will ask the questions.
- Cover process and questions.
- Use questionnaire to check completeness.
- Arrange for a note-taking scribe.
- Observe operation firsthand.
- Arrange for follow-up if necessary.

Post–site visit activities
- Debrief team and gain consensus on observations.
- Send thank-you letter.
- Prepare trip report.
- Distribute findings report to affected parties.

Figure 4.2. Conduct of a benchmarking site visit.

Many organizations are not only increasing their own benchmarking activities but they are also experiencing increased numbers of incoming benchmarking teams from other companies. In this case some understanding of the effective way to handle incoming and outgoing benchmarking requests is necessary. This can be in the form of a set of descriptive guidelines or a flowchart of the anticipated steps. Examples are shown in Figures 4.3a and 4.3b.

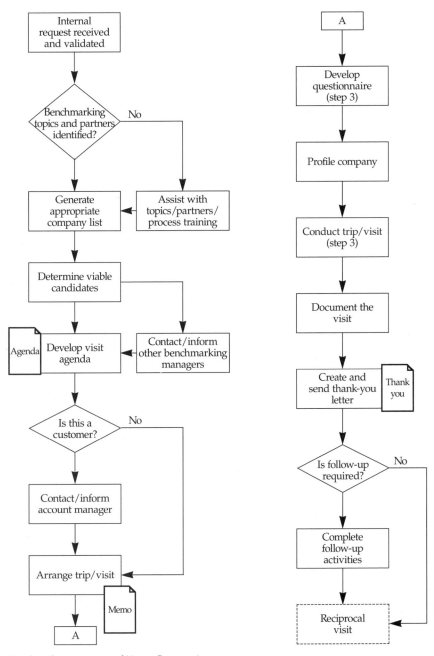

Used with permission of Xerox Corporation.

Figure 4.3a. Benchmarking process flow—internal requests.

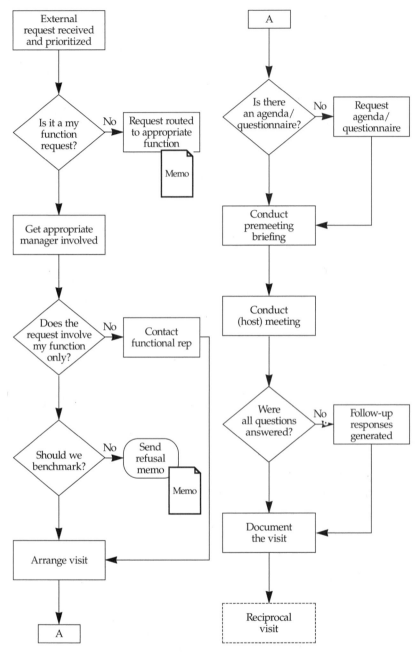

Figure 4.3b. Benchmarking process flow—external requests.

A standard questionnaire is also helpful so that individual teams will all return with the same questions asked in a common format. Most often, the questions are those covered in a who-we-are document.

Create a Site Visit Summary Report

A site visit summary report can be the traditional written text in a chapter-by-chapter format with an executive summary. This would normally cover the following: introduction and background; key assumptions; investigation findings, including a comparison of internal and external practices; assessment of the opportunities; financial implications; recommendations; conclusions; and exhibits.

With the emergence of the quality movement there are alternative ways of reviewing progress and summarizing projects. The primary mechanism is the storyboard, as mentioned in chapter 2. This is a way to reduce, to a concise picture-and-word description, the entire project on a single sheet of paper. The storyboard usually includes the following: makeup of the team; reason for its existence or needed improvement; focus of the benchmarking study (an identified process); companies benchmarked; key measures selected and other facts supporting the investigation; process-to-process analysis and documentation of the best practices; solution and planned changes; expected results; and impact on priorities and next steps.

This concise picture of approximately six to eight quadrants of chart, composed of both schematic drawings and textual summaries, allows the team to summarize the project in a quick fashion. The storyboard can be used to stress key points for formal presentations and reviews. It can also be used as a single-page status report.

Software to Assist in Benchmarking Documentation

In addition to the wide variety of mediums already used to document benchmarking—including the written page, videotape, audiocassette, and training materials—software is emerging. There are several reasons why software is a logical extension to other mediums and why its prominence is expected to grow. Among software's benefits are its ability to systematically gather data, to provide ready reference to the correct procedure and key points for conducting benchmarking investigations, and to automatically prepare comparisons and status or final reports.

With the advent of the portable PC it is common to take it on benchmarking visits. The ability to quickly reference the key considerations about any of the process steps is a significant capability for the team who wants a ready reference in the field. It is conceivable that quick reference guides on some of the more important topics, such as the conduct of a site visit or the preparation of a questionnaire, could be programmed for easy access and as quick reminders of key learning and major fail points. In this fashion the team would always have its bible available.

One of the more onerous tasks in conducting team activities is to capture the work output in an administratively effective fashion. Participants are too familiar with documenting the team's activities on wall charts and then having to reproduce or type them for analysis and filing purposes. A software application could make capture of the team's deliberations straightforward and could go a long way to bringing some structure and discipline to the activity. This assures consistency of not only approach but also results and replication. The software often contains a computerized version of the charts and matrices commonly used to capture benchmarking data and information. With headings and keywords already inserted they would be road maps for the team to follow. At any point, a question about why this item, why this step, or where is this leading could be answered by help menus.

Given that the data and information were gathered with some structure, they can now be compared, analyzed, and displayed with some structure. Processes would be documented consistently; process-to-process comparisons would be complete; summaries of comparisons across several benchmarking partners could be made; and the display of data could become automatic in bar, pie, and trend charts. It is possible that the end result would reflect itself in a storyboard summary of the team's efforts.

While the software application to benchmarking activities will take time to fully develop, it is a logical extension to use this important quality tool. Other quality tools are being converted to software and setting the precedent. Combined with various other mediums, software makes a powerful mechanism for management briefings and awareness, team training and learning, and the assurance that a level of discipline will be brought to benchmarking activities to assure consistent and replicable results.

Follow a Code of Conduct

It is imperative that benchmarking teams follow a code of conduct. Several versions exist. Individual companies and organizations have guidelines for information exchange. Several external organizations have codes for the conduct for their members' activities. These options are available for others to use as models.

Teams need a code as a ready reference to the appropriate conduct of their activities. The guidelines should cover three areas: protocol, legal matters, and ethical concerns. One code of conduct is available from the International Benchmarking Clearinghouse (IBC). Those teams that need such a document should conduct their own search and tailor it to their needs. More details and the address of IBC are in the chapter 6 section titled "Develop Guidelines."

Benchmarking professionals have gradually developed a protocol for their activities. This includes the way contacts will be made, the preparation and negotiation of agendas, the confidentiality of data exchanged, and the courtesies before, during, and after visits. One accepted guideline would be that information obtained from another organization would not be shared with others or presented in public forums without prior consent of the origin organization. This only makes good sense. If information is going to be exchanged, the parties need to know the level of confidentiality. Additional information-sharing guidelines include the following:

- Document intent and results.

- Follow established protocol.

- Justify the reasons and have written objectives.

- Document actions taken and how they benefit customers.

- Follow a code of conduct.

- Incorporate process into internal guides for benchmarking.

In a similar fashion the parties need to know what legal constraints are placed on them during their information exchange. This generally means no discussions of prices or market and no information that would allow one to directly construct pricing or market information. This is avoided by concentrating on the business processes. Most discussions of processes naturally stay away from matters of pricing and markets.

It is appropriate to have, as part of the protocol between the participants, a written set of objectives and a written agenda for the information exchange. This provides an audit trail for future reference.

Ethical matters also need attention. The ground rule should be that information should not be asked for if the organization is not willing to share it in turn. *Don't ask for what you are not willing to share.* Also, all parties should be aboveboard and candid about the purpose of the exchange and should appropriately represent themselves and their organizations. One way to do this is to use the accepted terminology of benchmarking.

These are sound bases on which to get agreement for an information exchange. In addition to there being internal guides and perhaps guidelines for dealing with outsiders—the most common being the press—the best policy is to consider a situation. If there was a report of a benchmarking exchange in a publication, would there be any reason for concern? This is the acid test of any ethical consideration on benchmarking.

Summary

- Create a data collection plan.
- Research internal sources.
- Search public domain sources.
- Research outside experts.
- Search benchmarking clearinghouses.
- Conduct original research.
- Consider the time and resources to conduct the study.
- Break down barriers to information sharing.
- Conduct site visits to best practice companies.
- Create a site visit report.
- Follow a code of conduct.

CHAPTER 5

Analyze the Performance Gap

*A general who wins a battle makes many calcula-
tions in his temple before the battle is fought.*

- Introduction
- Tools Useful in Process-to-Process Comparisons
- Display Data for Ease of Analysis
- Decide Which Practices Produce the Best Results
- Combine Best-of-the-Best Work Practices from All
  Observations
- Validate Best Practices
- How to Recognize Superior Practices
- How Best Practices Emerge
- Recommendations and Approaches to Implement Best
  Practices
- Summary

Introduction

It is useful to put the gap analysis into perspective by discussing a few analogous examples. Of course, the most traditional gap analyses are financial ones. Typically, quarterly or annual earnings are reported. The comparison is to the prior year or month. Most internal presentations are variations on this theme because management is constantly interested in change and is always searching for ways to improve. So there should be no mystery on how to conduct a gap analysis because there are many examples to learn from and to adopt. Now, however, analysts need to be creative and innovative.

There are examples of analyses that are closely related to benchmarking and are, therefore, instructional. One is from a government application called interfirm comparisons and the other is from a TQM initiative.

It is interesting that several governments, but not that of the United States, provide a service that is much like the first part of benchmarking. This service makes interfirm comparisons for those in a given industry. At the request of a firm, information is derived from financial and operating results of participants in the industry. A consultant visits each firm, collects data and information, and adjusts it where necessary to ensure comparability. The data are arrayed to evaluate the given firm with those that have superior results in each ratio group. Then, recommendations are made for performance improvement. Each study is presented in the form of operating ratios and becomes the basis for evaluating operating performance, improving productivity, and increasing competitiveness.

This is a gap analysis done on results measures of carefully selected performance ratios. It would be part of a complete gap analysis. What is missing, but increasingly being pursued as a follow-up activity, is tracing the gap back to the business processes that yielded the results. This would involve mapping the processes and making the comparison on a process-to-process basis.

The second example of gap analysis is derived from TQM initiatives. It is characterized by the comparison of the firm's current state to its desired state. The current state is defined by current practices, and the desired state is defined by the benchmark best practices. Given the gap, the objective is to understand the difference between the current and desired states and to understand the basis for needed improvement. Getting to the root cause of the differences and then adopting or adapting the best practice to close the performance gap are the next tasks.

Quality tools used to analyze the gap include root cause analysis, prioritization matrices, cause-and-effect diagrams, and all charts and graphs appropriate to analysis and display. This is a robust and powerful set of tools; in fact, it provides the most comprehensive approach to gap analysis. These tools should be appropriately used with innovativeness by the team.

What drives gap analyses? In addition to the search for better practices, there are often *stretch goals* with which organizations will challenge themselves. These are targets that the organization knows it will need in order to sustain the magnitude of change necessary for success and to get the organization to find entirely new ways to redesign its processes. Benchmarking is critical to locating and developing imaginative new approaches to meet these stretch goals. Motorola's well-publicized Six Sigma program for the reduction of its product defect and error rates is the most prominent example of a stretch goal. This was a challenge that Motorola knew it needed to pursue to become recognized as having world-class products. It has driven Motorola to conduct a substantial amount of benchmarking, and, therefore, gap analyses.

Other organizations have accepted similar challenges in key competency areas. The use of 10X or 100X programs are indicative of Motorola's approach. Organizations are being asked to find ways to improve key deliverables by a factor of 10 or 100. Here again is the need for benchmarking and the understanding of how to improve through gap analyses.

There are behavioral aspects to a gap analysis. It is a source of creativity and incentive for the organization to change. The tension and creative energy developed during the analysis phase should not be discounted. After carefully conducting the first three steps of the benchmarking process, this energy is now a payoff. What are the better practices? Why are they better? How can they be adopted or do they need to be modified? What will be the implications for the organization? What size change will be required?

The gap analysis is the ultimate benefit statement for the benchmarking effort, and, as such, will provide a source of energy and insight into the potential for continuous improvement. So the energy that this step provides to the organization to possibly, even radically, change itself should not be overlooked. In fact, it should be carefully planned. The objective should be to creatively adapt the best practices and innovatively implement them, not just copy them.

Tools Useful in Process-to-Process Comparisons

Before proceeding it is helpful to discuss the tools and techniques useful in gap analysis. The full range of tools is displayed in Figure 5.1. Each technique is cross-referenced to the appropriate steps of the 10-step benchmarking process. For those organizations active in the TQM/CQI movement the tools should be readily recognizable.

Where can the tools be found? Many are described in the GOAL/QPC *Memory Jogger* and *Memory Jogger Plus+* books and reference guides. Some of them come from internally developed techniques and are unique to the organization, yet recognizable to the quality professional. Some have been developed

Tool/technique	Steps									
	1	**2**	**3**	**4**	**5**	**6**	**7**	**8**	**9**	**10**
Activity network diagram	✓							✓		
Affinity diagrams	✓	✓	✓					✓		
AHP maturity index				✓						
Brainstorming	✓	✓	✓			✓	✓	✓		✓
Cause-and-effect diagram (Ishikawa)	✓	✓		✓			✓	✓		✓
Check sheet	✓	✓	✓	✓				✓	✓	✓
Control charts								✓	✓	
Flowcharts	✓			✓		✓		✓		✓
Force field analysis	✓	✓				✓	✓			
Interrelationship diagraph	✓							✓		
Interview techniques	✓	✓	✓		✓	✓		✓	✓	
Matrix diagram		✓	✓	✓	✓	✓	✓			
Multivoting	✓	✓				✓	✓			
Pareto diagrams	✓	✓		✓	✓			✓		
Policy deployment	✓						✓			
Prioritization matrices		✓		✓				✓		
Process documentation	✓			✓				✓		
Project management	✓	✓	✓	✓	✓	✓	✓	✓	✓	✓
Quality function deployment	✓			✓	✓			✓	✓	
Questionnaire/survey prep'n			✓			✓				
Quick reference guides/checklists	✓	✓	✓			✓	✓			
Radar/spider chart				✓	✓	✓	✓			
Root cause diagram	✓			✓	✓		✓			
Run charts				✓	✓		✓			
Scatter diagram				✓	✓					
Selection matrix		✓	✓	✓						
Tree diagram	✓					✓		✓		
Z chart				✓						

Figure 5.1. Tools and techniques for the steps of the benchmarking process.

and championed by select authors. Some are techniques that are as old as modern management itself.

While the tools and techniques in Figure 5.1 are conveniently cross-referenced to the 10 steps of the benchmarking process, they could just as easily be grouped into two sets: (1) charts, graphs, and diagrams; and (2) analysis activities and techniques. One set includes the approaches used to analyze the data and information and the other consists of the display methodology.

For gap analysis purposes, the following deserve mention: flowcharts and process documentation; matrices; radar or spider charts; AHP; and Z charts. Two deal with process-to-process comparisons, and three deal with the display of measurement data.

Flowcharts, process documentation, and matrices Traditional flow-charts are used to document a process to show its key steps and how each step is performed. There are alternatives to flowcharts, including arrow or data flow diagrams, mapping, FAST diagramming, and structured analysis. There are also computer software packages to assist with the effort and reduce the drudgery. Flowcharting, however, is the most well understood and traditional method used for process documentation.

Four outcomes are needed from the flowchart: a picture, a narrative, a description of what is done, and a description of how it is done. While there are other characteristics that fully document a process, such as identifying the customer, these are the very basics. The flowchart itself provides the picture. Its level of detail should be determined by the process-knowledgeable team members. Each step of the process should have a narrative description, and each narrative should include two explanations—what is done at that step and how it is done.

Once the process is flowcharted, the key steps along with process and results measurements can be displayed in traditional matrix format. The most common format arrays the process steps down the rows and uses the columns for the data and information of the different benchmarking partners. This matrix then becomes the basic document to display practices and to analyze and judge which practices are best.

Spider charts, AHP maturity index, and Z charts One of the dilemmas that benchmarking professionals face is how to show analytical data, or benchmarks, in which there are multiple measurements. It is rare that one single measure can suffice for a complicated process or, worse, a group of processes, such as from order taking to bill collection. Attempting to represent the performance of the process with a single measurement is nearly impossible if not bordering on the misleading. In addition, most processes are characterized by both pre-, in-, and postprocess measures and results measures. Therefore, the challenge is to display multiple measures and their associated benchmarks to indicate the gap. At least two approaches have been used successfully.

One approach utilizes the spider or radar diagram (see Figure 5.2). This diagram displays multiple measures as the spokes on a wheel. It requires that the measures be normalized, essentially converted to *percent accomplishment.* The current performance data points and benchmark data points are then connected. The resulting diagram effectively and succinctly displays the gaps. It is readable and understandable even by nonanalytically inclined individuals.

The AHP maturity index is a variation on the multiple measures display (see Figure 5.3). Here the multiple measures are weighted and converted to a single index. In similar fashion both current performance and the benchmark data can be indexed and the gap displayed. Both spider charts and the AHP maturity index are useful in displaying numerical gap information.

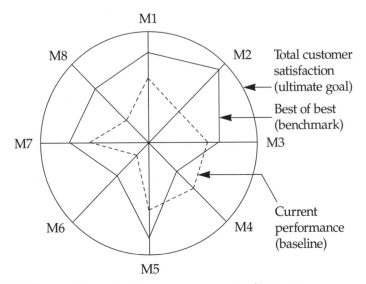

M1, M2, . . ., M8 are eight key measurements of interest.

Source: *Benchmarking: A Practitioner's Guide for Becoming and Staying Best of the Best*, Gerald J. Balm, QPMA Press, Quality and Productivity Management Association, Schaumburg, IL.

Figure 5.2. Spider or radar diagram.

The Z chart, first used at Xerox, is useful to display another characteristic of gap data; that is, where the gap is measured at a point in time (see Figure 5.4). Remember that performance does not stand still. Benchmarks and performance data change over time. So there must be a mechanism to show progress prior to a benchmark, the results of the benchmarking exercise, and the progress over time after the benchmark was established. The Z chart shows that the benchmark data may change because the industry changes and that the current performance is chasing a moving target. It is the one-time measurement and the closing of the gap over time that leads to a full understanding of the gap.

MI Comparisons

Profile	Wt	Base IBM	A	B	C	D	E	F	G
Process	0.275	2.2		−1			−1		
Define	0.360	2.3				−1	−1		
Understand	0.210	2.3	−1	−1				−1	
Simplify	0.141	2.4	−1	−2		−1			+1
Repeatable	0.120	2.0	−1	−2	−1		−1		−1
Flexible	0.094	2.0					−1		+1
Portable	0.076	1.4	−1	−1			−1	−1	
Methodology	0.253	3.2			+1	+1	+1		+1
Total quality control	0.272	3.1	−1	−1	+1		+1		
Production cycle	0.225	3.5		−1	+1	+1	.		+2
Continuous flow manufacturing	0.285	3.7	+1		+1	+1	+1	+1	+1
Modeling	0.134	2.8	+1	+2		+2	+2	+1	+2
Requirements	0.094	2.5							
Manufacturing competitive analysis	0.067	2.3	−1		−1				
Integration	0.213	2.0							
Scope	0.253	2.3		−1	−1	−1			
Presentation	0.230	2.1	+1						
Modular	0.201	1.8		+1			+1	+1	+1
Change	0.169	1.8							+1
Information system	0.140	1.7	+1	+1	+1	+1			+1
Management system	0.143	2.8		+1		+1		+1	+2
Owner	0.237	2.8	+1	+2			−1	+2	+2
Organization	0.188	2.7	+1	+2		+1	+1	+2	+2
Information management	0.167	2.4	+1	+1	−1	+1	+2	+2	+2
Computer-integrated manufacturing plan	0.167	3.1	−1	+1	+1	+1	+1		+2
Resource	0.111	3.1		+2		+1	+1		+2
Forum	0.069	3.1		−1	+1	+1	+1		+2
Business case	0.069	2.0	−1	+1					+1
Technology	0.117	2.4		+1			+1		+1
Discover	0.264	3.0	−1				+1		+1
Solution	0.230	2.2	−1	+1		−1		+1	+1
Data management	0.162	1.9					+1	+1	+1
Communications	0.136	2.1		+1					
Open system architecture	0.119	2.5		+1					
Enabling structure	0.085	2.1		+1					+1
Total (weights)		2.5	2.5	2.4	2.3	2.3	2.3	2.1	1.7

Reprinted from the April 1991 Issue of *Manufacturing Systems*. Copyright 1991 by Hitchcock Publishing Company.

Figure 5.3. AHP maturity index.

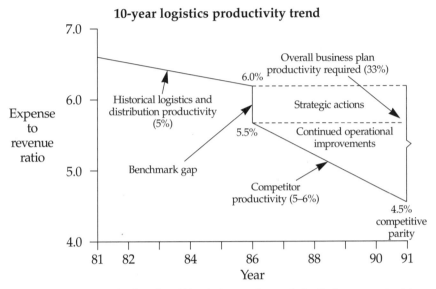

10-year logistics productivity trend

Figure labels within chart:
Expense to revenue ratio (y-axis)
Year (x-axis)
Overall business plan productivity required (33%)
6.0%
Historical logistics and distribution productivity (5%)
Strategic actions
5.5%
Continued operational improvements
Benchmark gap
Competitor productivity (5–6%)
4.5% competitive parity

• Unit costs were calculated as if logistics performed similarly to competition and converted to a single summary statistic; expense to revenue ratio.

• The result is an approximate 16% productivity gap compared to state-of-the-art operations or competitors studied thus far.

• During the next year, competitors will also be pursuing productivity, assumed to be 5–6% and equal to distribution's historical productivity.

• The results show distribution must pursue a combination of continuing, historical productivity efforts as well as undertake significant strategic changes.

Used with permission of Quality Resources.

Figure 5.4. Z chart.

Display Data for Ease of Analysis

The essentials of the gap analysis can now be applied to specific situations using the best practices matrices. At the highest level of detail, that includes a matrix consisting of the attributes and measurements documented in the rows compared to that of the companies shown in the columns. The last column would be the team's assessment of the best practice.

The data in the rows have been summarized from the helicopter view of the matrix. While one page is shown for example purposes, the matrix could actually span several pages. A representative example is shown in Figure 5.5.

Key summary business information to judge the comparability of the attributes and to provide background profile information is tabulated in the rows. Some statement of the environment within which the company operates is often necessary to establish its progress in continuous improvement activities or other relevant settings. The main body of the matrix shows the details of the processes. Not only are the current processes documented but any future, emerging, or planned changes are also shown.

A section on both results and process measures exists. While the example shows these in the last row at the end of the matrix, they could, if fact, be woven throughout the matrix next to the relevant details of each process.

The columns are established for the subject company and its benchmarking partners, however many that may be. Finally, a statement of the best practices is made.

What is the key content of the matrix? The business profile and environment provide information to judge relevancy. So the primary content is the practices documented at each step of the processes and the vital few key measures. This is the heart of the matrix. It is usually a statement—just a few key words—of what the practices are. It is understood that the details exist in some other records. This statement allows team members to quickly comprehend the practice and thus be able to judge its worth and to select the best practices to emulate.

The various sections of the matrix will now be discussed in more detail. It is understood that only sample items are covered and that the team may elect to cover more in its final document.

The business profile section could cover the organization's structure, key products or services marketed, and selected items

Attribute/measurement	Subject company	External comparisons			Best practices
		Company A	Company B	Company C	

• Business profile
  —Organization
  —Products
  —Sale method					

• Environment/culture
  —TQM proficiency
  —Empowerment					

• Processes
  —Order entry
  —Warehousing/delivery
  —Invoicing/collection					

• Future opportunities					

• Process measures
  —Cycle time
  —Defect rate
  —Orders/day					

• Results measures
  Satisfaction level
  —Percent satisfied
 	
  Business results
  —Return on investment					

Figure 5.5. Summary structure of gap analysis.

of information that would be of interest in judging what is driving the business processes. The one selected in Figure 5.5 is sale method and could have included commissions or sales force structure. What would be of interest to document in the matrix? Using the organization as an example, whether it is flat or hierarchic, how many management levels there are, and is it typically a centralized or decentralized operation?

The section dealing with environment and culture portrays the internal and external business climate. The external climate includes some key summary statements of the industry and competitive climate, such as where this company fits in terms of size, product array, and aggressiveness of marketing programs. Equally of interest is the internal business climate. This is portrayed by some statement of maturity in pursuit of a quality initiative and perhaps some cultural indicator such as empowerment. It could also indicate the existence of, and statement of intent, through vision, mission, goals, objectives, and direction pronouncements.

Between the business profile and environment sections of the practices matrix, the team has documented the basic information about the benchmarking partner. This provides the reason, rationale, and justification of the appropriateness of the comparison.

The heart of the matrix is the process-to-process comparison. Here each major process and subprocess is broken down in detail adequate enough to describe the process for analysis. The level of detail would be left to the process owners and operators to decide. Some guidelines might include the following:

- Set the level of detail low enough to highlight significant steps, but high enough so that the team is not dealing in minutia.

- Balance the details among the steps in the process.

- Size each step small enough to perform a cost analysis.

The objective is to describe the processes step-by-step and to have this information become the details in the columns. This is both a qualitative and quantitative exercise. For each step described in a column, there is an associated practice documented in the matrix slot for each benchmarking partner. These comparisons are assembled from the visit reports and partner company information. They describe the operating practices of others compared to the subject company. What is desired is the composite of all the practices compared to that of all partners— by step of the process. These are basically qualitative statements of the practices found at other, exemplar organizations. They describe, in key terms, the practice found. They act as summary statements of the practice. It is assumed that the details of the practice are documented elsewhere.

The quantitative information captures selected measures at key points in the process. The easiest way to visualize this is to examine the generic process diagram again. It consists of the inputs, process steps, outputs, and results. This model provides guidance on where in the process selected performance measures should be documented. This leads to identifying the appropriate in-process performance measures. What is desired is a select number of performance measures that are the key indicators of the process output. This is not an exercise of being comprehensive. The process measures will be used along with the quantitative data to assess the significance of the practice and to help determine which practice is the best. The performance data can be either embedded in the process comparison or summarized at the end.

The description of the process to this level of detail is the primary basis of sourcing the best practices, but with one qualification. The process is documented as of a stated date. But processes change. They are improved. Therefore, the matrix should document not only the current but also the proposed changes. While these may only be in the form of planning data and information, they are of added importance since they indicate future opportunities for continuous improvement of the process. They may also indicate strategic direction not incorporated in the current definition of the process.

With the matrix now completed, the team can address the issue of which practice is the best for each process step. Thus, the team can build a best practice process.

Decide Which Practices Produce the Best Results

The performance data and keyword statements of the practices are now selected and arrayed. Thus, the team turns its attention to examining the findings. This is the analysis of the gap in practices to source and obtain agreement on which is the best. The approach is one of exercising the criteria for judging superior practices while remembering that the organizations selected for benchmarking were found after extensive research. In other words, the companies were selected because they most likely have best practices. This was determined through significant research. They are the best practice companies with which to begin.

The team now scans across the practices and judges them by several superior practice criteria. There are also other general criteria that can be useful. These include the following:

- What is the impact on the business?
- How easy is it to implement the practice?
- Are results near-term or long-term?
- Are the results tactical or strategic in nature?
- Do the results tie directly to a specified goal or priority?
- Do the results give only moderate or major leverage on those priorities?

- Are the results controllable?
- Do the practices complement other initiatives and activities already under way?

An example of the matrix analysis applied to quality processes is shown in Figure 5.6.

At this stage of analysis, the in-process performance measures become a primary guide to determine the best practice. It is

Areas	Subject company	Company 1	Company 2	Company 3
Communications	Top down Quality quarterly	Top down Communication plan	Periodical Story-boarding	Video network Quality corner
Inspection	Team excellence	10X, 100X, and six sigma	10X defects and cycle time	7 core measures
Recognition	Teamwork award	Excellence progress	Recognition plan	Recognize any team
Training	3–6 days, all employees New employee training	All managers and employees Market-driven quality	Team leaders Quality education	All employees Quality education system
Process steps	9-step quality improvement process 6-step problem solving	8-step process Root cause analysis	Process quality management and improvement Quality improvement team	9-step Crosby, 6-step
Skills and tools	Interactive skills Cost of quality	Transformational leadership Quality function deployment	7 basic quality tools Defect definition	Group dynamics Deming seminar
Guidelines	Management behaviors	Nothing formal	Purpose agenda, limit	Meeting effectiveness

Figure 5.6. Matrix analysis applied to the quality improvement process.

obvious that if the in-process measures were selected to yield the overall outputs and results desired, they should weigh heavily in the decision. Another consideration, however, is to judge the selection of the best practice from the viewpoint of what satisfies internal and external customers most.

It is assumed that the reason for improving the basic work processes is to ensure that they are the best; and the reason that they must be the best is to ensure that they satisfy customers. It is through the best practice processes that an organization comes in contact with its customers and is seen by its customers as having the best practices. Therefore, the organization is seen as user-friendly and ultimately eager to do business. Thus, taking the perspective of satisfying upstream customers and downstream suppliers is another consideration for selecting the best practices.

Combine Best-of-the-Best Work Practices from All Observations

At this stage the team can assemble the best-of-the-best work practices into the process. This contrasts the current state of the process and its desired state. Performance gaps can be identified. The supporting and hindering implementation factors that will influence acceptance of the best practice process can also be identified. The new, revised performance measures, based on acceptance of the new practices, can be calculated, and a recommendation for acceptance, a schedule of actions, and the timing for implementation and next steps can be formulated.

At this stage the team will critically examine, debate, and consider the implications of the benchmarking findings. There may be practices in the process where the subject company is the best in class. That fact should be made known to senior management. Invariably, however, the comparison will show that there are other companies that are exemplar. The task is to carefully understand why. How are the benchmarking partners operating their process? What are the differences in practices? Why do the differences exist? How can the newly found best practices be applied to the subject process to make it the best? These are all part of the analysis of the gap and questions that will invariably be asked during the findings review.

If the approach is stopped at this stage, because much is expected at this step of the team's activities, then the value of benchmarking is lost. It is true that many of the practices will be readily, easily, and totally implemented exactly as they were found. There is, however, another requirement in the analysis and formulation of best practice processes. At this stage the new-found practices should be creatively adapted and innovatively implemented.

Here, the creative talents and innovative ideas of the team should be engaged to see how, in implementing the best practices, they are further improved. It is here that the input from customers, suppliers, process owners and operators, and the team's commissioning manager are brought into the analysis. Everyone sees what additional modifications and adaptations could be brought to bear on the newfound best practice that, when implemented, would give the organization superior performance, if not competitive advantage. It is through this further enhancement of the gap analysis that the true worth of benchmarking becomes fully understood.

The value of benchmarking is to find the best practices, but the power goes further. It is to creatively implement, not just copy, those best practices. So it is in this definition of benchmarking that an organization will set itself above the rest.

Validate Best Practices

At some point in the analysis of the gap there is a need to validate the practices, to run more than just a sanity check on the findings. In fact, the validation is an important part of the analysis to ensure that all parties are informed. Using the process model again, the most important individuals to gain validation from are the upstream customers, downstream suppliers, process owners and operators, and the commissioning manager or the customer of the benchmarking investigation. Each will be discussed in turn.

Customers and end users It is ultimately the customer of the process outputs that is the most important individual validating the worth of the best practices. If processes are being improved to enhance customer satisfaction, then the customer is the final judge. If the organization truly sees its business processes as major contributors that will enhance the organization's image as being user-friendly and that will be used by customers to determine their choice of organizations, then the customer must be consulted and must judge the worth of the best practices.

A typical way of accomplishing this is to develop a statement of the best practices and get customers to rate them. The first rating ranks the practices to determine the customers' order of preference. A second rating assigns the practice a numerical score to determine its importance. This information is invaluable to the team in formulating its final recommendations. The input could readily be obtained by a focus group. At the same time the customers could be asked if they saw any creative adaptation of the practice suitable for implementation.

Suppliers In similar fashion suppliers should validate best practices. More importantly, however, suppliers should comment on how any changes to a process will affect their inputs. If the process will operate differently then invariably suppliers' inputs will be different. Suppliers are also a good source of ideas on creative ways to implement best practices, since they see a wide variety of uses of their inputs.

The obvious example is software suppliers. With the broad client contacts they have, and the interest in having their application remain state-of-the-art, software suppliers are prime contacts to validate best practices and to comment on their implementation feasibility.

Process owners and commissioning manager It is obvious that the process owners and knowledgeable operators would have key insight into the operability of the best practices, especially if the operation has been doing some benchmarking over a significant time period. If the operators had been maintaining contacts with others interested in the same process, there is significant basis to contrast practices and to comment on the best ones found.

The obvious example is where senior managers make a concerted effort to visit with counterparts and to speak to others about their operation. Over time, this builds a consensus view of the major process trends and practices. At a minimum, managers would have the network through which to confirm and validate the practices.

How to Recognize Superior Practices

There are at least six ways to judge the superiority of different practices. There may be others, but these six are used collectively to determine the best practice from an array such as one documented in a matrix. The methods are discussed in the following sections.

The Practice Can Be Validated from Several Sources

One reason for conducting benchmarking with more than just one company is the distinct probability of finding the same best practice repeated. This indicates that the practice is a preferred way to operate. It is another reason why benchmarking should be conducted with three to six carefully researched and selected companies.

This was clearly the case in some catalog company bench-marking studies. One best practice was to capture the dimensions and weight of each item in inventory. This seemingly wasted effort, captured when items were received at the beginning of the process, had pervasive consequences for process streamlining and downstream efficiencies. In marketing, the item weight was displayed to advise customers of their shipping costs. Thus, customers could choose postal delivery, expedited air shipment, or surface package delivery, and they could decide the speed and cost of delivery. In shipping, the weight became a standard accepted by the delivery services so charges could be calculated for the items plus the packaging instead of having to weigh each individual shipment. In quality assurance, the entire contents of the packed shipping container could be passed over a scale and validated against the calculated weight to ensure 100 percent, order-filling accuracy.

The Practice Is Clearly Superior or Leading Edge
Even a casual observer passing a retail checkout counter would not debate that the bar code scanning of items is more efficient than manually entering each item number into the cash register. This is a clearly superior practice, which the nearly untrained eye recognizes.

If the full ramifications of bar code use were explained then there would be little question about its superiority. For example, bar code scanning permits point-of-sale item data capture. Thus, items can be replenished overnight, which markedly reduces inventory costs. Bar code scanning also automatically permits correct and timely price updates thus foregoing significant manual labor.

The Quantified Opportunity Is Large

As part of the process documentation it is expected that key performance measurements will be collected. If the performance measurements indicate a significant difference between the subject company's practices and those of the benchmarking partners, then that fact should indicate the existence of a potential best practice. If the data are comparable then there is strong evidence of a best practice.

This was the experience of the Xerox benchmarking team the first time it looked outside the industry for best practices. This classic case study compared the Xerox distribution function with that of L. L. Bean. When the key performance measure was quantified and compared, Bean was found to be picking its orders three times faster than Xerox. This order of magnitude difference could only be explained by the existence of better, if not best, practices. In fact, that is exactly what was found.

With all the articles, books, and other documents now in the public domain there are many case studies that illustrate the order of magnitude differences that others have found in their benchmarking studies. Even a cursory review of that information indicates that this experience is not uncommon. In fact, order of magnitude findings are exactly what many organizations are seeking.

Expert Judgment Validates the Practice

Process owners and operators are experts at what they do. They know their operation and its strengths and weaknesses. If they have been observant and know what is changing in their function, perhaps by conducting some benchmarking, then they are in a good position to judge a practice. A word of caution, however, is in order. While process owners and operators may be exceptional experts by virtue of their responsibilities, they may not have the perspective of what is happening outside the industry.

So there are other experts that should be consulted. The most obvious ones, of course, are the analysts that are frequently quoted on the happenings at a particular company. These individuals have a select number of companies that they watch, are briefed by senior management, and are quoted in the media when major company events take place. In similar fashion there are consultants that have made a career of a particular field, like direct marketing or computer software. These individuals can be consulted for their expert opinion on the best practices found.

In fact, it is common for a team to have its findings submitted to an independent third party for just that purpose. This should not adversely affect the team's efforts. In fact, if the team has conducted its investigation carefully, then the report by an outsider should be nothing but a confirmation of the benchmarking excellence practiced.

The Practice Is the Organization's Core Business

The delivery of innovative products and services to the marketplace is likely the core business of most enterprises. Billing, the creation of an accurate invoice, is not the core business of most organizations; it is a cost of doing business. Thus, reasonable efforts are made to maintain invoice accuracy and timeliness.

To some organizations, however, billing is their core business or is seen as such. In the banking, brokerage, and credit card business, maintaining an accurate statement is paramount to the business. Customers will not stand for inaccuracies in their financial accounts. So the accuracy and timeliness of these documents is central to satisfying customers. As such these organizations have to ensure that best practices are incorporated in their processes.

Thus, when judging best practices it is essential to find those organizations that perform the activity as the core of their business. These are the organizations that should be benchmarked.

The Practice Is Preferred if Its Outputs Are Offered for Sale

The ultimate test of a best practice is if it is preferred by others and they are willing to pay for it. This circumstance occurs when an organization has a best practice process that is second to none. The organization is so confident of its abilities that it offers the process for use at a price that compensates the organization plus earns a profit, and that others actively seek to use the process and pay for it. In this instance the organization is acting as a service bureau.

With the increase in outsourcing this is becoming an accepted approach. Organizations are recognized as excelling at what they do, whether it is operating copy centers, food services, cleaning and maintenance services, computer centers, or hotel franchises. An industrial or service organization may also elect to offer a best practice process to others for a fee.

These are organizations that are proficient enough to start offering processing to others. They may have a cost base and processing cycle that are preferred by others. The advantages to the providing organization are that its expenses are lowered by spreading fixed costs over a larger activity, and that providing the activity does not interfere with the mainline business activity. To the accepting organization, the offer of a turnkey operation of some segment of its business also holds the opportunity to have faster processing and lower costs as a result of the combined operations. Offering best practices for sale to others is an excellent way for an organization to keep its process on the leading edge through the test of market competitiveness.

How Best Practices Emerge

It is instructive to consider how best practices emerge or evolve as a precursor to deciding the most productive areas to search. These considerations have primarily to do with how industries develop and how innovation evolves. Giving some thought to these two avenues of potential best practice sources could give some insight into where the greatest potential lies, especially in developing the candidate list of organizations.

Different industries develop at different rates. While it probably has not been proven statistically, an active observer of the development of best practices would quickly conclude that certain industries advance faster than others. One has only to look at the history of the computer industry, and in particular the development of the personal computer, for an example. The amount of computing power in a personal computer now exceeds that of many mainframes of only a few years ago. The implications for the manufacture of these small devices, and the advancement of the materials used in their construction, hold significant potential for those pursuing the improvement of product delivery or manufacturing processes and the development of materials used in those processes.

Another way to consider how best practices evolve is to recognize that some organizations or industries are acknowledged leaders at certain processes because they are the core competencies. The competency of error-free documents in bank, brokerage, and credit card statements is an easily recognized example. In many respects what has to be asked is, who is the exemplar at a particular activity, operation, and process? Then this model can be studied and understood, and eventually its best practices can be adopted.

Another way to find best practices is to consider that through innovation and engineering new ideas will always be forthcoming because advancements in technology always generate new ideas. Consider where technology is changing at a rapid pace. For example, this might lead to the pharmaceutical or scientific instruments industries. The key to understanding the practice and transferring the knowledge will heavily depend on the detail of the processes under investigation. The more detailed, the more credible the comparison and the opportunity for finding and adapting the best practice. The challenge is then how to implement the practice.

Benchmarking will not replace any of these basic trends. They will always exist. The challenge for benchmarking professionals is to use these rationales and approaches to source best practice organizations to visit and to get their own organizations to see the possibilities of the practice transfer. There will still be the need to innovatively and creatively implement the best practices.

Recommendations and Approaches to Implement Best Practices

The final phase of the gap analysis is to prepare a report on the best practice process and recommendations for its implementation. The purpose of the report is to share the findings with process owners and operators, upstream customers, downstream suppliers, and the benchmarking project's customer. The report not only details the best practice process but also discusses the new goals and objectives that would be set by adopting the new process. In addition, implementation strategies and some indication of the needed improvements to implement the new process are also covered. Finally, the creative adaptation of the best practice in the new process is developed. This is the capstone chapter of the report.

Summary

- Examine other gap analyses for analogies.
- Consider tools useful in process-to-process comparisons.
- Display data and practice information for ease of analysis.
- Decide which practices produce the best results.

- Combine the best practices to produce a best-of-the-best practice.
- Consider how to recognize best practices.
- Validate best practices.
- Develop recommendations and an approach to implement the best practices.

Section 2:
The Leadership and Management of Benchmarking

CHAPTER 6

Benchmarking Leadership and Management Process

Supreme excellence consists in breaking the enemy's resistance without fighting.

- Establishing a Benchmarking Program
- Supporting a Benchmarking Program
- Sustaining a Benchmarking Process
- Summary

Benchmarking activities can be classified into two distinct processes—the user process and the management process. The user process is the exercise of the benchmarking steps, often recognized as the 10-step benchmarking process. It is used as a map to follow by the benchmarking team. The management process consists of all the other activities required to ensure that effective benchmarking investigations are conducted and results are implemented.

There are several ways to examine the benchmarking management process. The process perspective covers starting, supporting, and sustaining the benchmarking process. This perspective is parallel to the user process, as it is also started, supported, and sustained. This is the traditional input-process-output model.

Another way to examine the benchmarking management process is to categorize the management activities as those that are needed to set up a benchmarking program and those that are needed to manage the activities over time. These later activities are the traditional investment-and-benefits approach to sustain the benchmarking effort.

It is also possible to describe the management process in terms of its owners and suppliers; its inputs and outputs; its source and destination processes; its customers; its customer requirements and supplier specifications; and its measurements, inspection methods, and resources. As part of this documentation a flowchart is created to provide a visual representation of the process.

Of all these ways to examine the benchmarking management process, the most useful one is the process perspective. Thus, the benchmarking management process should categorize management activities into establishing, supporting, and sustaining a benchmarking program.

Establishing a Benchmarking Program

Key components of establishing a program include developing a strategy statement, setting expectations, providing management awareness, establishing a competency center, developing guidelines, and establishing a network. Each of these components is examined in the following sections.

Develop a Strategy Statement

At any one point in time, large organizations have many improvement initiatives underway. These can include TQM, statistical process control, quality function deployment, and many others. These are all focused on the reduction of errors and the prevention of defects for overall continuous improvement. Benchmarking is another quality initiative that can be pursued to change and improve an organization's operation with particular focus on improvement of the business processes.

When benchmarking is introduced, employees need to know where it fits in with the existing initiatives. Employees also need to have some rationale for why benchmarking is being pursued. Thus, a strategy statement is very desirable. Not only will it indicate the what and why for benchmarking but it also goes a long way toward legitimizing benchmarking. Those responsible for benchmarking should be able to state what its strategy is and should gain acceptance from senior management.

One strategy might be the outgrowth of an organization's pursuit of quality and continuous improvement through business process improvement. High-performing business processes allow an organization to anticipate and react to customer needs more quickly and better than others, and consequently deliver leading-edge customer satisfaction. Thus, customers are eager to do business with the firm.

If that is the stated perspective of the organization, then a complementary benchmarking strategy statement could be as follows:

Benchmarking goal To improve customer satisfaction and business results by continuously searching for and incorporating best practices in work processes

Benchmarking strategy To continuously improve work processes to produce better outputs by

- Focusing major benchmarking efforts on finding and implementing best practices in key work processes
- Maintaining a critical few benchmark summary output measures as indicators of progress

This strategy rationale is a direct outgrowth of the organization's stated objective of improving work processes. The benchmarking initiative is specifically linked to the rationale. In effect, it puts the organization on notice that superior customer satisfaction and business results are delivered by outputs from high-performing work processes; and these processes are based on methods or practices that are the benchmark, namely the best in industry and increasingly world-class.

Set Expectations

Second only to having a strategy statement is for management to have some stated expectations for the benchmarking activities. There are at least two considerations: (1) Management wants the benchmarking activity to be continuous and the basis for continuous improvement, not a one-time event. (2) There are specific management deliverables expected that are requirements for tracking the status of benchmarking activities and for inspecting the benchmarking process. An example of such a direction-setting statement is shown in Figure 6.1.

How benchmarking activities will become continuous must be considered. The key to this need is identifying existing, continuous management activities. While many can probably be cited there are three activities that are common to most organizations—creation of a business plan, development of an annual or operating plan, and ongoing operations review. It is logical to have benchmarking a specific requirement in each activity to ensure its permanence and continuity. It is in these documents and activities that benchmarking should be reported. An example of using benchmarking and benchmarks in the planning process is shown in Figure 6.2.

In the business plan, benchmarking supports the focus on priorities and developing objectives to meet customer requirements. The questions supported by benchmarking are as follows:

Product benchmarking is conducted to establish product planning and development guidelines.

Process benchmarking is conducted to achieve world-class work processes that will satisfy customers.

Performance benchmarking is conducted to establish rational goals and performance measures.

Benchmarking is **incorporated into the planning process** to ensure its continuity and its institutionalization in the organization.

Benchmarking is **part of business process management** to ensure that processes are based on incorporation of best practices.

Benchmarking is **used to provide** objective, external comparisons and fact-based decisions.

Figure 6.1. Direction-setting statement.

- How does the subject company compare to the competition?
- What opportunities can be identified to gain an advantage?
- What strategies and best practices have been considered?
- What are the performance goals needed for the next three to five years?
- What are the key processes that drive these goals?

In the annual or operating plan the focus is on specific objectives and on validating the process capability to implement best practices. Questions answered by benchmarking include the following:

- What gaps should be closed this year?
- How will the gaps be closed?
- How long will it take to close the gap?
- How much of the gap will be closed this year?
- What best practices will be incorporated?

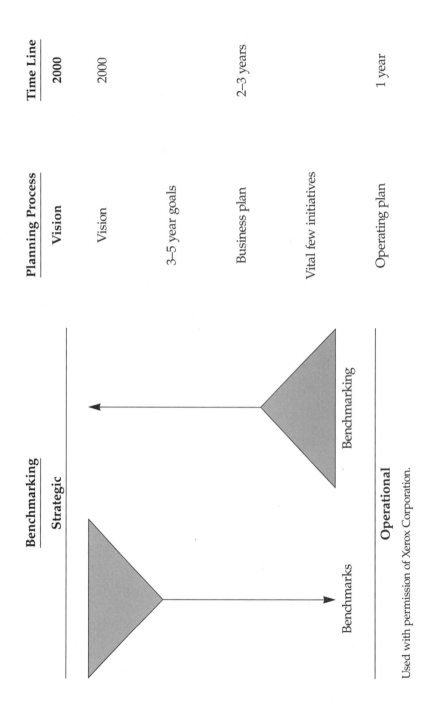

Benchmarking		Planning Process	Time Line
Strategic		Vision	2000
		Vision	2000
		3–5 year goals	2–3 years
		Business plan	
		Vital few initiatives	
	Benchmarking		
Operational		Operating plan	1 year
Benchmarks			

Used with permission of Xerox Corporation.

Figure 6.2. Benchmarks and benchmarking in the planning process.

Since the focus of operation reviews is on action plans, concentration should be on the vital few practices and inspection. Questions supported by benchmarking are as follows:

- What progress has been made toward the benchmarks?
- What are the vital few best practices on which to concentrate?
- On what basis were these prioritized?
- Are adequate resources being devoted to benchmarking and specifically to implementation of the best practices?
- What are the results of implementing best practices?

The specific management deliverables expected in these documents and reviews must be considered next. These deliverables are stated as five requirements: (1) a strategy statement; (2) identification of key products, services, and processes benchmarked; (3) reporting of a vital few performance measurements maintained as benchmarks; (4) a prioritization of benchmarking activities; and (5) contribution to business results.

The strategy statement has already been covered and should be easily documented for review. There should be some effort to display, in a rational and cascaded way, a tree-type diagram to identify the processes to be benchmarked. If the organization has the business process focus on its continuous improvement efforts, it is assumed that there is some logical process classification scheme. Thus, benchmarking activities can be tied to the key processes for improvement that year.

A select few performance measures should be maintained as benchmarks for purposes of tracking progress. These would be of two types: a set of common measures that all functions report, such as expense to revenue; and a set of optional measures tailored to the functional area, such as billing quality for the administrative area or sales productivity for the field sales organization. There is one consideration, however, for the optional measures: Should these be high-level business measures or should they be specific business process measures? The experience of the author is that the tailored measures should be those vital few in-process measures that support the key processes of the organization. High-level business measures should be the organization's output or performance measures.

The prioritization of key benchmarking activities is another requirement to ensure that the maximum return is achieved for every organization objective. This activity can take several forms. It can be a tree-like analysis or a hierarchic classification of processes; however, there must be some picture of how the selected benchmarking activities cascade from priorities to objectives to vital few benchmarking investigations. The prioritization criteria can be set by consensus, expert judgment, or a company objective such as customer satisfaction. AHP can also be used to prioritize the key benchmarking activities.

The last management requirement is to show how benchmarking activities contribute to business results. This can be effectively done by a reporting matrix that covers the focus of the benchmarking activity; the excellent companies visited; the best practices found; and how the findings were implemented. In the business plan this information would be reported for completed studies as well as for planned, future activities, with the later noted as tactical or strategic in nature.

Provide Management Awareness Training

Management awareness for benchmarking is required. Managers will need to know what benchmarking is so there is a consistent understanding throughout the organization. This serves as a common basis on which to make decisions about starting benchmarking activities. The rationale for specific content and preferred training delivery methods are covered in chapter 7.

The objective of management awareness is to perform a readiness check for establishing and sustaining benchmarking. Questions managers should ask include the following:

- Does everyone know what benchmarking is?
- Are the necessary prerequisites available to start benchmarking?
- Is there senior management support?
- Are the necessary skills and competencies available to support benchmarking?

Establish a Competency Center

Organizations and benchmarking teams need assistance. They may need facilitators or trainers, consultants, and someone to be responsible for the benchmarking program. The person placed in a competency capacity is responsible for many of the topics covered in this chapter. Where that person comes from, what skills he or she possesses, and to whom this person reports are important considerations.

Most organizations do not have a benchmarking manager position. So there is no source of qualified individuals. Therefore, the position is usually filled from within the organization through a preferred route. The organization can grow its own benchmarking manager, and there are many benefits for doing so. First, a capable, credible individual, as judged by his or her peers, is selected. Second, the person that has been in the organization can relate the need for benchmarking to internal priorities and give tailored examples. Finally, the individual can be made competent in benchmarking through training or networking with others.

The candidate benchmarking manager should have a background in some, if not all, of the following skills: analysis, library research, quality process, problem solving, process documentation, facilitation, training, and project management. Operational knowledge is also important so the new manager can relate to problems that have been tackled and that could have been solved more readily with benchmarking. The ability to relate to operational problems and to anticipate where problems might yield to benchmarking, and the capability to convince managers to devote the resources to pursue benchmarking, are critical. At the same time the candidate should be knowledgeable in and capable of influencing the organization and management to make benchmarking an ongoing pursuit as a necessary quality tool.

The candidate can readily acquire benchmarking skills through several avenues. First, there are publicly available training courses to attend. These are helpful not only to train the individual but also to see firsthand what training would best fit the organization's teams and culture. Second, there are public seminars and conferences on benchmarking where the candidate can hear about others' experience in pursuing benchmarking. These provide a cross section of comparative approaches and experiences that can be the basis for formulating a tailored benchmarking program. Third, there are numerous articles and books about benchmarking, which serve as references to how others have pursued benchmarking and which relate case studies and testimonials for marketing benchmarking internally. Finally, the candidate can network, and more importantly visit, with the few experienced counterparts in other companies to get firsthand insight into their benchmarking programs.

Given that the organization accepts benchmarking as a quality tool for continuous improvement, the benchmarking manager should be in a high-level position that reports into a quality organization. This is also desirable at the group or division level. At some point, however, the benchmarking competency needs to reside, even if on a part-time assignment basis, in an operation.

At this point the position could report to a planning group or an engineering group or it could become stand-alone.

The responsibilities of the benchmarking manager include the following:

- Maintain wide outside contacts for benchmarking.

- Pursue a defined benchmarking strategy.

- Lead benchmarking teams.

- Lead the network of individuals representing their organizations for benchmarking.

- Provide benchmarking training or see that it is done effectively.

- Act as a resource on the benchmarking process.

- Ensure that benchmarking activities are prioritized to those that will return the greatest benefits and to those that fit with the organization's objectives, mission, and vision.

- Report benchmarking's progress to all appropriate parties.

But the real value of the competency center and related operational network, described in the next section, is to be the focal point and forum for sharing experiences. It enables the benchmarking representatives to remain close to the operation.

Develop Guidelines

The organization needs to develop guidelines for managers and teams conducting benchmarking. The guidelines ensure some semblance of consistency and are the standard procedures for handling benchmarking activities. These guidelines usually involve information sharing, visit protocol, and ethical, legal, and nondisclosure considerations. It is extremely beneficial to have these guidelines documented and available to benchmarking teams and their commissioning managers. While these guidelines are often in the form of job aids or quick reference guides, the ultimate guideline to stress is good judgment. There is no substitute for sound business judgment. In many cases managers should ask: If this were to appear in the local newspaper would it be cause for concern?

Guidelines for information sharing should start by stating that no information will be shared that is proprietary or seen as restraint of trade. Matters of price, market, and market share are not the focus of benchmarking in which best business practices are pursued. Therefore, proprietary matters are usually avoided by the very nature of the benchmarking investigation.

Following this general tendency, experience shows that the following rule is most practical: The organization will share information in equal measure to that shared with it on a mutually agreed topic. This is one-for-one sharing. If the organization has documented its process as the basis for information exchange, then it is expected that the benchmarking partner will share equal information on the same process with particular emphasis on the differences in practices. Often an organization will want to benchmark one process but finds the partner interested in another. To the extent that it is mutually agreed, this exchange is also beneficial and acceptable.

Where information is deemed sensitive or of a competitive advantage either organization may elect not to discuss that topic. It is an accepted practice to set some topics aside by mutual agreement. The benefits of pursuing the remaining common interest topics have proven to be of enough interest to continue the benchmarking activity. There is a word of caution, however, on setting some topic aside. By doing so the organization is telling something to the partner. Either the topic is seen as a competitive advantage, or there is some concern for the quality of the information. The latter does not reflect well on the organization. Thus, not discussing the information has revealed something anyway.

Visit protocol also needs guidelines. Some accepted procedures for handling incoming and outgoing requests are necessary. Since many of the benchmarking activities will be conducted between major customers, suppliers, or other significant organizations, these relationships should not be placed in jeopardy. Also, there is simply the need to have the contacts handled efficiently, with the least bureaucratic hassle, to ensure that requests are promptly responded to and that the correct parties are brought together. Lastly, every inquiry provides a benchmarking opportunity. Ultimately, an organization should put its best foot forward in any external exchange.

One successful practice calls for a benchmarking representative in each function. These individuals make up a network for handling benchmarking activities. A backup contact may be someone in a quality capacity. These benchmarking designees coordinate external requests, which should be directed first to the appropriate functional representative. That person makes the initial decision on whether the visit should take place and, more importantly, based on knowledge of the organization, can contact the respective operations to determine if there is any mutual interest.

Where the organization has a direct sales force, the account managers should be aware of any benchmarking requests from customers. Similarly, the organization's buyers should be aware of any benchmarking contacts with suppliers. Account managers can help determine the seriousness of the contact and the correct unit or organization to handle the request. Account managers can also provide any background information that might help the account relationship and avoid any sensitivities.

Lastly, documenting and archiving the contact outcome in some central or easily accessed source should be considered. This serves as a source of contacts for future visits and avoids embarrassment and duplication of efforts. The archives also store status reports, which explain the extent of benchmarking activities.

For further information on benchmarking guidelines, the code of conduct subscribed to by the members of the IBC may be helpful. The IBC is a service of the American Productivity and Quality Center. Its code was developed from the contributions of several prominent organizations in benchmarking and their professionals. Contact the IBC at 123 North Post Oak Lane, Houston, Texas 77024; telephone 713-685-4666 and facsimile 713-681-5321.

Establish a Network

Organization structure is one of the major considerations for managing benchmarking. What structure has proven most effective in the subject organization? Most organizations form networks from their functional benchmarking representatives. These networks not only serve the need to source and update benchmarking activities but they also fulfill the need to disseminate benchmarking information and requirements throughout the organization. There may also be a need to conduct work on the benchmarking program, gain consensus on direction or decisions that affect benchmarking, and develop positions and documents to further direct and expand the program. Hence, an internal benchmarking network is most worthwhile. A mission statement for a typical network is shown in Figure 6.3.

Supporting a Benchmarking Program

Key components to support a benchmarking program include identifying champions for benchmarking, commissioning teams, providing team skills training, documenting the processes, qualifying partners, and following the 10-step process.

Our mission is to promote, gain understanding, support the use of, and improve the practice of benchmarking for the operation, business divisions, respective functional organizations, and process owners so that customer satisfaction and business results improve through the incorporation of best practices in our products, services, and business processes.

Used with permission of Xerox Corporation.

Figure 6.3. Internal benchmarking network mission statement.

Identify Champions

Organizations need champions for major programs that bring about change—and benchmarking is no exception. Benchmarking is an important change process, and selected champions should be designated, so that when change activities are anticipated benchmarking will be considered. The champion's role, however, should go beyond simple sponsorship. It should be based on advocacy—challenging the organization on why benchmarking was not considered in major decisions and showcasing success stories as a basis for motivating the organization to aggressively pursue benchmarking. A secondary role of the champion is to prepare the organization for order of magnitude change.

One of the important roles of the champion should be to advocate the pursuit of benchmarking by focusing activities on the business processes. Experience shows that this application of benchmarking has the highest payback. Therefore, the champion should ensure that business processes are identified, classified in some hierarchical structure, and prioritized for purposes of concentrating on those with the greatest return or leverage of organizational priorities. Given this focus—concentration on improving the basic business processes—the pursuit of benchmarking will become clear. It is the incorporation of the best practices in the business processes that deliver the expected business results.

Commission Teams

Given that benchmarking activities have been prioritized to the vital few business processes, the teams that will conduct the benchmarking need to be commissioned. Members need to be selected; team size and skills mix need to be considered; team operation must be agreed to; the scope of the project must be defined; and arrangements for removing organization roadblocks should be made known. These are the responsibilities of the person commissioning the benchmarking team.

Who commissions teams? That is best answered by determining who the customer of the benchmarking is. It is effective to go through at least the first few steps of a traditional quality process in the start-up of any benchmarking team effort. Determining (1) the output, (2) customers, (3) their requirements, and (4) specifications to meet the requirements are essential first steps. It is the customer identified by this process that, in most cases, is the person to commission the team. He or she also agrees to the output, requirements, and specifications. In other words, if no customer can be identified for the output, or the customer does not agree to the four points, there is no justification for the work.

Teams rarely function effectively if they consist of more than 9 to 12 members. Three to six are preferred for benchmarking. Larger teams can be considered but will most likely break down into smaller subgroups in practice. Members of the team should have a good mix of skills. An absolute requirement is that representatives of the process be included on the team, if not be given leadership of the team.

The team should have direct operational experience in the process under study. The focus should clearly be on implementing the process improvements that will produce better results. The process operators are most capable of bringing this capability to the team.

In addition to being knowledgeable of the process, team members should possess analytical, research, process documentation, and team facilitation skills. This last group of skills is particularly needed during start-up. Analytical skills call for team members with engineering or technical backgrounds, and research skills include an interest in conducting information research.

The team should use an accepted process model, such as the 10-step Xerox process. This should be based on agreed-to rules established in advance with the customer. The rules should include the scope and boundaries of the investigation. Most often, this can be described in terms of business processes, such as order taking but not proposal development and negotiation.

Lastly, organizational roadblocks must be removed since benchmarking based on processes invariably crosses through several functions. Thus, understanding the potential effect of the implementation of the best practices on those organizations is needed. Adequate treatment of this topic is best covered in the implementation phases of the benchmarking process. See chapter 4 for more details.

Provide Team Skills Training

Just as managers must understand the benchmarking process, commissioned team members must have the skills training to conduct benchmarking investigations. Benchmarking is very much a methodology but it is also a skill, and the methodology can be taught and the skills can be simulated. Therefore, teams should be trained, preferably at the time of need. The primary focus of the training should be on identifying what to benchmark and whom to benchmark against, and on reviewing all the data and information sources.

The rationale, content, and delivery methods for team training are completely covered in chapter 6. The objectives should be to get teams jump-started on the benchmarking process, namely the first three steps, and to have them look ahead to the next two steps where they will determine the performance gap and revise the operational goals and measurements. The remaining steps of the benchmarking process can be self-taught or covered in a working session with a facilitator.

Document the Process

Benchmarking must be started by documenting the work process that is the focus of the investigation. There are many reasons for this important step, and they include defining the scope of the project, understanding the appropriate key measurements, and having a clear understanding of the way the work is conducted. There may also be some not-so-obvious reasons for this step.

One of the tasks will be to convince the identified benchmarking partners that they should participate in the study. Experience indicates that having a documented process is a significant incentive for others to participate. The process documentation will show a level of preparation far beyond what the other participants have.

The basic reason to have a documented process, however, is so that a credible comparison can be made. There is no more credible basis for comparison than indicating how the work is done. This acts as a baseline. When this documentation is not done, only random information is gathered. This results in the frustrating, if not impossible, task of trying to compare the external practices in any meaningful way to the internal practices.

There are many ways to document the work process, and these are completely explained in chapter 2. The documentation can vary from the minute detail to the overview, but there are some basic requirements. The minimum includes a picture of the process; a word description of the process; and a word description of the step-by-step procedure (what is done) and the practice at each step (how it is done). Beyond these basics, the level of detail can be changed to complement the level of analysis. Usually, the process owners and others intimately involved in the process can determine the level of detail needed.

Qualify Partners

Benchmarking knowledge varies considerably from that of the naive to the highly experienced. This is not an indictment of the individual, but it can be a problem when a company is asked to become a benchmarking partner by an inexperienced newcomer who may be just starting. Under these circumstances some qualification or screening is appropriate. This includes a discussion of the newcomer's level of preparation and the partners' code of conduct.

While the content of the code of conduct has been covered, its preparation has not. It is perhaps unreasonable to expect that those wanting to benchmark will have recognized the need for documenting its process as a prerequisite. But a telling factor in the preparation will be whether the newcomers have thought through the subject adequately enough to have prepared a questionnaire. If so, that would be the minimum requirement. If not, it is reasonable to request one. This will at least show some thoroughness in preparation to ensure an effective information exchange. A properly documented process is highly desirable and may be essential for complicated topics.

Preparation always pays off. This includes understanding the basics of the partner's business. At a minimum the relevant databases on the company, by name and topical area, should be extracted. This level of preparation will only enhance the potential for getting the other party to participate. Also see the section titled "Breaking Down Barriers to Sharing Information" in chapter 4.

Follow the 10-Step Process

The need for consistent, replicable results argues for a standard way to conduct benchmarking. There are benchmarking processes that have 9, 10, and 12 steps, and probably others with every variation. But what is important is that there be one process and that it be followed during the initial benchmarking and recalibration.

The accepted process is the road map to ensure credibility in comparisons and consistency in results. Credibility is gained when it can be shown that a standard process was followed. Consistency in results is important in recalibrating benchmark data and information.

Sustaining a Benchmarking Process

Sustaining a benchmarking process over an extended period of time, say years, includes securing external assistance, developing a handbook for managers, showcasing successes, role modeling, inspecting for use, and recognizing and rewarding benchmarking excellence.

Secure External Assistance

It is often expedient to use external resources to conduct benchmarking. The alternatives vary from the large, recognized management consulting firms that have benchmarking practices, to those firms that have benchmarking as their sole or primary area of expertise, to individuals who have extensive experience and will act as consultants. Using outside assistance, however, should be carefully considered. The types of external assistance resources and examples of each are shown in Figure 6.4.

In the past, the principal benefit of using outside consultants was to provide confidentiality so that the benchmarking partners would participate in the studies. Many would only participate if their data and information were masked. With the widespread recognition that benchmarking has today, driven by the Malcolm Baldrige National Quality Award, there is less concern about open sharing of information. Therefore, outside resources usually provide added assistance to accomplish the following:

- Reduce the time to conduct benchmarking investigations.

- Provide ready contacts as a direct result of their consulting practice.

- Provide special skills, such as a specialization in a high-tech industry.

- Quality consulting organizations
  —Company-specific, such as QualTech and AT&T

- Associations and nonprofits
  —Clearinghouses and centers, such as the American Productivity and Quality Center (APQC), International Benchmarking Clearinghouse (IBC), and the American Management Association (AMA)

- Consulting firms
  —General, such as audit and finance
  —Specialists, such as management consulting
  —Individuals, such as subject experts

- Conference organizers
  —Multiorganization events, such as one by *Industry Week*

Figure 6.4. External assistance alternatives.

There is also a growing use of third parties to facilitate consortia; that is, ongoing benchmarking activities with the same partners sharing information at regular intervals over an extended time period, perhaps several years. In these activities there is a need to have an impartial third party arrange the exchanges, facilitate the agenda and discussions, and bring the partners to closure on the best practices.

There are special cases where the third party conduct of a benchmarking investigation is not desirable. The reason is quite important. Benchmarking is not only the finding of data and information on best practices but it is also, more importantly, a learning process. *Benchmarking is a learning experience, not just a data-gathering effort.* The value of benchmarking comes from seeing how companies achieve their benchmark performance levels. It is a way by which organizations and individuals are exposed to new ways of doing things. Benchmarking sensitizes practitioners to the fact that there may be others who are doing things differently and probably more effectively. Therefore, participation on the team (at a minimum) by representatives of the process, or leadership of the benchmarking activities (most desirable) by the process owners is highly desirable if not imperative. If outside resources are used they should supplement the internal team. When the underlying benefit of using outside resources is evaluated, the usual conclusion is that they have reduced the time to conduct the benchmarking study.

Another important consideration, which emphasizes the learning aspects of benchmarking, dispels the myth that performance measurement data are all that are needed. Knowing the practices that deliver the results is the key to world-class leadership.

Develop a Handbook for Managers

Since benchmarking is not conducted continuously by all managers or process owners, those in a competency capacity must repeatedly answer the same fundamental benchmarking questions. Even though there may be a network of competent individuals who are organized to see that the organization does benchmarking right, some of the essentials still slip through the cracks. For instance, calling the appropriate contact, conducting the barest essential library search on the topic and target company, and documenting the process first are tasks typically "forgotten."

To forestall the questions, and to proactively place in the hands of managers some guide to turn to, a managers' benchmarking reference guide is very useful. Content of the guide should not duplicate materials already available for the 10-step process. The guide serves as a reference to available materials with a short abstract on what they contain. It consists of readily accessible job aids and examples of what to do to effectively conduct benchmarking.

The development of the managers' resource guide is completely covered in chapter 8. For explanation purposes here, the guide should contain the following:

- Reason for the guide
- The unit's benchmarking strategy
- Roles and responsibilities of participants
- Essentials of getting started
- Visit guidelines and referral process
- Conduct of a site visit
- Information-sharing guidelines and legal considerations
- Identification and documentation of key processes and measures
- Use of technical libraries
- How to archive benchmarking documents

- Training and resource materials
- Operation of benchmarking networks
- Definitions
- Appendix with sample forms and letters

This 50- to 60-page booklet is a reference guide that can be used to prevent mistakes in the benchmarking process and to drive consistency in its approach. The audience for such a document is the process owners and their benchmarking teams and those conducting or contemplating benchmarking activities. In the final analysis, however, the beneficiaries of the resource guide are all managers in the organization.

Showcase Successes

There is no one way to let organizations outside the benchmarking study see the business process under investigation and the best practices found. But showcasing success stories and case histories is an important activity in expanding and intensifying benchmarking throughout the organization. This is a powerful means to recognition and serves to stimulate the benchmarking activities of others. This includes cataloging benchmarking documents for others' reference; making the results available in some abstracted form for consideration and replication by other similar functions; reporting results at internal seminars and external presentations as appropriate; distributing internal communications from progress reports to formal project reviews; and reporting benchmarking results in business plans, operating plans, or budgets and at operational reviews. All of these tasks are described in detail in other chapters

One way to showcase successes is through the internal network of benchmarking representatives and their activities to become the champions of benchmarking within their respective organizations. This is illustrated in Figure 6.5.

Benchmarking effectiveness strategy team (BEST) network of locally based functions and business units

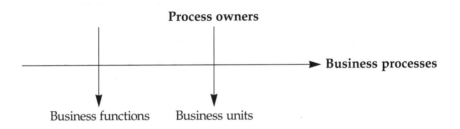

Process owners

Business processes

Business functions   Business units

Representatives act as focal points and competency contacts for key benchmarking studies

Figure 6.5. Benchmarking direction and coordination.

Role Model

Managers should take every opportunity to cite best practices derived from benchmarking. This puts the organization on notice that it is an important and effective way to justify operations. It also sensitizes the organization to the needed external focus to remain competitive. Process reengineering, benchmarking, and best practices should be lexicons that come easily to all managers interested in improving their operations.

Managers should use benchmarking examples in communications sessions and as a basis for speeches. Those communications channels can be extensive as shown in Figure 6.6. Senior managers can provide visible evidence of support for benchmarking when they use the term in their internal and external communications. These can vary from incorporating benchmarking activities into monthly program reports, to asking that benchmarking team results be reported at progress reviews, to

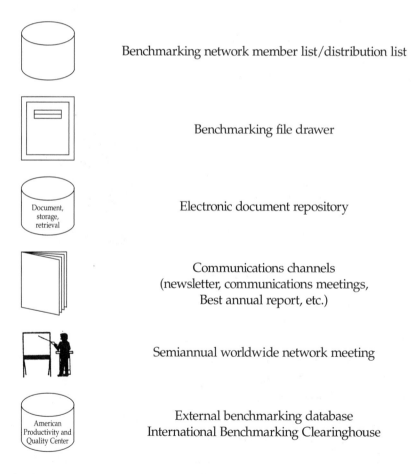

Figure 6.6. Benchmarking communications channels.

analyzing the benchmarking program in internal assessments. No opportunity should be missed to embed the word *benchmarking* in key messages to the organization by working in advance with the executives' speechwriters. In this way the executives show that they walk the talk, or act as they exhort.

Benchmarking is a learning experience. It is the accepted way to learn from others to gain innovative insight on how to change the organization. No senior executive should miss the opportunity to stress this message.

Inspect for Use

Like all processes, benchmarking must be inspected at appropriate intervals for effective use. This can be done at two levels: inspection of the number and type of benchmarking projects; and inspection of the effective use of the 10-step process. What is important is an understanding of the process focus, the companies visited, the best practices found, and what was done to implement them. When inspecting the process, a checklist can be used as an effective tool that serves as a self-assessment by the team or as an evaluation by the project's customer.

The most telling inspection is by senior management, and the benchmarking question is, how is this known? When major decisions are considered senior managers can be coached to ask the benchmarking question. The response expected is that the recommendation is based on the best practices found. There can be no more credible basis on which to justify an operation or recommendation. If managers have taken the time to find the best practices and have creatively implemented them as the basis for changing an operation, then they have done their best.

One such way to inspect the benchmarking activity is through a simple status report that quickly summarizes the studies to date. An example is shown in Figure 6.7. A summary

Organization name
Benchmarking plan summary

Focus of visit	Company visited/ date	Best practices found (Subject company or partner)	Follow-up/ status	Findings implemented	Type*	Process affected

*Benchmarking types: **I** = informal; **F** = formal (uses 10-step process); **S** = strategic; **T** = tactical

Figure 6.7. Benchmarking plan summary and status report.

document used for archiving the benchmarking studies is shown in Figure 6.8. An inspection checklist is shown in Appendix F.

Recognize and Reward

Achieving excellence in benchmarking requires that managers use the array of recognition options and rewards that most organizations have. While some organizations may set up a special award for excellence in benchmarking, it is equally effective to use the existing options to recognize superlative performance

The one exception to this experience is when a benchmarking team has been commissioned to conduct a highly visible and critically important benchmarking study of a key multiprocess project. Where that type of program and team are set up, and individuals are relieved from current duties to work on such a cross-functional effort, it may be appropriate to spell out what the rewards will be if the team is successful in accomplishing the objectives during the specified time frame.

What is ultimately desired is that the benchmarking activities be seen as the "benchmark" for benchmarking. The astute manager will know how to use the recognition and reward options creatively to continue the benchmarking initiative.

Another way to recognize the organization for benchmarking achievement is to consider competing for an external award. The most prominent are those offered by the IBC. Included here are awards to individuals through contributions to research, awards to teams in benchmarking study excellence, and awards to organizations for overall excellence in benchmarking activities.

Summary

- Managing the benchmarking process includes establishing, supporting, and sustaining the program.
- Develop a strategy statement.

	Control #: (Document filer's employee # – sequence #)
Contact Name:	Date study started: Date study completed:
Organization:	Phone:
E-mail address:	Study name:
Business process and code:	Benchmark company:
Priority goal impact:	Benchmarking type:
Keywords:	Strategic or tactical:
Primary customer:	
Objective of the study:	
Best practices found/key findings:	
Resulting actions taken:	

Figure 6.8. Benchmarking summary document.

- Set expectations for the benchmarking activities.
- Provide management awareness training.
- Establish a benchmarking competency center.
- Develop guidelines for information sharing, visit protocol, and ethical, legal, and nondisclosure considerations.
- Establish a functional network of internal benchmarking professionals.
- Identify benchmarking champions.
- Commission benchmarking teams.
- Provide team skills training
- Document the process.
- Qualify benchmarking partners.
- Follow the 10-step benchmarking process.
- Secure external assistance to supplement internal benchmarking team efforts.
- Develop a handbook for managers.
- Showcase successes and case histories.
- Have managers role model benchmarking in their activities.
- Have managers inspect for benchmarking use.
- Recognize and reward exemplar benchmarking efforts.

CHAPTER 7

Training

Order to disorder depends on organization.

- Internal Training
- Training Techniques
- External Training
- Summary

Training is essential to effectively conduct benchmarking activities. No individuals or teams should be allowed to contact other organizations or go on benchmarking visits unless they understand the essentials of benchmarking. The most effective way to gain this understanding is through some form of training. There are two ways training and experience with benchmarking can be obtained. One is through internally developed and delivered programs, and the other is through externally developed programs of which there are many alternatives.

Internal Training

Introduction

Experience in delivering benchmarking training indicates that there are at least three audiences that need it. They are (1) awareness training for managers and executive teams; (2) cross-functional skills training for those wanting the basics of benchmarking; and (3) team training for commissioned benchmarking teams. If benchmarking training courseware is developed for either of the skills training conditions, the same materials can be condensed and will satisfy the management awareness need. The training alternatives with their key characteristics are shown in Figure 7.1.

Management Awareness Training

The audience for management awareness training is all managers or those who will be responsible for seeing that benchmarking is done. The purpose of the training is twofold: (1) To orient and make all managers aware of what benchmarking is and what it is not, so there is a common understanding at all management levels; and (2) to have management teams knowledgeable enough to facilitate the benchmarking process through to its successful conclusion. Thus, there can be some assurance that a consistent approach will be followed and the expected benefits from benchmarking activities will be achieved. Course objectives for such training include the following:

- Provide management awareness of the benchmarking process.

- Provide knowledge and skills to use the process.

- Enable managers to become role models in planning benchmarking investigations and in implementing best practices.

	Awareness	Refresher	Team skills
Audience	Managers	Mixed cross section	Functional teams
Focus	Orientation/awareness	Benchmarking process starter skills	Identified team topics
Objective	Understanding, manage process	Skills	Project application
Content	Information only	Knowledge, some skills	50 percent project specific
Case study	None	Standard case study	Individual projects
When	Any meeting	On demand	When topic defined
Class size	Unlimited	20–30	15–20
Time	3–4 hours	1 day	2 days
Delivered by	Quality managers	Trainer/subject matter expert	Trainer/subject matter expert
Materials	Field materials	Field materials • Exercises • Video • Library • Project planning	Designed course • Prereading • Workbook • Instructor guide

Figure 7.1. Types of benchmarking training.

- Enable managers to become proficient in inspecting benchmarking projects.
- Help managers understand benchmarking's relation to total quality.

The content of the training is primarily information about what benchmarking is and responsibilities for successfully starting and managing it. Usually this can be done in an information exchange session, not requiring skills exercises to reinforce understanding. The training can and should cascade through the organization at scheduled events, such as staff meetings and other communications sessions.

The audience size can be unlimited. The training session should last three to four hours and should be broken into two sessions. The topics covered include the following:

- Background information on why benchmarking is important
- Definitions and examples
- The process to follow
- What to benchmark
- Whom to benchmark against
- Data and information sources to access
- Specific success factors and pitfalls for pursuing effective benchmarking activities

A typical agenda to use for this training session is shown in Figure 7.2.

If a standard set of materials is developed and supplemented by a talk track, then most managers and quality professionals should be able to deliver this type of awareness session in their organization. If not, then the benchmarking-competent professional can provide the initial training and those in a quality capacity could follow and become the next level of trainers.

```
┌─────────────────────────────────────────────────┐
│                      Agenda                       │
│  • Benchmarking chronology                        │
│  • Relationship to total quality                  │
│  • Benchmarking benefits                          │
│  • Benchmarking strategy                          │
│  • Definitions                                    │
│  • Types of benchmarking and examples             │
│  • The benchmarking process and phases            │
│  • What to benchmark                              │
│  • Whom to benchmark                              │
│  • Information sources and study conduct          │
│  • Roles and responsibilities                     │
│        —Managers                                  │
│        —Process owners                            │
│        —Teams                                     │
│        —Competency centers                        │
│  • Success factors and management expectations    │
│  • Decisions needed                               │
│        —Resource commitment                       │
│        —Approach selected                         │
│        —Results expected                          │
│        —Timing                                    │
│  • Inspection checklist                           │
└─────────────────────────────────────────────────┘
```

Figure 7.2. Executive briefing on benchmarking agenda.

Cross-Functional Skills Training

For companies that are beginning or at an intermediate stage of their benchmarking activities, there is a need to train a cross section of individuals and organizations with different backgrounds and knowledge levels. Their focus and interest are beyond awareness training. They need the skills so that they can confidently return to their respective organizations following training to start and conduct benchmarking. Often these individuals do not have the time to devote days to training. They are, however, interested in jump-starting on the essentials and finding references to additional assistance as needed. The specifications for cross-functional training are outlined in Figure 7.3.

The objective of this training is to understand the most important steps of the benchmarking process and to obtain starter skills. Therefore, emphasis is on the first three steps of the process with particular attention on the extensive data and information resources available. This involves understanding what the information resources are and how to access them. Most individuals in an operational capacity have lost touch with the extensive public data sources or the mechanisms for accessing them. There is a need to review these sources so a structured information and data-gathering plan can be developed.

The content of cross-functional training includes not only knowledge on benchmarking but also skills in exercising the basic steps; that is, what to benchmark, whom to benchmark, and how to conduct information searches. The skills training can conveniently concentrate on a standard case study for each of these steps. Since there would be no commonality in the participants' backgrounds, the case study should be selected with some care. It should be familiar to all.

The case studies that have proven most successful are those that are indicative of a small business operation that participants come in contact with regularly. Therefore, the operation of a restaurant, video rental store, and auto dealership are appropriate. In particular, the operation of a repair service is an excellent topic for a case study. A more difficult topic is one that is a common business function or process, such as training; however, the functional business topic, in which all participants are familiar with the subject matter, is hard to find. The least desirable case

- **Participant value**
  —Benchmarking training skills and knowledge
- **Workshop focus**
  —Jump-start
  —Understand key steps in the process
- **Method used**
  —Six modules
  —Prereading
  —Video introduction
  —Presentation and discussion
  —Three simulation exercises
  —Personal project planning (optional)
  —Key learnings and fail points
  —Invited guest speaker for library services
  —Question and answer time
  —Quiz
  —Course evaluation
- **Objectives**
  —Be able to start a benchmarking investigation (the planning phase) and know where to go to find information and assistance
  —Use materials and prereading
  —Be able to remember the three key process steps, the four types of benchmarking, and up to five sources of information
  —100 percent class participation
- **Source of materials**
  —Two-day benchmarking for quality improvement workshop
  —Benchmarking books
- **Instructor's abilities**
  —10 years experience conducting benchmarking investigations
  —Author of book on benchmarking
- **Review**
  —Use a variety of methods to develop knowledge and skills
  —Remember process steps, key types of benchmarking, and major information sources
  —Be ready to conduct a benchmarking study

Figure 7.3. Cross-functional training specifications.

study is a forced business topic where participants must struggle to understand the operation before being able to discuss it for benchmarking purposes. The one exception is if a number of participants just happen to come from one function. They can be given the option of concentrating on an issue for that function. An example of such a case study structure is shown in Figure 7.4.

Class size must now be considered. The ideal is to organize the class into teams of four to eight members. There should be no more that eight teams. Each team activity can be different by structuring its benchmarking focus under some predetermined umbrella topics like customer requirements, services provided, processes used, and critical success factors. The teams would then select the topic of their case study within one of these areas. Contrasting the results among the teams' efforts is then a major portion of the learning.

Cross-functional training can usually be delivered in a day. It is the kind of training to which most organizations can afford to send participants. Many of these individuals will then return to start benchmarking projects and will be able to supplement their activities with internal benchmarking competency assistance as needed.

Cross-functional training can be offered on demand, at the time of need, since it is only a day long and the format is well structured. Delivery is preferably done by a subject matter expert, a competent benchmarking professional, or someone who has done benchmarking. These trainers are preferred, because, invariably, there will be extensive questions about benchmarking techniques that will need answering. Having the experience of conducting benchmarking investigations and being able to relate them to examples within the organization makes this delivery relevant and credible. An outline of the day is shown in Figure 7.5.

Exercise 1

Team organization
1. Agree on a team discussion leader, scribe, and timekeeper.

Instructions
1. Assume you are the manager of a video store for a major franchise.
2. Attached are major topic areas of interest to benchmarking.
3. For one of the two topics assigned, develop a list of specific items to be benchmarked within the topic.
4. Prioritize the list. (Hint: Brainstorm a list and vote to select the top items.)
5. Develop a measurement that best reflects each item's output. For example: For an item called "fast checkout," selected within the category of customer requirements, the measurement might be number of customer checkouts per hour.
6. List the subgroup's top three items on a clean worksheet for presentation purposes.
7. Select one item to benchmark and flowchart the business process involved.
8. Agree on one person (not the discussion leader) to briefly describe the process followed and to present the results.

Information provided
1. The attached worksheet
2. Article on the video store marketplace <u>for background information and reference</u>

Exercise 2

Team organization
1. Agree on a team discussion leader, scribe, and timekeeper.

Instructions
1. Assume you are the manager of a video store for a major franchise.
2. For one of the three items selected in Exercise 1, agree on a description for one item of importance to benchmark.
3. For the item, develop three to six examples of whom you would benchmark against
   a. For internal benchmarking
   b. For competitive benchmarking
   c. A functional industry leader

Figure 7.4. What to benchmark: Video store case study.

4. Determine if there is an applicable <u>generic process benchmarking</u> comparison. If so, note it.
5. Agree on one person (not the discussion leader) to briefly describe the process followed and to present the results.

Information provided
1. The attached worksheet
2. Article on the video store marketplace <u>for background information and reference</u>

Exercise 3

Team organization
1. Agree on a team discussion leader, scribe, and timekeeper.

Instructions
1. Read the first page of the attached article on the video store marketplace.
2. List on the worksheet the number of discrete <u>items</u> of data and information mentioned that would be of interest to benchmark.
3. Discuss the items to ensure a complete list.
4. Read the second page of the article.
5. List on the same worksheet the <u>sources</u> of additional data and information mentioned that would be useful to contact for benchmarking.
6. Discuss the items to ensure a complete list.
7. Count the items in each list and note the number at the bottom of the worksheet.
8. Are there any unique sources of information?
9. Agree on one person (not the discussion leader) to briefly describe the process followed and to contrast the number of items and sources found by each team.

Information provided
1. The attached worksheet
2. Article on the video store marketplace <u>for background information and reference</u>

Figure 7.4. *(continued)*

Franchising

By Ripley Hotch

The videocassette rental industry did not exist before 1978, when a company called Video Station opened a small store in California. Says Robert Moffett, who once worked for the company: "The first year they had net profit of $98,000, so you knew there was franchise potential."

Indeed there was. Moffett, now president of Los Angeles-based Video Biz, whose more than 250 stores make it one of the 10 biggest VCR franchise chains, has seen the number of rental stores balloon to almost 20,000—3,000 to 4,000 of them franchises.

The eight-year boom has been fueled by the runaway market for home videocassette recorders, which enabled people to see movies when they wanted, in their own homes. Figures are hard to come by—as Byron W. Boothe, chairman of Popingo, Inc., Wichita, Kans., one of the larger video franchise chains, says, "One of the things about a new industry is it's hard to get your arms around statistics"— but various industry estimates put the number of VCR households in the United States at 30 percent.

Hit hard by the trend have been movie theaters and cable television, both of which have suffered losses of audience and revenues since the video boom began. A recent study for Merrill Lynch, Inc. by analysts Wilkofsky Gruen Associates, predicts that the videotape rental and sales industry will reach an annual retail volume of $20 billion by 1995—more than triple expected movie box office revenue. The biggest beneficiaries of the trend, besides the Japanese manufacturers of VCRs, have been stores that rent video tapes.

The sales curve on videocassette recorders is leveling, says Ira Mayer, executive editor of Los Angeles-based Video Marketing Newsletter, which tracks the industry. Sales of 12.6 million are projected for this year, a slight increase over 1985. But, Mayer says, "although the rate of growth is stable, when you look at the percentage of households added, it's enormous. VCR sales are adding 10 percent of households a year through 1988, and you're looking at two thirds of households by the end of the '80s."

The size of the market has attracted

Shopping for rental movies to watch at home has become an established habit in the 30 percent of American households with videocassette

recorders. Competition among franchisors to supply videocassette tapes to the rental market is intense.

PHOTO: KEN TOUCHTON

greater competition—hundreds of new stores and even hundreds of chains (some have only a few outlets). That means, say industry leaders, that there will be a major shakeout, but that there will continue to be a huge business for retailers who are resourceful in dealing with the new realities.

Most observers believe the video rental and sales industry will be profoundly changed in the next few years. That means that someone who is considering a major investment in a franchise—and the cost can be up to $250,000 with franchise fees, inventory and remodeling—needs to be very careful about the chain he chooses.

No one is more positive about the trend toward consolidation than Ron Berger, president of National Video, Inc., Portland, Ore., with 624 stores the largest of the franchised chains. He predicts that the strong will get stronger and the weak—particularly the independents who are not members of any kind of chain—will fall by the wayside. Berger predicts that 5,000 U.S. and Canadian video retailers will fail in 1986. Of the top 10 franchisors, he says,

"at least five will not be here a year from now, and it will be much worse for guys below that." Berger's NVI is taking over Pop & Card, Inc., an Oklahoma-based franchisor, and is looking for other acquisitions.

Robert McIntosh, a former executive with Adventureland Video, Inc., of Salt Lake City, and now a franchise consultant, says: "Video franchising has seen its day. Two or three years ago everybody wanted to get into it. I think you'll see mergers and conversions, or people will have a regional chain of 50-75 stores and be satisfied with that."

Big franchisors, though they agree there will be a consolidation, say franchisors are in the best position not only to survive, but to prosper. The big losers, they say, will be the mom and pop video retailers.

"It's kind of like a little market competing against a big supermarket," says Moffett. "They don't have the buying power; it's pretty tough for the independents."

Popingo's Boothe, one of the most aggressive franchisors, insists that the

Figure 7.4. *(continued)*

Videocassette rental stores are facing a shakeout. Franchisors are trying innovative approaches to make sure they survive—and prosper.

industry will "grow by leaps and bounds as VCR sales go up," although he also sees consolidation ahead. "There will end up being about three national video franchisors," he says.

Boothe says that the "real growth in the next 18 months will be in the how-to categories—exercise, or how to cook, those kind of things. You're going to see an educational bent to a lot of them: coaching for the Scholastic Aptitude Test and things like that.

"I saw one of my children's test scores improved 40 percent by watching an SAT coaching tape. A lot of investment dollars will be poured into making those tapes." Boothe says Popingo will be getting into videotape production and even into creating computer software.

A major move by convenience stores to open video clubs—7-Eleven is opening its first "Movie Quik" videotape clubs in stores around Washington—is viewed as a minor threat.

Doug Reed, a spokesman for Dallas' Southland Corporation, parent of 7-Eleven, says the primary reason the company is getting into video rental is that "it is an emerging need on the part of our consumers, who have expressed a desire to rent movies in a convenient, inexpensive manner."

In other words, he says, it is a natural extension of the convenience store business. Each store will carry around 200 titles. "The two advantages," says Reed, "are 1) you can rent and return movies 24 hours a day, seven days a week; 2) they are sensibly priced. They will be 99 cents Monday through Thursday and $1.99 Friday through Sunday."

Bill Ditch, an area franchisee of Video Biz in Florida, says the convenience store outlet will be limited because "7-Eleven can't carry enough titles. The average club member will rent 200 movies a year. How many do I have to carry to have 200 you want to see? That's four a week."

Franchisors see supermarkets as a bigger threat—Berger says they will eventually capture 25 percent of rentals—and are fighting back by opening kiosks or ministores themselves within supermarkets or department stores.

"We're very heavy into grocery

chains in California, Nevada and Arizona," says John Bosworth, referral coordinator of Adventureland. "Why have a competitor when it can be you?"

National Video is offering its "Movie Express" kiosk option as a franchise in itself. Another National Video innovation, "Pay Per Transaction," is being closely watched by others in the business.

The concept attempts to solve the recurring complaint of video rental outlets—not enough movies—by forging an alliance with movie producers. In a test now going on, selected National Video franchisees pay a studio $6 for cassettes of a new movie up to two months before it goes into general release. The franchisees share all rental revenues on the cassettes with the studio on a 50-50 basis.

Berger says the program will reduce wholesale prices of cassettes, which he says are artificially high; allow the public quick access to hit films; and assure studios of a steady share of rental income, thus encouraging them to produce more—and possibly better—films.

Other video franchisors are not so sure it will work that way.

Moffett worries that studios, which have been known to dictate what percentage of the gross theater owners got, will do the same to video stores. "And then the video stores will be working for the studios. What assurances are there that the split will stay at 50-50? Berger may be playing with dynamite."

Such innovations, though they may not assure the health of individual chains, suggest that strong franchisors will be in the best position to take advantage of a widespread American desire to watch movies at home. **NB**

Reprinted by permission, *Nation's Business.* April 1986. Copyright 1986, U.S. Chamber of Commerce.

Figure 7.4. *(continued)*

Benchmarking for Superior Performance Workshop
Benchmarking: Finding and implementing best practices.

Introduction
- Objectives of workshop

Background
- Benchmarking defined
- Types of benchmarking
- Strategy, relationship to TQM
- Recent example studies

Benchmarking process
- Overview of 5-phase, 10-step process
- Case study exercise (the video store)

What to benchmark (step 1)
- Guidelines and approach
- Understand and document the work process
- Case study exercise (the video store)
- Relationship to L. L. Bean

Whom to benchmark (step 2)
- Guidelines and approach
- Best competitors or functional industry leaders
- Case study exercise (the video store)
- Relationship to L. L. Bean

Information resources (step 3)
- Navigating the information resource maze
- Information sources (what are they?)
- Information searches (how are they conducted?)
- Case study exercise (the video store)

Planning a benchmarking investigation
- Conducting a site visit
- Preparation, conduct, and debriefing
- Gap analysis (steps 4 and 5)
- Guidelines, approach, and tools
- Look ahead to implementation (steps 6–10)

Figure 7.5. Workshop outline.

Managing benchmarking
- Establishing a benchmarking program
- Supporting a benchmarking program
- Sustaining a benchmarking program

Summary and evaluation
- Quiz: Benchmarking myths

Reference material
- Bibliography of benchmarking information
- Learning points and key faults
- Inspection checklist

Figure 7.5. *(continued)*

In addition to the structured exercises around the case study, there are other methods that make cross-functional training effective. These involve individuals not usually associated with training.

If a video of a senior executive discussing the need for benchmarking can be found, it serves as an excellent introduction and proof statement. If an internal source cannot be found, there are an increasing number of external, credible experts. They are found in universities, through consultants, or through benchmarking clearinghouses.

Bringing in the information search expert to cover accessing public databases is another, proven training method. The company's resource librarian could also be a participant in the training. The benchmarking trainer should cover what the various sources of data and information are, and the resource librarian should cover how to access them.

Thus, the end objectives of cross-functional training are

- To be able to start a benchmarking activity

- To know where to find information and assistance

- To be skilled at the important steps of the benchmarking process
- To understand the different types of benchmarking and their benefits and expected outcomes
- To understand the key sources of information

Benchmarking Team Training

As companies become more mature in their benchmarking programs, and as managers become more skilled in their ability to commission and facilitate benchmarking projects, a different type of training becomes necessary and is usually requested. In particular, when organizations understand the worth of focusing their productivity and continuous improvement efforts on work processes as part of an ongoing quality initiative, conducting benchmarking on a process team basis has proven to be highly successful.

In this instance the audience consists of preselected functional teams made up of process owners and operators. Some of the team members will have been selected because of their specific knowledge about the work processes and others for their analytical or other research skills. They are commissioned to conduct a benchmarking investigation by a responsible manager or sponsor who indicates the general area of investigation but not necessarily the specific, highest-priority process. It will be the team's work to analyze its operations and ensure that the selected topic or work process will coincide with the function's mission and goals and will yield the greatest payback in performance improvement.

About half of the content of this team training is project specific. The team exercises are based on the work process selected, not on an abstract case study. The approach has four phases: team selection; workshop to analyze the operations and identify industry leaders; on-site research to plan and undertake site visits; and an optional workshop to analyze best practices and implement findings.

Course materials include the standards for highly structured training. These consist of the following:

- Prework for the participants to prepare for the workshop so that they are familiar with the key concepts

- Preview of the benchmarking process to help focus on priority objectives

- Classroom materials to guide participants through project exercises, group discussions, and project steps

- Instructor materials containing lesson plans and all student materials used

This formal training is delivered on a scheduled basis. Management agrees to the focus of investigations. Class size is usually limited to 30 participants organized into five teams. Training lasts two days for the first workshop and an additional day for the second, optional workshop. The instructor must be a qualified individual with benchmarking experience.

Training Techniques

There are some fundamental training techniques that are effective. They will be covered here as a group and left to the trainer to implement as appropriate.

Training should be based on the proven sequence of tell, see, and do. This is similar to the old navy adage of "Tell them what you're going to tell them. Tell them. Then tell them what you told them." The points need to be reinforced. The "tell" portion of the training should be a short tutorial. The "see" can best be accomplished through an example or case history. The "do" step has participants apply what they learned to their chosen benchmarking topic.

In benchmarking training, experience shows that certain places need special attention. If a process focus is taken, what to benchmark will require an exercise in documentation, most likely using a flowchart of the process. It is often instructive to have a common example to gain proficiency. The one that seems most understandable is the application to a retail counter check-out. This is an almost universal experience.

Another place where special attention is needed is in the understanding of the different types of benchmarking. The best way to get that instilled is by having participants work through an exercise of developing, for a selected topic or process, whom they would benchmark against using the four types of bench-marking—internal, competitive, functional, and generic.

There are training situations where role modeling is useful, particularly in the preparation and execution of a questionnaire. If a process description or questionnaire is developed, then the interview process that will take place during the site visit can be simulated. One team can represent those being visited and another group can represent the visiting team. The teams can simulate a site visit, ask the questions, and then debrief after-ward. This exercise usually reveals that not nearly the depth of information is asked for what is available. This exercise is invalu-able in preparing the team to make efficient and effective use of the site visit.

With the prominence of benchmarking there is now course-ware available. It has been prepared by several organizations and, in some instances, shared with others who have improved the content. Any organization contemplating benchmarking training should seriously consider not developing new materials but rather taking the existing materials and tailoring them to its specific use. There is also a wealth of media for reinforcing train-ing, including courseware, software, videotapes, audiocassettes, reference materials, bibliographies, and some media that are still evolving like on-line databases. Cross-references to key points can also be added in the text being used. The training should summarize key learnings and major fail points. It could involve a quiz, and it should definitely have an evaluation.

Lastly, the benchmarking trainer or facilitator should, because of the applied nature of the subject and materials, be someone who has done benchmarking. Since this individual is most likely not an experienced educator, he or she will need to be trained. This means taking a "train-the-trainer" course, observing some training sessions, and then conducting a few under the supervision of a qualified benchmarking trainer before going solo.

External Training

Introduction

In addition to the training that can be delivered internally to the organization there are external offerings and events. These should be considered depending on their usefulness in accomplishing a specific purpose. There are at least three reasons for considering external training events.

1. Send individuals to external training sessions when there is not the class size required for the critical mass internally.

2. Use external offerings when an individual has been designated to become the benchmarking competency person or program manager for the organization and that individual wants exposure to others' benchmarking approaches.

3. Use external training when the organization wants to assess the worth of the external event for potential use internally, since many of the events can be customized and delivered on-site.

Often external events are divided into different levels of expertise to serve as a guide to their use. They include basic or beginner level, for those organizations just starting with little or no knowledge about benchmarking or those at the beginning stages of a quality initiative. The intermediate or semiskilled level is for those individuals with a working knowledge of benchmarking or for organizations that have embarked on a benchmarking or quality process and want to implement a careful plan. The advanced level is for those who have successfully implemented benchmarking and need additional skills to perfect it.

The same offerings mentioned for internal training are also available for external training. Fee-based quality solution organizations, associations, consultants, universities, and professional meeting or event organizers all offer management awareness, cross-functional skills, and benchmarking team training options. Additional external training alternatives include benchmarking strategy seminars, conferences, workshops, study missions, and on-demand, customized team facilitation and consulting. These are briefly covered in the following sections.

Strategy, Organization, and Management
The strategy approach taken by companies embarking on benchmarking can be shared with interested audiences. This is a major learning activity for those just starting. They have an opportunity to learn from others that have successfully implemented a benchmarking process. The strategy approach includes the following:

- Organization and management of benchmarking
- How benchmarking fits into TQM, continuous quality improvement, and business process management
- Infrastructure for managing benchmarking
- Use of networks, competency centers, education, and training
- How benchmarking eventually becomes institutionalized

- Management responsibilities of establishing, supporting, and sustaining benchmarking
- Assessment process for defining the current state and the desired, endpoint state of the organization
- Vision of what benchmarking should be

Customers for strategy approach training are senior, department, and division managers; senior quality professionals; process owners; and newly appointed professionals interested in getting benchmarking started and integrated into other continuous improvement activities. Their principal requirements are how to implement benchmarking in their organizations. This includes getting it started, it sustaining over time, and eventually having it institutionalized. Trainees gain insight from others' experiences and thereby markedly reduce the time to implement benchmarking. Given the interest not only in the topic of benchmarking but also in the national, state, and regional quality awards in which benchmarking is an essential requirement, the ability to learn strategies for successful benchmarking management is significant. On the basis of the organization's experience, it could formulate its own training adaptation for internal deployment and justification.

Conferences

Conferences provide a comprehensive way to quickly expose attendees to a wide variety of benchmarking experiences. These are sponsored by clearinghouses, associations, and professional meeting and event management firms. They normally cover one to two days and consist of presentations by benchmarking professionals. Each presentation is about one hour and covers a defined topic. Eight to 10 presentations are given each day. Often the topics are structured to minimize the overlap as much as possible. Providing this is done, conferences can be rich sources of learning from the experts and of networking. In fact, the informal networking at conferences can be the single greatest benefit.

The content of presentations generally includes positioning benchmarking within the organization, getting senior management support and buy-in, tutorials on how to conduct benchmarking and experience in doing so, and different organizations' experience and key learnings and fail points. Expanded subtopics include positioning benchmarking with other TQM and continuous improvement activities, and integrating benchmarking into an operational approach that will ensure its continuation and institutionalization.

Several organizations often describe their experience during the presentations. Organizations include manufacturing and service companies but are now expanding to include financial services and health care, government, and educational institutions. The latter increasingly show the robustness of the benchmarking approach and its application and adaptation to all types of organizations that need to improve. Consultants and their client experiences are also included in these presentations.

Ideally, the conference audience is composed of managers of divisions and operating units, quality professionals, potential benchmarking team leaders, and benchmarking managers. Their justification for attending would be to gain insight to, enthusiasm for, and information on benchmarking. Then they could return to their respective organizations and adopt a benchmarking approach or enhance an existing one to the organization's mores and culture.

Workshops and Seminars

One-day workshops or seminars are of interest to heterogeneous groups that want to be exposed to benchmarking in some depth beyond awareness but do not want to be focused on preselected team topics. These workshops often take the character of the jump-start training delivered to internal organizations. The objective of workshops is to give refresher skills, often to intermediate-level knowledgeable organizations. Providing the seminars are adequately structured, there is an opportunity to provide meaningful information on benchmarking. The difficulty in their delivery is rationalizing the differences in content with awareness, strategy, and team training offerings. Reaching the right audiences that already have some appropriate benchmarking understanding and having the training meet their needs are also difficult tasks.

Study Tours and Missions

Benchmarking is a topic that attracts study missions. These are groups that have an interest in a specific topic and arrange for organizations to host them and share experiences. Usually the groups are from other countries or companies. Study tours are a structured way for visiting groups to be exposed to benchmarking in a comprehensive way focused solely on their needs. These sessions include awareness and management of benchmarking and, sometimes, panels of experts to bring firsthand information from a functional area on some focused topic.

Team Facilitation and Consulting

Most external organizations are prepared to offer on-demand team facilitation and consulting for the proper pursuit of benchmarking. This can include individualized attention to specific team questions about approach; helping teams with procedural problems; and the audit and inspection of team activities for conformance to the 10-step process. It may also include several visits to the team, such as after its training on the first steps of the process, after the team has completed the planning phase, or while the team is analyzing the potential performance gap.

Customers of team training and facilitation include organizations that are starting benchmarking and want to have assistance in the start-up phase, possibly with some of the initial showcase benchmarking efforts, and teams starting benchmarking or perhaps ones that have failed or have been discouraged in their results and are seeking guidance. Their requirements include firsthand benchmarking experience and the ability to relate to personal dealings with points of success and failure. Having contact with other benchmarking professionals and assistance from others starting benchmarking would be a major reason to seek out this type of assistance. A key is to exhibit a professional approach and to have a proven methodology.

There should be no difficulty justifying the value of consulting to the organization because the facilitator has a proven track record. The key, however, is ensuring that the team does the work and the facilitator truly acts as a coach. There is a real danger in having the facilitator become so involved that he or she tries to run the benchmarking study.

Summary

- Use awareness training for managers and executive teams.
- Use cross-functional skills training for those who need basic and intermediate benchmarking skills.
- Use team training for commissioned benchmarking teams.
- Have experienced benchmarking professionals conduct the training.
- Supplement internal training with video presentations and guest speakers.
- Use tell-see-do training techniques.
- Provide exercises in documentation and role modeling.

- Use existing benchmarking courseware and adapt the materials to the firm's condition.
- Use strategic training approaches for managers, senior quality professionals, and process owners.
- Utilize external training options including conferences, workshops, seminars, study tours, missions, team facilitation, and consulting.

CHAPTER 8

Managers' Resource Guide

Therefore, the skillful commander takes up a position in which he cannot be defeated and misses no opportunity to master his enemy.

- Reason for the Guide
- Benchmarking Strategy
- Roles and Responsibilities
- Getting Started
- Visit Guidelines and Referral Process
- Conduct of a Site Visit
- Information Sharing Guidelines
- Identification of Key Processes
- Information Searches
- Knowledge Base and Archiving
- Training and Resource Materials
- Networks
- Definitions
- Appendix
- Summary

A great quantity of benchmarking material is starting to accumulate. There are hundreds of journal articles on the topic. Several books with various perspectives are on the market. Training courses are available. Videotapes and audiocassettes exist, and software is starting to appear to help teams conduct benchmarking. Last, but not least, many organizations have prepared their own internal documents to further explain benchmarking. Many of these are excellent.

For managers interested in benchmarking essentials, and for process owners interested in how to get started, this volume of material can be bewildering. Therefore, a guide to the essentials is needed. The managers' resource guide is not a compilation of all that has been written about benchmarking, but a synopsis that abstracts the key points, provides quick references to selected subjects, and subsequently creates a document order number, title, telephone number, or other reference that enables users to find the appropriate details.

By using the guide, managers and team leaders will know the key considerations for effective benchmarking, and they can find out where to go for additional material. This chapter describes the content of a managers' resource guide. A description of one such guide is shown in Figure 8.1.

Reason for the Guide

The reason for the managers' resource guide should be clearly stated. It provides managers with a source of quick reference information to start and conduct a benchmarking investigation, and it provides additional resources to pursue as the benchmarking study continues. This includes key points about the 10-step user process as well as management considerations that make benchmarking successful.

Introduction—An overview of benchmarking's importance to the organization and how this guide can aid your benchmarking efforts

Strategy—Benchmarking's impact on quality improvement initiatives

Roles and responsibilities—A summary of key benchmarking suppliers and customers

Getting started—The essential first steps to ensure a successful benchmarking effort

Benchmarking requests—How to handle benchmarking requests

Benchmarking visit guidelines—How to plan and conduct a benchmarking visit

Information sharing—Legal guidelines to prevent antitrust concerns; rules to ensure benchmarking is fair and beneficial to both parties

Key processes—The business processes that should be understood before researching other companies

Library services—The primary research center for benchmarkers; a summary of research and archive services available from the library

Document search and retrieval—How to use software to research and retrieve documents, and to file benchmarking reports

Training and resources—A list of training available for benchmarkers

BEST network—A description of the benchmarking effectiveness strategy team's (BEST's) role in promoting benchmarking; a list of BEST members

Appendix—Supplemental information, including a benchmarking inspection checklist, samples of benchmarking correspondence, lists of questions used by benchmarking teams, a code of conduct from the International Benchmarking Clearinghouse, and a bibliography

Used with permission of Xerox Corporation.

Figure 8.1. Sections at a glance.

Benchmarking and the Company

How benchmarking has contributed to a company's quality initiatives and pursuit of continuous improvement is described in the guide. It is important to remind readers that benchmarking is a quality tool. How benchmarking contributes to any goal setting, such as 100X or six-sigma programs, or its contribution to the improvement of key work processes, is also described in the guide.

Benchmarking should be mentioned not just as a process for finding best practices but also as a learning experience. Looking outside the company or industry provides a fresh perspective on better practices that can be used to pursue improvement. Benchmarking's contribution to achieving satisfied customers is an important relationship to detail in the managers' resource guide.

The increased interest in benchmarking derived from the pursuit of quality awards is another important perspective to mention. Many of these awards have specific benchmarking requirements. Perhaps reference to other companies' pursuit of benchmarking would be important to the subject company.

The managers' resource guide must stress the essentials of benchmarking and how it is critical to achieving customer satisfaction. Studying the processes of others determines how to make improvements that will ultimately achieve stated company-wide goals.

Corporate Benchmarking Directives

Any company pronouncements on benchmarking should be covered in the managers' resource guide. These may be derived from performance improvement initiatives. They include 10X programs, improving critical outputs, setting and validating key performance measurements, focusing on business process improvement, establishing feature and functional benchmarks for products, and objective, external comparisons for internal operations.

Who Should Use the Guide

The intended audience for the guide should be identified. The audience might vary depending on the skill level of the organization or the maturity of a quality pursuit. Most likely the audience includes all managers, all functional benchmarking representatives, and all process owners and operators.

Special attention, however, should be given to cascading the guide or its availability through the organization so that those contemplating a benchmarking investigation, or those who want to become more knowledgeable about this important quality tool, know the guide exists and is available to them to conduct benchmarking effectively and efficiently. The guide is there to help do benchmarking right and to avoid difficulties.

Key Points

The basic structure of the guide is an outline of the key steps of the benchmarking process. It shows how to gather data and prepare for a benchmarking visit. The guide provides the appropriate legal and ethical cautions for information sharing and proper protocol.

A reminder of what the guide is not is important. It is not meant to be a compilation of all that has been written. It is a supplement, not a replacement, to the many available benchmarking resources. A section at the end of each chapter of the guide should reference where to find details or whom to contact for additional assistance.

Early in the guide's introduction, it is wise to rationalize the need for the guide and to preview its content. Included here are key comments about ethics and that benchmarking is a mutual exchange of information that should remain confidential to all involved parties unless otherwise stated.

Readers should be reminded that value is derived from understanding how others have achieved their performance. Benchmarking does not concentrate on the measurements but on the practices. That is important.

The need for discipline and structure in preparing for an information exchange must be stressed. The key essentials of careful preparation by documenting the process under study, involving the process owners and operators, and concentrating on the practices of others must be emphasized.

The Benchmarking Process

It is appropriate to cover some essentials of the 10-step benchmarking process in the first sections of the guide. Details could be cross-referenced to later sections. Such things as defining the purpose of the study and the expected use of the results are important not only from the customer's viewpoint but also from a historical viewpoint, especially, if at a later date, there are inferences of possible impropriety. Examining the subject company's work processes as the baseline for comparison to others must be stressed. Careful planning of visits, buy-in from process owners, and following guidelines for information gathering should also be emphasized.

The Manager's Role

The roles and responsibilities of the major benchmarking parties are covered in the guide; however, the responsibilities of the manager interested in having benchmarking done or in commissioning teams must be covered early.

Benchmarking Strategy

Each organization should determine its benchmarking strategy statement. There should be some rationale for benchmarking in relation to the organization's goals and objectives or in relation to the other continuous improvement initiatives. Everyone in the organization must understand at the outset of any benchmarking activity where it fits in the overall scheme of things. This should be stressed in the managers' resource guide.

Mission Statement

It is presumed that benchmarking has some purpose that complements other initiatives within the organization. It may be that the organization is pursuing benchmarking to support a larger operational mission or key priorities. If so, there is a need to succinctly state that purpose.

Focus of Strategy

The strategy for implementing the benchmarking mission should then be articulated. One variant of finding and implementing best practices logically focuses benchmarking on improving business processes.

If this is the case then some description of the scope of the mission tied to organizational goals is an appropriate statement of strategy. How the strategy's success will be measured should also be mentioned. Most likely, some vital few, high-level performance measures will be used.

Finally, the outcome expected from the strategy must be stated. This can best be accomplished by articulating the end-point or desired benchmarking state.

Approach, Deployment, Results

The next task is to provide some insight into how the mission and strategy statement will be carried out. This is best explained in the Malcolm Baldrige National Quality Award's discipline of approach, deployment, and results.

The approach may be a centralized pursuit of benchmarking or it may cascade to the operational units with them carrying forward the activity. Therefore, support activities, such a competency center, network, or other resources, should be mentioned in the managers' resource guide.

Deployment most likely will mean that specific benchmarking studies are underway. It also means that training is available to make those undertaking benchmarking proficient in the process.

Results can best be discussed by showcasing successful benchmarking studies. These would cover the focus of the investigation, the process being improved, the companies visited and rationale for selecting them as partners, the best practices found, and their implementation strategies for specifically stated business impact. This later material can be effectively documented in tables indicating the overall quantity, type, and results along with selected narrative descriptions of completed studies.

Roles and Responsibilities

A critical element in pursuing effective benchmarking is to understand its users, resources, and assistance providers. It is rare to find benchmarking assistance from one central source. Therefore, understanding what different individuals and organizations do, and do not do, is important. All this should be explained in the managers' resource guide.

Rationale

The most straightforward description is to discuss customers and suppliers of benchmarking studies. Each of these will have specific outputs and their roles and responsibilities can be discussed. The same descriptive approach can be taken with groups such as networks, libraries, and clearinghouses.

In this text, the outputs of customers and suppliers are discussed in the following sections. The roles and responsibilities are discussed in Appendix G.

Customers

The primary customers for benchmarking activities are senior functional managers, senior divisional managers, and process owners and operators. In the managers' resource guide, their roles and responsibilities can be discussed as a group since they are similar. The major outputs of these benchmarking customers include ensuring that

- Teams are properly commissioned.
- Boundaries are established.
- Outputs are determined.
- Key milestone dates are established.
- Status reports are agreed to.

Suppliers

The suppliers of benchmarking studies should be described in the managers' resource guide. Since it is assumed that benchmarking is conducted through teams commissioned to focus on an identified area, they will need assistance provided by suppliers. At a minimum, the suppliers to the teams are a corporate-level benchmarking competency; a division-level benchmarking competency; a functional benchmarking representative; a benchmarking network; the benchmarking team itself; an information center or library; and individual resources. There may be other suppliers depending on the specific organization structure and company culture. Their outputs are described in the following sections of the managers' resource guide.

Corporate benchmarking competency Experience dictates that unless there is someone responsible for benchmarking it will not happen. The company-level role is mostly related to information.

One possible output for such a position is a companywide communications network. Most large organizations now have an internal benchmarking seminar that is run for the entire corporation. At the same time, a newsletter focused on benchmarking could come from this company-level position.

Division benchmarking competency At the major divisional level, either based on geography or product line, some coordination of the benchmarking effort is needed primarily from an operational perspective.

Assigned outputs of the divisional benchmarking competency include

- Running an operational network of those involved or of those who represent their organizations for benchmarking

- Coordinating incoming and outgoing benchmarking requests

- Maintaining electronic networks and other files of benchmarking information including a best practices library

Benchmarking network It is often desirable to coordinate benchmarking activities through an operational network that meets at regular intervals to update activities, reduce redundancies, and produce work. Members of the network are representatives from each of the major functional units or other organizations that have been designated as the benchmarking contact.

Specific outputs include coordinating cross-unit benchmarking; promoting and communicating the need for benchmarking; contributing to the planning process and business plans; continuously improving the benchmarking process itself; and developing whatever support materials and services are needed by the organization.

Functional benchmarking representatives These are individuals, either assigned full-time or part-time, to be the functional representatives for benchmarking within their respective units. These are the individuals the teams turn to for assistance. They are the members of the benchmarking network and the "lightning rod" for benchmarking.

Specific outputs include maintaining the status of team activities; linking the team's focus of activities to the unit's objectives; helping teams identify companies that might have best practices; facilitating the formation of teams; and, ultimately, ensuring benchmarking results are achieved through implementation of the studies' findings.

Benchmarking teams Of course, the teams perform the benchmarking investigations. Their outputs include refining the focus of the investigation; obtaining agreement on the customer requirements for the study; documenting the process to be studied; conducting the investigation; documenting and reporting the findings; obtaining concurrence on the changes to be made and the plan for achievement; and archiving the results of the study.

Information centers and other internal resources There may be still other organizations, such as the librarian and other internal experts, whose roles and responsibilities need to be covered in the managers' resource guide. Because of their importance, these should be presented in a separate section of the guide.

Getting Started

This section of the managers' resource guide shows teams how to start a benchmarking study. Teams need a primer on what to do first. They should be given a list of essential steps. This will lead them to the details of the process. Figure 8.2 illustrates a typical list from the managers' resource guide that can be given to the teams at the start of their studies.

Visit Guidelines and Referral Process

There is a need to document how to handle incoming and outgoing benchmarking requests. Users should also be reminded of the proper protocol for handling site visits. Many of these tips can be portrayed in flowchart form for quick comprehension.

- **Conduct preliminary research.**
  - —Select the topic.
  - —Ask for assistance.
  - —Contact the library.
  - —Canvas internal experts.
  - —Access internal documents.
  - —Review bibliographies.
- **Conduct secondary research and examine the following sources.**
  - —Trade periodicals
  - —Professional associations
  - —Consulting firms
  - —External industry experts
  - —Software providers
- **Select benchmarking criteria.**

Figure 8.2. Task list to help benchmarking teams get started.

Company Contacts

With the growing interest in benchmarking, it is prudent to have some guidelines on handling outgoing benchmarking requests. This way the contacted companies will view the process as best-in-class and will, therefore, be willing to participate in a study. Benchmarking requests can come from many different sources and from all levels of an organization. Thus, the guidelines ensure that the requests are properly handled and adequately planned and executed.

The guidelines should spell out, in company-specific terms, who is responsible for what and who else should be notified of the contact. There are untold accounts of sales reps with customers, and purchasing agents with suppliers, that when advised of an impending benchmarking visit, have either been able to markedly aid the process or head off a potentially sensitive situation. The managers' resource guide should translate these opportunity and risk situations into company-specific actions, as well as other analogous situations.

External Requests

When external organizations express an interest in benchmarking the same, counterpart need for predefined handling is, perhaps, even more crucial. The incoming requests quite often do not identify the correct internal unit to contact, or there is overlap with several units. So the level of coordination is greater with attendant risks. In all cases it is wise to have a principal contact and a backup identified.

If there has been a network established within the firm, then the network often becomes the coordinating body to pass referrals to the right organization. It must be understood, however, that if such a handoff happens, the recipient will follow through. Some documentation of the visit should eventually be sent to the unit's benchmarking representative for future reference. All this should be detailed in the managers' resource guide.

Conduct of a Site Visit

While several books detail what to do to prepare for a site visit, the essential steps should be summarized in the managers' resource guide to maintain consistency and uniformity and to prevent pitfalls. The essentials include what to do before, during, and after a site visit. These steps do not need a great deal of narrative and generally can be presented in outline form. Preparation must be stressed; that is, there should be clear expectations for well-prepared trips that are detailed enough to understand the better practices sought.

Visit Prerequisites

It goes without saying in benchmarking circles that returning from a site visit with defensible best practices rests on adequate preparation for the visit. This includes determining and documenting the purpose and intended use of the information, and having a thorough knowledge of the business process involved and some background knowledge of the company to be able to speak knowledgeably about its business.

Adequate Preparation

The following key points should be discussed in the managers' resource guide.

- Initial research should be conducted. If the company is a customer or supplier the appropriate account manager should be contacted.

- The most appropriate person to contact in the partner firm must be determined. Generally, it is most effective to contact the individual in the counterpart function.

- The contact person should then be called and sent a letter. In it, the specific purpose of the visit and topics to be discussed are outlined.

- A clear statement of the purpose and use of the data and information is prepared. This statement provides a common agenda for the partners, ensures that the appropriate individuals are present, and ensures that an efficient information exchange can take place. This statement might be important later if the visit is reviewed for possible sensitive issues.

- A detailed process description and/or questionnaire, to ensure all the relevant data and information are gathered, is now prepared. The questionnaire should only be sent if it is requested so that there will be no chance of it becoming a deterrent.

- The optimum team size must be determined and justified. The who-we-are documents should be prepared. These quickly acquaint the benchmarking partner with major responsibility areas, organizational structure, and other relevant information, data, and statistics.

Note that the actual time spent visiting the partner firm is small in relation to the overall benchmarking study time line. Thus, it is essential that the team be well prepared.

During the Tour

The following details of the tour should be discussed in the managers' resource guide. The procedure for note taking should be determined. Obtaining clarification of observations and information should be stressed in the guide. It is often appropriate to leave the option of calling back to follow up, to validate the information, and to verify interpretations. As appropriate, a reciprocal visit or tour should be offered.

Wrap Up

A thank-you letter is always proper protocol. Debriefing is also essential. Individuals retain different information and observations. They should be discussed as quickly after the visit as possible to gain consensus based on fresh recall. The trip should be documented in a formal report.

Visit Documentation

Guidelines on what to document are worthwhile. This ensures some semblance of uniformity of information, but more importantly, it serves as the basis for archiving the information for reference by others.

Informal Visits

Under selected conditions informal benchmarking may be conducted. This often occurs when executives meet to see if there are, in general, significantly different practices being used and to confirm the need for a formal benchmarking study. These forerunners of a more disciplined, detailed, process-to-process comparison are worthwhile but should not be confused with effective benchmarking. In the managers' resource guide, the point might be stressed through a matrix comparing the two approaches and expected outcomes.

Information Sharing Guidelines

A key section of the managers' resource guide should be devoted to covering the legal and ethical guidelines and the protocol for benchmarking. Individual firms and outside third-party organizations have prepared such guidelines. They generally deal with the dos and don'ts of information sharing, the use of nondisclosure agreements, benchmarking within the same industry, and benchmarking information confidentiality. The key points can be captured in the following sections of the guide: legal guidelines, ethical guidelines, and protocol and courtesy guidelines.

Identification of Key Processes

Assuming the organization will be pursuing benchmarking through the improvement of the key business processes, then a section on how the processes are related is appropriate. How the processes are identified, documented, and prioritized should be described in the managers' resource guide. A process classification for cross-referencing the benchmarking studies is one primary outcome.

How the business processes are linked to and directly contribute to the organizations' priorities should be described. The scheme for how the organization arrived at this stage and the relationship to benchmarking should be explained. *There can be no more compelling reason for benchmarking than focusing it on business process improvement that directly supports the organization's goals and concentrates on the vital few, prioritized processes.*

Business Process Management and Improvement

The organization's approach to process improvement, its classification scheme, process listing, and all process owners should be described in the managers' resource guide. This provides the reference to business process management that underpins the benchmarking effort.

If not specifically covered elsewhere in the guide, the preferred approach to process documentation should be covered. The approach to determine the summary performance measures should also be described and might include flowcharting, arrow diagramming, mapping, and other techniques.

The methodology for determining the key summary performance measures, whether pre-, in-process, postprocess, or output measures, should receive some attention to ensure consistency in understanding and approach. If there are any general guidelines for the focus of process measurements, they should be covered in the managers' resource guide. They include such things as concentrating on customer satisfaction, quality, cycle time, cost effectiveness, and the appropriate asset measurements.

Key Process Prioritization

While benchmarking focused on business processes is necessary for achieving business results, it is not sufficient. The organization should be able to show that it has prioritized its processes to directly leverage and improve results. This may not be the role of the benchmarking competency professional but it is that person's role to ensure that the prioritization is done. Only then can there be assurance that benchmarking is actively contributing to the organization's stated goals. These points must be stressed in the managers' resource guide.

Information Searches

Since the capability of an information center or library is a major contribution to benchmarking efforts, its services should be described in detail in the managers' resource guide. Not only is the library an important resource for benchmarking research, but it is also the likely repository for any archived benchmarking documents.

The main holdings of the library should be described. These might include commercial databases, industry publications, special reports, books, software, and many other materials and services. How the library accesses the materials should be explained.

Services offered by the library must be described in the guide. These might include the following:

• Public services, such as assistance with the identification of keywords for the benchmarking focus or topic and actual conduct of the information search

• Traditional library services, including acquisition of materials and possibly reproduction and storage of materials on other mediums

• Database services, including indexing, abstracting, and cataloging of internal and external documents

• Benchmarking assistance, such as access to a bibliography that is annotated for content

Knowledge Base and Archiving

The importance of the benchmarking knowledge base and archiving must be detailed in the managers' resource guide. Managers need to be aware of these archived documents because they store completed studies that will assist future teams in their efforts and because they provide a knowledge base of best practices.

Document Search and Retrieval

The process for filing documents, retrieving them, and searching should be described in the managers' resource guide. Searches can be simple, based on keywords, or they can be complex using modifiers. Retrieval may be on the basis of full text, key section, or keyword. Filing may depend on whether the document was originally in electronic form or scanned in as text. A report summary capability from the search should be described in the guide.

Best Practices Knowledge Base

Some knowledge bases include full text. In some fashion the benchmarking studies' final reports, presentation charts, trip reports, and other relevant documents should be cross-referenced so that users can find the details of the study. Most best practices knowledge bases, however, are composed of abstracts of the full text. The relevant items that need to be in the abstract include the following:

- Date of the study
- Company name, division, and location
- Persons contacted and their job titles
- Benchmarking team members
- Subject or focus of the investigation
- Business process studied
- Description of the best practices found
- Reference to where the full documents are stored

The procedure for filing an abstract should be described in the managers' resource guide. If this includes electronic filing, it is wise to give a flowchart description of the process, including a reference manual of steps.

Training and Resource Materials

A description of the types of training available and the internal and externally relevant resource materials should be documented in the managers' resource guide. The primary reason is to ensure that training is available to teams before any substantive benchmarking is conducted. A secondary reason is to show the wide variety of resource materials available.

Training

The types of training may vary from organization to organization, but there seems to be some consensus on at least three types—management awareness, cross-functional skills, and benchmarking team training skills. These should be explained in the managers' resource guide.

Resource Materials

Resource materials are becoming increasingly extensive. They deserve abbreviated descriptions in the managers' resource guide. This way individuals can select them either for training or reference in conducting benchmarking projects, or for purposes of internal and external benchmarking discussions.

Resource materials could include the following: overhead slides and training materials, such as prereading, participant guides and instructor guides; supplementary materials, such as internal publications describing benchmarking or other useful references; and videotapes, audiocassettes, and software.

A comprehensive bibliography on benchmarking citing the value of the various sources is invaluable. For example, some sources have listings of companies cited for best practices. Others have case histories of completed benchmarking studies.

Networks

Increasingly, benchmarking professionals in an organization are linked through formal, operational networks. This is the way benchmarking is updated and coordinated within the organization, and it is the way information on expected results are passed into the organization. The firm's network should be described in the managers' resource guide.

Internal Networks

Internal networks of individuals charged with the responsibility of representing their organizations for benchmarking purposes need to have some structure. That includes a mission statement, a set of goals or reasons for existence, and yearly objectives. The operation of the network should be described in the managers' resource guide because the network will be a major resource and competency contact for those conducting benchmarking. Describing the network's outputs is a productive way to describe its operation. One output might be an annual report on the prior year's activities to give it some sense of accomplishment and recognition.

External Networks

There are a select few organizational networks being established to share information and contacts and to set up benchmarking activities. These deserve mention in the managers' resource guide, since they provide a little-known resource, and possibly a major opportunity for conducting benchmarking effectively, especially if the company is already a member of the organization.

Definitions

Either at the outset of the managers' resource guide or shortly after its justification, a set of definitions about benchmarking would bring some common understanding to the topic. While there are many ways to gain that understanding, the following have shown to be needed for most audiences.

Describing benchmarking as distinguished from benchmarks is important to understanding best practices. Another useful way to describe benchmarking is through the following layered approach.

Benchmarking needs to be described through how it is conducted; that is, focused on products, services, and business processes with well-developed performance measures. The types of benchmarking should be described; that is, internal, competitive, functional, and generic, and the focus of benchmarking—either strategic or operational—should be explained. Lastly, how benchmarking can be applied, namely, as problem-based or as process-based, should be detailed.

Appendix

An appendix of materials for reference and example completes the managers' resource guide. The appendix includes, but is not limited to, the following:

- Any codes of conduct
- Benchmarking process inspection guide
- Benchmarking status matrix
- Sample nondisclosure agreement
- Sample letters of introduction and thank-you for a benchmarking investigation
- Sample standard questions developed for an organization
- Sample of key bibliographic references that are annotated for content
- Any process classification schemes or taxonomies
- Other documents of importance to the organization

Summary

- Create a managers' resource guide to abstract key benchmarking points, to provide quick reference guides, and to subsequently generate a reference that shows users where to find additional information.
- Describe how benchmarking contributes to the company's quality initiatives.
- Include in the guide any corporate benchmarking directives.
- Describe the key points of the 10-step benchmarking process.
- Include in the managers' resource guide the company's benchmarking strategy and mission statement and how they are carried out.

- Describe the roles and responsibilities of all parties in a benchmarking study including customers and suppliers.
- Show teams how to start a benchmarking investigation.
- Describe in the managers' resource guide all benchmarking visit prerequisites, guidelines, and protocol.
- Detail information sharing guidelines and how to identify key processes.
- Include in the guide how to conduct information searches using library services.
- Describe the types of training and resource materials available.
- Detail the company's internal and external benchmarking networks.
- Include in the managers' resource guide key benchmarking definitions and sample documents in the guide's appendix.

CHAPTER 9

The Future of Benchmarking

One defends when his strength is inadequate, he attacks when it is abundant.

- Lexicon and Classification—The Software of Benchmarking
- Template—The Hardware of Benchmarking
- Networking—The "Peopleware" of Benchmarking
- Rapid Organization Learning
- Benchmarking Excellence
- Summary

When talking about the future one should be cautioned by the words attributed to Mark Twain: "I always hesitate to make predictions, especially when it involves the future." In many respects that is what is facing benchmarking. Because of the interest in this business improvement topic and because of the multiplicity of organizations and individuals using benchmarking, it is still in a state of evolution. Since there are many new techniques being developed and used, it is probably more appropriate to talk about benchmarking milestones instead of an endpoint vision. One way to look at the future of benchmarking is to consider those milestones as major learning points in benchmarking management. Another is to consider some of the evolving challenges that will eventually have to be solved to make benchmarking a mature business tool. That is what is covered in this chapter.

Lexicon and Classification—The Software of Benchmarking

Lexicon

There needs to be a widely accepted *lexicon* or language of what benchmarking is and is not. There is still confusion about the definition and types of benchmarking and how it can be applied. Part of this confusion results from new authors trying to bring a different slant to benchmarking to distinguish their brand from that of others. There is plenty of room for opinions; however, somewhere the fundamental definition needs to have some permanence. With this in hand authors can give their various views on a common theme.

The most likely place where this standard definition should appear is in some recognized quality institution. This could be an association, institute, clearinghouse, or center. The definition could also be embedded as a standard in the many quality awards being implemented. Ultimately, then, an organization like the National Institute of Standards and Technology would be the keeper of the benchmarking definition. This could easily be done through a white paper and could be made part of the training that the quality examiners and judges receive. Through this process, a consistent message would evolve and become accepted.

Classification

Just like there is a SIC code for industries, there needs to be an accepted classification of the business processes or at least the vital work processes. There are many organizations that do essentially the same thing; however, because of some convention internal to their industry, the process is called something different. All one has to do is consider customer satisfaction to recognize the different interpretations. This is a burden on the benchmarking activity. There needs to be some way of quickly getting to a common definition of processes so that the benchmarking can begin and so that the findings can be implemented to get the results.

The classification should be process-oriented, that is, taking the horizontal—not functional or vertical—view of the organization. The classification system should

- Take the customer's viewpoint.
- Be simple to use.
- Be defined in layperson's language.
- Be understandable in its construction.
- Show all natural interfaces and relationships.
- Be based on a hierarchic view of the enterprise.

The classification system would be flexible and, therefore, easily revised as new information is uncovered and adapted. A process-focused and customer-driven taxonomy of work processes is the most effective basis for quickly defining and agreeing on topics of common interest.

The classification should be used as a diagnostic tool to understand the business of the organization, namely how the work is done. It should become the plan for improvement. It would be the framework for resolving industry-specific terminology. It would become the main basis to reduce duplication of the benchmarking effort. The classification would provide for the identification and improvement of the boundaries and handoffs between processes, which are often the locations of inefficiencies. The classification would become the way to creatively view the business.

Template—The Hardware of Benchmarking

In addition to the definition and classification, there needs to be a growing body of knowledge of how to do benchmarking well. This involves understanding the basic processes that organizations run and focusing on the practices in those processes. So a *template* also needs to become widely accepted. Without it benchmarking will become anyone's approach and that will feed confusion. Eventually, without a template, benchmarking will fall into disuse as another management fad. Thus, the template is the hardware of benchmarking.

Part of the difficulty in developing a benchmarking template is management's impatience with the ability to find best practices quickly enough to feed the rapid pace of change. There is a major disconnection between the need for change and the time to search for best practices. What may evolve is the ability to do quick benchmarking. This could arise either from the technology of computer networks, telephones, facsimiles, and satellites, or it may evolve from the ability to conduct not only formal benchmarking, as in the 10-step process, but also the legitimizing of informal benchmarking. The later could become a do-it-yourself ability to study others in a slightly more disciplined way, such as when senior executives visit each other and discover new approaches to running organizations. What can only be hoped for is that formal benchmarking, done by process-owning teams, will follow. This would tie down the detail necessary for the implementation of best practices.

Networking—The "Peopleware" of Benchmarking

The use of networks, consortia, clearinghouses, common interest groups, exchanges, knowledge bases, and other "peopleware" of benchmarking must constantly evolve to keep this important tool sharp. Fortunately, with the level of interest not only in the various segments of the economy but also in cultures around the globe, there is enough variety, inquisitiveness, and innovativeness that benchmarking will be a robust field for some time to come.

Networking may involve an electronic network of external benchmarking professionals or an electronic bulletin board or a distribution list to find partners interested in improving the same process. The bulletin board can also be used to announce items of interest or to disseminate information on services and media for benchmarking. The ultimate goal would be to electronically match one's interest in a given business process with an expert process owner, who would then be willing to share the best practices in exchange for keeping a world-class business process current. The challenge will be to keep in touch with the partner to share the evolving, varied techniques. Thus, only through the evolution of software, hardware, and peopleware will benchmarking rise to a higher plane of acceptance and use.

Reengineering

The difference between benchmarking and process reengineering, or other new initiatives that invariably catch management's attention, needs to be distinguished. The best way to do this is to deal with their definitions. Reengineering has come to mean the *radical redesign of business processes.* The working definition for benchmarking is *finding and implementing best practices.*

Is one approach replacing the other? If reengineering is process redesign to fundamentally alter how organizations deal with their customers and suppliers, then how are the new practices that will become the basis of the new design found? That would seem to be the role of benchmarking. Thus, benchmarking is essential to reengineering. So benchmarking is still a necessary, stand-alone quality tool.

The radical redesign of business processes is not a necessity. But finding better practices to be the source of continuous improvement is, whether it radically affects business processes or not. That fact needs to be continually reinforced, along with the fact that benchmarking of business processes, used by line managers, is the way to get desired results.

Rapid Organization Learning

Xerox undertook its first formal benchmarking study in 1980. That study changed the company in a dramatic way. Compared to foreign manufacturers, Xerox had nine times as many suppliers; had seven times as many product defects; took twice as long to develop and deliver products; and took five times as long to set up a production line. Organizations cannot deal with this magnitude of competitive crisis. There needs to be continuous learning. Organizations need to figure out how to rapidly learn and transfer knowledge in the context of becoming a constantly knowledgeable, learning organization.

This would not be an unbridled, random activity. It would be goal-directed and would support the achievement of the enterprise's overall priorities. It would be the basis on which the organization would learn from others to supply insights to drive creative thinking. It would leverage critical success and competency areas. Once best practices from continuous learning were embedded in the work processes, they would achieve organizational goals.

This learning involves the internal transfer of best practices. The organization has to find the mechanisms and foster the motivation for continuous learning. The problem is not with the mechanisms. There will always be ways to document an idea, a practice, or a method that is considered better. The problem is with the motivation. The challenge is how to foster the willingness of every organization member to, first, want to volunteer a best practice, and second, to want to search out, understand, and eventually adapt for use the best practices proposed by others.

This is a substantial challenge and one that is not easily solved. It is, however, in the process of being benchmarked to gain understanding and insight to what will make organization learning successful. Perhaps some of the answer lies in the key factors for successful change shown in Figure 9.1.

Benchmarking Excellence

How is benchmarking excellence attained? How will we recognize it when we see it? At least four factors must be considered.

Key factors for successful change
- Believing there is a **need** for change
- Determining **what** should be changed
- Developing a **picture** of how the organization will look after the change

How benchmarking makes change successful
- The gap between internal and external practices creates the **need** for change.
- Understanding industry best practices identifies **what** must be changed.
- Externally benchmarked practices, developed from others, give a **picture** of the endpoint after change.

Benchmarking desired state
- Effective use of benchmarking is persistent throughout the organization.
- There is a conscious need to find and implement best practices.

Figure 9.1. Benchmarking change management.

1. The management process; that is, the things that are done right to establish, support, and sustain benchmarking activities

2. The rationale taken with benchmarking; namely, it will be how the business is run

3. Increased recognition of the link between benchmarking and other business process improvements

4. Understanding that benchmarking does not stand alone, but, in fact, is hooked to other initiatives to continuously improve

Ultimately, however, attaining benchmarking excellence will come down to how credibly management uses benchmarking to get results. It must continue to be seen as a key quality improvement tool—one that is intensified, expanded, and institutionalized. The direct relationship of benchmarking and operational results will prove its worth. Only then will benchmarking attain the level of excellence along with all the other quality tools. This means benchmarking has to be seen as a key tool to drive competitiveness, support customers, and make organizations and operations effective.

Benchmarking must come to mean learning from others. Organizations, individuals, and leaders need to accept this. We are in the knowledge and learning age, which is rapidly accelerating. Ultimately there may be no other way to learn that will keep pace with change. Organizations cannot afford more competitive crises from not keeping active pace with the outside world. That is fatal. Benchmarking can have no higher purpose than to be known as the effective way to pursue rapid learning and to obtain knowledge to change how we work—and how we all work differently!

Summary

- Benchmarking is still an evolving process.

- A widely accepted lexicon, the software of benchmarking, must be developed, and a widely accepted, flexible classification of business processes is needed.

- The classification system is used as a diagnostic tool to reduce duplication of benchmarking efforts and to provide identification and improvement of the boundaries between processes.

- A widely accepted template, the hardware of benchmarking, must be developed.

- Networks, the peopleware of benchmarking, must be used. This may include electronic networks.

- Reengineering is the radical redesign of business processes. Benchmarking is essential to reengineering.

- Organizations need goal-directed, rapid, continuous learning to stay competitive.

- Excellence is attained through the credible management of the benchmarking process.

Section 3:
The Case Studies

CHAPTER 10

Materials Only Differentiated Service at AT&T

Prepared with the cooperation of Paul Klemchalk, MODS process manager, AT&T Network Systems, Morristown, New Jersey

Who can determine where one ends and the other begins?

- Background
- Customers and Requirements
- Organizations or Industries Benchmarked
- Best Practices Found
- Actions Taken
- Implementation
- Planned Changes
- Conclusion
- Summary

Background

During the past several years, AT&T had the unique opportunity to change from yesterday's monopolistic, domestic telephone company to today's competitive, international telecommunications company. In 1992, AT&T Network Transmission Systems received the Malcolm Baldrige National Quality Award. AT&T provides worldwide communication services and network communication systems and products.

AT&T's network is made up of switching, transmission, cable, energy, operations systems, and wireless products. Together, they provide AT&T's communications backbone. These products are required to install new systems (system service orders) and to support maintenance of less-current networks (material only orders). AT&T Network Systems headquarters in Morristown, New Jersey, has a product line of over one-half million unique items. This case study focuses on the material only (MO) products, which number more than 30,000 active items and more than 100,000 inactive products.

AT&T's primary domestic customers are the Regional Bell Operating Companies (RBOCs) and several large distributors. They order complete systems that include installation services as well as MO products that the customers install themselves. Therefore, provisioning MO orders is required for the maintenance and timely delivery to the customer installation crews. Subsequently, delivery of the MO product is critical to AT&T's customers' business and their overall satisfaction.

Thus, a way had to be developed to provide MO product in a timely manner at a reasonable cost. This process is known as the Material Only Differentiated Service (MODS).

Goal/Objective

AT&T's goal was to achieve customer satisfaction for on-time provisioning performance by establishing differentiated levels of service that consider and align customer requirements, customer expectations, product provisioning capabilities, business requirements, and competitive market intelligence. AT&T's objectives were to develop the following:

- A MODS customer communications package that outlines AT&T's efforts to improve service performance

- A product segmentation process that assigns a MODS service level indicator to each MO product

- A customer expectation alignment process that focuses AT&T people, processes, and products to meet customers' current and changing needs

Focus/Topic

In January 1993, a quality improvement team (QIT) was formed to analyze and develop a solution to this dilemma. The team's mission was driven by AT&T's *Process Quality Management and Improvement Guidelines,* also known as PQMI.

AT&T's quality policy states that quality excellence is the foundation for the management of AT&T's business and the keystone of its goal of customer satisfaction. Therefore, it is AT&T's policy to

- Consistently provide products and services that meet the quality expectations of customers

- Actively pursue ever-improving quality through programs that enable each employee to do his or her job right the first time

Team Operation

A team of 14 experts was assembled with representatives from each of the following business units: switching, transmission, network cable systems, operation systems, energy, purchased products, marketing and sales, logistics, and asset management. This diverse group of people, with their perspectives and experiences, covered the complete order processing universe. Using AT&T's *Total Quality Management Guidebook*, this methodology directed the team's activities and became the foundation for the MODS process.

The team's efforts included the following:

- Conducting customer and sales team interviews
- Conducting customer-specific order histories
- Conducting an AT&T internal benchmarking analysis
- Conducting external benchmarking analysis
- Developing a gap analysis of AT&T benchmarks
- Conducting product revenue and volume data analysis
- Applying all successful benchmarking information learned in the MODS program

These in-depth activities were then incorporated into a QIT document, which became the team's strategy and its implementation plan (see Figure 10.1). Thus, the QIT document focused the team's effort on three deliverables.

1. Customer communication package
2. Product segmentation process
3. Customer expectation alignment process

Customers and Requirements

AT&T's customers wanted the following:

- Reliable delivery intervals that reflect AT&T's actual capabilities
- AT&T's commitment to meet these published delivery intervals

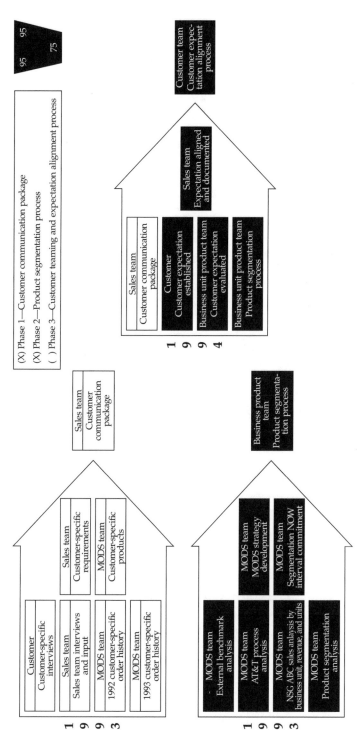

Note: ABC sales analysis involves the examination of all revenue-producing items. *A* items are high-volume, high-revenue products that account for 80 percent of total MO sales. *B* items are mid-volume, mid-revenue products that account for 15 percent of MO sales. *C* items are infrequently purchased items and account for 5 percent of MO sales. Used with permission of AT&T Network Systems.

Figure 10.1. MODS process overview.

- AT&T's advance notification of a jeopardy situation
- An effective voice in the negotiation of customer-identified critical product intervals

AT&T's customers recommended that

- AT&T should make a delivery commitment and honor it.
- AT&T should differentiate service levels based on its provisioning capability.
- AT&T, with its customers, should jointly identify customer-critical products and should mutually determine acceptable product intervals.

Need/Reason for Improvement

External Customers were confused and frustrated. Their delivery expectations regarding AT&T's MO provisioning capabilities and commitments were not met. Additionally, there was no consistent policy or process to enhance and improve AT&T's network systems' traditional provisioning process other than to expedite everything at significant cost and effort.

Internal Organizational perception found inconsistent communication and lack of coordination among many groups. This contributed to discrepancies in product responses and delays in provisioning products.

Clearly, a major effort was needed from both internal and external perspectives. Sales teams were not synchronized with manufacturing realities, and manufacturing realities were inconsistent with customer expectations. Additionally, there was a lack of uniform policy or process when establishing, maintaining, and changing delivery intervals (see Figure 10.2).

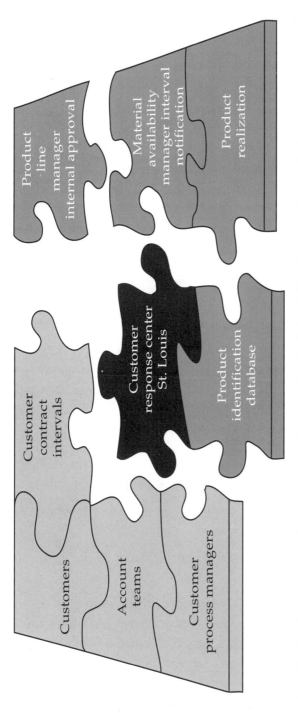

Issue: Functional groups are not effectively communicating or coordinating their activities with one another to collectively bring together customer expectations and the Network Systems' capabilities.

AT&T needs to
1. Internally segment and synchronize product interval information across all quote-to-cash organizations.

2. Externally implement customer partnering teams (customer, sales, and business unit members) to manage the customer expectation alignment process. This process will identify active MO products and align Network Systems' capabilities (at the product level) with customer interval expectations.

Used with permission of AT&T Network Systems.

Figure 10.2. Current situation.

Organizations or Industries Benchmarked

Three corporations cooperated with AT&T in its benchmarking effort. Companies A, B, and C are all high-technology manufacturers. Company A makes computers; Company B manufacturers copiers and related equipment; and Company C produces heavy equipment. Each organization had become a best-in-class company while overcoming many difficult business situations.

AT&T had a keen interest in Companies A and B because their industries and business backgrounds were similar to that of AT&T. Company C was of interest because of its successful winback situation in its industry and because it had a product line of several hundred thousand parts. These products supported Company C's current and less-current equipment that was still in operation and that was still valued by customers.

Each benchmarking partner provided AT&T with access to their experts through conference calls and, later, during site visits. These companies provided business knowledge of complex issues and potential solutions. They also provided the personal support and encouragement at a point when individual inspiration was needed.

Current Process

AT&T's current segmentation process set three levels of service for MO products. They are

1. Available NOW—Products to be delivered to the customer within one week.

2. Available to INTERVAL—Products to be delivered to the customer within the advertised interval (AI). The minimum interval in this class was two weeks. Every product had a published AI that AT&T would deliver and meet.

3. Available to COMMITMENT—Products with unpublished AIs since each product is a made-to-order item. The interval is to be determined (TBD) by availability of materials.

This segmentation establishes three service level expectations with the highest expectation of delivery within one week and the lowest expectation to be determined. This lowest level of service implies custom manufacture.

Available-NOW products have been mutually agreed to by the customer and by AT&T to be time-sensitive, critical products. Available-to-INTERVAL products are important, but not time-critical; however, the delivery intervals are longer due to the complexity of a scheduled manufacture cycle. Available-to-COMMITMENT products are custom-made items with an unscheduled manufacture cycle. For this lowest service, a commitment needs to be determined, and this date is not immediately available to the customer as with NOW and INTERVAL products.

Key Measures and Facts

AT&T Network Systems Group (NSG), with over one-half million products, has taken a major step to improve service and delivery performance of communications products. Starting in January of 1995 the entire NSG business will be restructured from traditional business units to customer business units. This massive change is indicative of the highest level of management commitment to the focus on AT&T's customers' needs and requirements for communication products and services. MODS is one of several initiatives being implemented to provide improved service and customer relations.

MODS was developed in 1993 (see Figures 10.3a and 10.3b). It is being implemented in 1994 across all business units and new customer business units. The Asset Management Organization, headed by vice president Bob Van Saun, was chartered to meet a

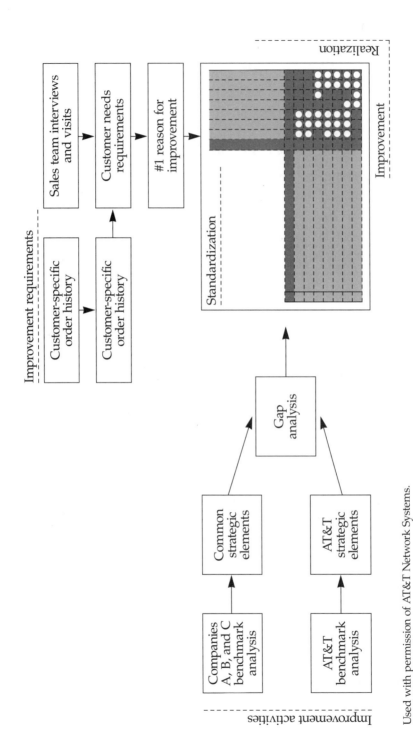

Used with permission of AT&T Network Systems.

Figure 10.3a. Standardization development.

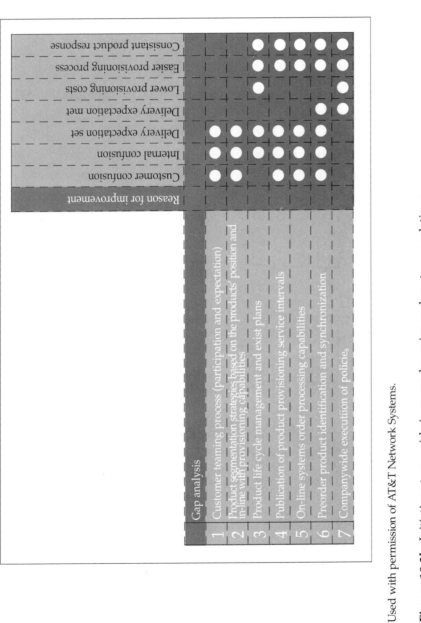

Used with permission of AT&T Network Systems.

Figure 10.3b. Initiatives to provide improved service and customer relations.

95 percent MO on-time performance metric in 1995 with 75 days of stock. This keystone (95, 1995, 75 days) required the development of a process, which became the MODS process.

Service level segmentation and the customer alignment process will allow AT&T NSG to focus on customer-defined critical products and critical product interval reductions. AT&T anticipates that MODS will improve MO performance metrics by 10 percent. Even more significant, MODS will reduce communications confusion between AT&T and its customers, thus resulting in improved customer satisfaction and increased business for AT&T. In addition, AT&T already sees its customers' anticipation and participation in the MODS joint efforts. AT&T expects the full MODS process to be realized through the customer expectation alignment process.

Process-to-Process Analysis

A gap analysis was performed against AT&T's internal and external benchmarks. This analysis indicated the need to develop and/or include the following:

- Proactive customer teaming
- Product segmentation strategies based on product life cycle (PLC), market needs, and competitive position
- Identification and segmentation of AT&T products according to service levels
- On-line systems order processing and tracking capabilities
- Companywide acceptance and adherence to product team policy decisions
- PLC management that includes the appropriate product exit plans

This analysis gave the QIT a baseline of the current situation and the direction it needed to pursue its improvement efforts.

Each area became a major component in the MODS process, and each is linked to address customer satisfaction concerns.

Best Practices Found

In reviewing the common strategic elements of AT&T's three benchmarking partners, the following proven policies and processes were discovered. These became the standard foundation set for developing the MODS strategy.

- Top-down corporate commitment to customer service
- Internal teaming of all stakeholders in the process
- External communication and partnering with customers
- Dynamic on-line, up-to-date product ordering information
- Short order fulfillment cycle times
- Reduced expediting efforts and their associated costs
- PLC management including exit plans
- Companywide knowledge and execution of PLC policies

Actions Taken

AT&T's external focus in 1993 was to document the customers and sales team's requirements and concerns. This list became the improvement requirements.

AT&T's internal focus in 1993 was to analyze its processes and product line to identify areas that needed improvement, replacement, or totally new processes. In general, it was found that organizations did perform their functions reasonably well; however, poor communications and documentation of customer expectations were not known to critical organizations. This was especially true of the provisioning intervals.

Communication, standardization, and documentation—across all organizations—needed improvement in order to deliver the product when the customer requested it. Thus, on-time product delivery became the key goal.

Externally, AT&T established its new MODS program such that customers participated in establishing their expectations on a product-by-product basis. This approach was well received by the customers, and, in fact, it generated a significant amount of enthusiasm and participation.

Internally, AT&T developed a product segmentation strategy that would classify products according to the velocity that they could be delivered. Once the segmentation process was complete, and the actual delivery interval standardized, the customer expectation alignment process began.

Implementation

Once AT&T's internal process and segmentation activities were stabilized, the sales team met with the first MODS rollout customer. At this meeting, the customer's actual order history was presented and reviewed. The customer identified the products that were critical to its business and reviewed the delivery interval previously established at AT&T.

During this meeting, service level segments were reviewed; that is, the segmentation levels of available-NOW, available-to-INTERVAL, and available-to-COMMITMENT products were examined. As a result of these meetings, customers' input and requirements on specific products and intervals were documented. This product list was then reviewed internally by AT&T's business unit product team. A second meeting was then set with the full customer team present.

During this meeting, the AT&T customer team reviewed the list of products and accommodated the customer's request where it was possible and where it made mutual business sense. In those instances when agreement was difficult, and no customer commitment was made to purchase the specific item, the best delivery interval that AT&T could provide was used. Since AT&T makes available over one-half million products that span decades in product life, stocking these low-volume products is not feasible from warehousing and financial perspectives. In those instances of unique usage or requirements, additional customer team meetings were scheduled and special agreements were developed.

Planned Changes

The customer expectation alignment process was developed to transition AT&T to an increasingly competitive and customer-focused environment. Since customer needs are always changing and evolving, AT&T envisions that the MODS process will be a continuous and iterative process aimed at achieving customer satisfaction today as well as tomorrow.

AT&T has historically been manufacturing-focused and is now moving toward being customer-focused and customer-driven. AT&T has become increasingly responsive to the marketplace and continues to listen to its customers and meet their expectations. An example of this is the transition from AT&T customer-ship-date to a customer-requested-on-job-date. Customers have requested delivery dates not ship dates. Therefore, all order processing groups, data support systems, and metrics had to be realigned for this simple change.

Conclusion

Benchmarking successful companies, segmenting products, and listening to the customers are good, strong business actions. It was, however, the interrelationship of these activities that lead AT&T to create an overall, integrated MODS strategy that combined people, product, and processes.

This case study illustrates how benchmarking, when integrated with several other critical activities, can greatly contribute to process problem solving. For AT&T's QITs, benchmarking is a powerful tool. The right managers—that is, stakeholders in the process—were involved, and benchmarking's very important position was set up early in their work.

The PQMI process is a critical ally of benchmarking. The PQMI process requires that

- The process owners are the key players in the study. All owners must be involved—even if there are 14 of them.

- Current processes are documented.

- Customer benchmark feedback data are collected and analyzed for gaps. Actual data versus customers' expectations must be examined.

- The QIT's collective wit is challenged for identifying opportunities for improvement.

- Competitive analysis is available.

- External best-in-class benchmarking produces both what is possible (that is, benchmarks) and how to achieve them (that is, action plans).

From selecting the right partners to conducting effective interviews, the benchmarking process is enhanced by this combination of thoughtful preparation.

From AT&T's first MODS benchmarking study and QIT, a subsequent QIT in the Information System development group was formed. This second team also visited AT&T's three benchmarking partners. Then this information system team documented its processes and learned how a vitally important support tool—the management information system—was developed. This type of companion benchmarking provides effective continuity of process development and implementation.

Summary

• MO products are time- and delivery-sensitive, user-installed products ordered through AT&T's centralized customer response center by RBOCs and major distributors.

• Problems in the MO process included lack of synchronization among sales projections, manufacturing realities, and customer expectations and a lack of uniform policy when setting delivery intervals.

• Customer requirements included the following: reliable delivery intervals; AT&T's commitment to meet published delivery intervals; AT&T's advance notification of a jeopardy situation; an effective voice in the negotiation of customer-identified critical product intervals; and differentiated service levels.

• The MODS process was developed to provide MO product in a timely manner at a reasonable cost. Its goal is to achieve customer satisfaction for on-time provisioning performance by establishing differentiated levels of service.

• The QIT's efforts included the following: conducting customer and sales team interviews, customer-specific order histories, an internal and external benchmarking analysis, and product revenue and volume data analysis; developing a gap analysis of AT&T benchmarks; and incorporating and applying all successful benchmark information learned into the MODS process.

• The QIT developed three deliverables: (1) a customer communication package; (2) a product segmentation process; and (3) a customer expectation alignment process.

• Gap analysis indicated the need to develop the following: proactive customer teaming; product segmentation strategies; product identification and segmentation; on-line systems order processing and tracking capabilities; companywide acceptance and adherence to product team policy decisions; and product life cycle management that included product exit plans.

• The foundation set for developing the MODS strategy included the following: top-down corporate commitment to customer service; internal teaming of all stakeholders in the process; external communication and partnering with customers; dynamic on-line, up-to-date product ordering information; short order fulfillment cycle times; and reduced expediting efforts and their associated costs.

• Communication, standardization, and documentation— across all organizations—were improved in order to deliver products when requested.

• The MODS process will improve NSG's MO on-time performance metrics by 10 percent. The MODS process will be realized through the customer expectation alignment process, which has become the cornerstone for MO customer satisfaction activities.

The following organizations and individuals contributed to this case study: AT&T Network Systems Group (NSG); the marketing and sales organization (MS&O); the order realization process (ORP) division; the asset management (AM) division; Robert L. Fox, measurements/product differentiation manager (AM); Bettie Jean Henry, MODS segmentation manager (AM); Darel R. Hull, manager, process reengineering and benchmarking; Paul Klemchalk, MODS process manager (AM); Ronald McKee, order process manager (ORP); Brud Patterson, customer process director (MS&O); and Robert Van Saun, vice president, asset management.

CHAPTER 11

Housekeeping System Cycle Time Reduction at The Ritz-Carlton Hotel Company

Prepared with the cooperation of Judy N. Kirk, quality leader, with process analysis prepared by Alan F. Galanty, cycle time advisor, The Ritz-Carlton Hotel Company, Dearborn, Michigan

> *All we need to do is throw something odd and unaccountable in his way.*

- Background
- Customer Requirements
- Organizations or Industries Benchmarked
- Best Practices Learned
- Actions Taken
- Summary

Background

The Ritz-Carlton Hotel Company successfully operates in one of the most logistically complex service businesses. Targeting primarily industry executives, meeting and corporate travel planners, and affluent travelers, the Atlanta, Georgia-based company manages 30 luxury hotels while pursuing the distinction of being the best in each market. The hotel company builds it success on the strength of a comprehensive service quality initiative, which is integrated into its marketing and business objectives.

Winner of the 1992 Malcolm Baldrige National Quality Award, The Ritz-Carlton Hotel Company operates business and resort hotels in the United States, Europe, Hong Kong, Mexico, and Australia. It has 13 international sales offices and employs 13,500 people. Restaurants and banquets are also marketed heavily to local residents. The company claims distinctive facilities and environments, highly personalized anticipatory services, and exceptional food and beverages.

The Ritz-Carlton, Dearborn is close to downtown Detroit, Michigan, and the city's airport and business district. It houses 308 guest rooms, including 15 suites. The hotel features full service and a la carte dining and over 20,000 square feet of meeting space, including two ballrooms and several conference rooms. A fitness center is complete with indoor lap pool and whirlpool spa. Additional hotel amenities include private concierge service, 24-hour room service, valet, and personal guest profile capability.

Focus/Topic

Through focus groups and independent marketing surveys, The Ritz-Carlton Hotel Company identified several hotel processes that were highly important to customers. These processes, however, were also given low satisfaction ratings. Thus, the company set out to accomplish several tasks at the corporate level.

- Identify what was important to customers and how they rated those features.

- Complete a gap analysis.

- Identify the primary processes and if the company had existing work areas or processes that were aligned to meet those needs.

The company learned two things: (1) There were primary processes common to any hotel, such as housekeeping and front office registration; and (2) there were vital support processes, such as purchasing and human resources for the selection of new employees.

From this research the customers of The Ritz-Carlton Hotel Company identified 19 critical processes as vital to their continuing business decision to loyally patronize the company's properties. Each of The Ritz-Carlton hotels elected one of these processes to investigate in a one-year research study. Then each hotel picked process teams, identified study boundaries, and ran the research process with help from corporate headquarters in Atlanta. This process involved cross-functional teams using a total team approach and scientific methods.

One of the 19 processes that customers identified was a "clean, fresh, fully stocked guest room." The Ritz-Carlton in Dearborn, Michigan, took on the housekeeping system with the goal of creating an error-proof, reliable process that could be standardized within the company to ensure 100 percent customer satisfaction.

Objective/Purpose

Customers indicated that they wanted their hotel services better, faster, cheaper, and with greater reliability than before. It was the aim of the Dearborn process team to identify and reduce waste through process analysis by simplifying, eliminating, and combining steps within the housekeeping system. This was done to meet The Ritz-Carlton Hotel Company's 1996 quality goals of

1. Six sigma

2. 50 percent cycle time reduction

3. 100 percent customer retention

Team Operation

The housekeeping system studied had boundaries of guest arrival through guest departure. The director of housekeeping was the process owner. The team consisted of those individuals active in the housekeeping system and impacted by any changes to it. Process team members represented the following organizations and individuals.

- Housekeeping, including room attendants, houseperson, and director

- Laundry, including laundry attendants

- Engineering, including preventive maintenance engineer/ painter

- Rooms division, including the executive assistant manager of rooms

- Total quality management, including the cycle time advisor, the quality manager/historian, and the quality leader acting as facilitators

The roles of quality leader and cycle time advisor are present in each Ritz-Carlton property as an investment in the company's competitive future. The quality leader advises on the total team approach, team building, and problem-solving techniques. The cycle time advisor contributes scientific techniques of data collection and analysis and statistical process control. Both persons act as change agents to encourage and embrace continuous improvement.

The housekeeping process team met for two-hour weekly meetings beginning in May 1993. Team-building exercises were discussed and practiced at these meetings. A mission statement, from the guidance team of hotel senior leaders, served as the focus of the process team's progress (see Figure 11.1). The team used consensus decision making and shared leadership as participative themes in the total team approach to cycle time reduction.

A nine-step quality improvement process benchmarked from Xerox Corporation gave structure to the process identification and analysis. Because of its emphasis on assembly, the Xerox Quality Tool Kit was readily applied by the Dearborn process team. Many hotel functions and processes involve assembling items.

Customer Requirements

By listening to the voice of its customers, The Ritz-Carlton, Dearborn process team learned what was wanted, needed, and expected in a guest room experience. It included the following characteristics.

- A clean, fresh, fully stocked room
- A guest room serviced right the first time
- Few, if any, interruptions
- Short interruptions when they do occur

The housekeeping process team will simplify, eliminate, and combine steps resulting in 50 percent housekeeping cycle time reduction and providing clean, fresh, fully stocked guest rooms "right the first time on time" efficiently meeting our guests' key requirements and ensuring 100 percent customer satisfaction.

Used with permission of The Ritz-Carlton Hotel Company.

Figure 11.1. Housekeeping process team mission statement.

- Consistent service provided for the stay over
- A room ready when the guest arrives
- A room cleaned at the guest's convenience
- Correct and timely honor bar billing (The honor bar consists of food and beverage items available a la carte in each guest room.)
- The assurance that guest's possessions are safe and secure
- Reduced housekeeping costs and labor

This last characteristic identified the need to eliminate waste. It was an internal customer requirement.

The process team's goal was to meet these external and internal customer needs with reliability, while reducing the overall housekeeping system cycle time by 50 percent. The customers' requirements and The Ritz-Carlton's measures of fulfilling those requirements are illustrated in the house of quality in Figure 11.2. Reduced internal costs would increase profitability and market competitiveness for the hotel. The savings would ultimately be shared with the hotel's ladies and gentlemen who contributed to it.

Note that alignment with The Ritz-Carlton Hotel Company's Gold Standards ensures that employees are "ladies and gentlemen serving ladies and gentlemen." This is considered the behavioral standard.

Organizations or Industries Benchmarked

Current Process

Consecutive, task-by-task work by one room attendant was the time-honored method of cleaning a guest room. Random sample observations of 30 housekeeping room attendants produced the pie chart shown in Figure 11.3. Analysis revealed that the bathroom-cleaning task was the most time-consuming of room-cleaning tasks and the obvious limiting factor.

Direction of improvement

Ritz-Carlton Measures (HOWs) vs. Customer requirements (WHATs)

Customer requirements (WHATs)	Importance	Defect rate (random sample)	Room cycle time	Possible number of interruptions	Occupied interruptions	Honor bar discrepancies/allowance rate	Number of guest room doors open at one time	Housekeeping productivity
Fully stocked room	4	◉					○	
Room serviced right the first time	5	◉		○	○	○		
Little if any interruptions	3			◉	◉			
Short interruptions when they occur	4		◉					△
Consistent service provided	5	◉				○		
Room ready when I arrive	5		○					○
Room cleaned at my convenience	4		○		◉			○
Honor bar billing correct and timely	5	△				◉		
My things should be safe/secure	5		△	◉			◉	
Reduced housekeeping cost/labor	5	◉	△					◉

Guest requirements for housekeeping / Ritz

Customer rating 1 2 3 4 5

Targets							
	# defects (110 items)	x minutes	# per guest—day	# per guest—day	# per 1000 guests	# doors open	# rooms/housekeeper

Technical assessment: 5 4 3 2 1

Absolute importance	131	113	92	78	87	45	76

Roof		Matrix		Weights	Arrows	
Strong positive	◉	Strong	◉	9	Maximum	↑
Positive	○	Medium	○	3	Minimum	↓
Negative	X	Weak	△	1	Nominal	○
Strong negative	#					

Figure 11.2. House of quality.

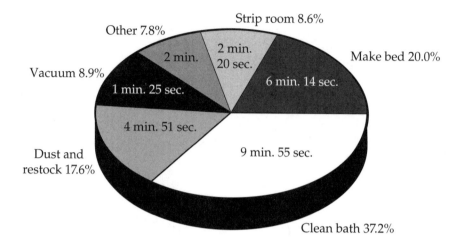

Average room cycle time 26 minutes, 45 seconds;
based on sample size of 30.

Used with permission of The Ritz-Carlton Hotel Company.

Figure 11.3. Five steps in cleaning a room.

The process team had already brainstormed the concept of simultaneous work; that is, multiple task completion by a number of room attendants in one guest room. Thus, the team-cleaning concept was born.

The process owner was fortunate to have seen a four-person cleaning team in action at a competitor's hotel in New York City. It referred the process owner to a sister facility on Maui, Hawaii, since this was the only hotel that used teams daily. While this experience served as an inspiration to the Dearborn team, investigating the competitor's team-cleaning process was neither a reciprocal benchmark nor a tutorial.

Process-to-Process Analysis

The greatest value of investigating the competitor's process was the practical application of team cleaning in daily practice.

Operational questions were answered and from that reality check the housekeeping team-cleaning system was customized to meet customer needs at The Ritz-Carlton, Dearborn.

The Pugh concept selection chart of cleaning alternatives facilitated the team pilot process (see Figure 11.4). Initially, four-person teams were piloted. After analysis and internal customer

Alternatives / Measures	1 person	4 person	3 person	2 person and honor bar attendant	Cartless plus 3 person
Cycle time	▲	+, +	+, +	+	+
Number of guest room doors open		−, −	+	S	+
Defects per room		+	+, +	+	+, +
Possible number of interruptions		+	+	S	+
Honor bar discrepancies and allowances		+	+	S	+
Number of occupied interruptions	Baseline	S	S	S	S
Productivity		+	+	+	+
Cost effectiveness		+	+	+	−, −
Reduce loneliness		+, +	+, +	+, +	+, +
Clear hallway		+	+	+	+, +
Time to implement		+	+	+	−, −
Probability for success (paradigm shift)	▼	−, −	−, −	−	−, −
Total		11 + 4 −	13 + 2 −	8 + 6 −	11 + 6 −

Used with permission of The Ritz-Carlton Hotel Company.

Figure 11.4. Pugh concept selection chart of cleaning alternatives.

feedback, three-person teams were found to have the greatest effectiveness within the housekeeping parameters of The Ritz-Carlton, Dearborn.

Key Measures

Key measures used to collect the baseline data on the reliability of the housekeeping system changes included the following:

1. Defect rate per room

2. Room cycle time

3. Possible interruption rate

4. Honor bar discrepancies and allowances

5. Housekeeping productivity (rooms cleaned per team)

6. Distance traveled

Baseline data collected through random sample techniques and plotted on statistical process control charts proved independent cleaning of a guest room resulted in the following:

1. 7.4 defects

2. A cycle time of 26.45 minutes to clean a room, plus 7 to 10 minutes to service the honor bar

3. Three standard interruptions of maid service, honor bar service, and turndown service

4. Chronic honor bar discrepancies

5. Productivity of 13 guest rooms per attendant

6. 525 feet, or about one-tenth of a mile traveled to clean a guest room.

Benchmarking Partners

Although it was an important discovery, finding the team-cleaning process at a domestic competitor's facility was unplanned.

The Ritz-Carlton, Dearborn team did adopt some of the competitor's practices. No other external benchmarking partners were sought.

The Dearborn team sought an internal benchmarking partner at the sister property in Naples, Florida. The Naples team provided new practices to reduce the logo fading and matching on the company's towels.

The Dearborn team also examined one of its member's hospital laundry experiences and elected to modify part of that process to Ritz-Carlton standards. This new practice reduced the handling of linen and terry items during the transportation and distribution processes.

Best Practices Learned

Key Findings

Key in the housekeeping study was the customer-supplier relationships vital to productivity. Housekeeping is the laundry department's primary customer. The entire housekeeping operation can grind to a halt if the supply of clean terry and linen is limited or interrupted. A great deal of time was wasted if room attendants received an inadequate supply of terry and linen items and were forced to go in search of more during their shift. This created slowdowns and rework to reenter rooms to replace missing items. A common practice was hoarding of supplies and hiding them, thus wasting up to 45 minutes daily while collecting materials vital to guest room cleaning.

To combat these recurring problems, a process change spearheaded by the laundry department to listen to the voice of its internal customer occurred. It was determined that the process from soiled to clean terry and linen was needed within the same day. If distribution centers on each guest floor could be stocked by the turndown attendants before the end of their shift, then supplies would be available for the room attendants at the beginning of their shift. Thus, this process would save 30 to 45 minutes per person per day.

After careful analysis and process identification, the laundry pilots were implemented to have sufficient terry and linen processed by 10 P.M. daily to allow for the stocking activity. Reliability of this process has not reached 100 percent, yet significant progress has been made allowing for increased room attendant productivity.

The industry rule of three par of terry was disproved during this study. The normal practice is to have one par of terry in the guest room, one par available for use, and one par in process from soiled to clean. Usage figures showed that hotel guests dirtied only 50 percent of the nine terry items placed in a room. It was learned through guest usage patterns that the hotel could function on 1.5 par of terry on the weekdays and 2.0 on the weekends. The outcome of this discovery was an annual savings of $60,000 in terry purchases.

The greatest paradigm shift of this process study involved the team-cleaning concept. Independent work by 30 individuals was totally impacted by such a change. The normal human response of resistance to accepted and practiced habits was experienced. Behaviors, which had up to five years to develop, were markedly changed. Individual pacing of work, singular patterns of productivity, and personal preferences were all under study. Best practices were revealed through observation, discussion, cycle timings, and work flow diagrams. These superior practices, or "knacks" as Dr. Juran notes, were identified and documented to standardize current best practices for efficiency and reliability.

Potential Opportunity for Improvement

Team cleaning of guest rooms held both tangible and intangible benefits. Tangible benefits included the following:

1. Reduction in room cleaning cycle time by 65 percent or 8 minutes with the added task of servicing the honor bar

2. Reduction in defects per room by 42 percent to 3.7, which translated to a higher reliability in cleanliness factor

3. Reduction of standard guest room interruptions by 33 percent due to combining of honor bar tasks with room cleaning

4. Reduction in time guest would be disturbed if occupying the room at the time cleaning was provided

5. Increase in the property and life safety for guests and staff due to fewer guest room doors being opened at any one time, as well as the presence of more than one room attendant within a room

6. Increase in productivity from 13 to 15 rooms per person and still increasing with resultant labor savings

7. Reduction in individual travel by 64 percent to 205 feet within a guest room

Intangible benefits of team cleaning included the following:

1. Reduction in loneliness from working independently

2. Increased teamwork through shared tasks and responsibilities

3. Increase in camaraderie and morale from working with others

4. Job enrichment through the team process, which provided coaching, feedback, and stimulation during repetitive housekeeping tasks

5. Increased communication among team members and between guests and team members

6. Increased effect of peer pressure to perform to standards, resulting essentially in self-directed work teams

7. Reduced monotony from switching roles throughout a shift

8. A stronger customer-supplier relationship between the housekeeping and laundry departments

Conclusion

The goal of reducing the housekeeping cycle time by 50 percent was realized and exceeded through this total team study. The external customers have expressed amazement while viewing the room-cleaning process and delight in finding their rooms completely cleaned in such an expeditious manner. A strong contributor to the success of the team-cleaning concept was involving people directly impacted by the housekeeping system and using their expertise to drive change. The benchmark was important to lend credibility to the team's possible solutions, as well as providing evidence of practicality to move forward in piloting teams.

The reduced process time delighted the hotel's customers in another important way. The front office staff benefited greatly from up-to-the-minute room availability. This was accomplished by team self-inspection and status updating directly tied to the hotel's room inventory computer. This practice allowed the front office receptionists to give customers the rooms they wanted. It also reduced the following:

• Customer queue time at the registration desk

• Delays at the front office because the right rooms were available when they were needed

• Defects and errors in out-of-inventory situations

Three important factors contributed to the success of this study.

1. Team meetings were held with the individuals and departments that were impacted by the study and its subsequent changes.

2. Daily lineups at the beginning of each shift served as a means of communication.

3. Staff members were involved and empowered to make changes and to pilot the same.

Two practices that did not work during this study were the following:

1. Small, incremental changes were met with resistance and a "what-next?" attitude. Combined, comprehensive changes were much more welcome by the staff.

2. Managers discussing the team's work and process changes was less effective than peer-to-peer coaching.

Actions Taken

Implementation

The implementation of housekeeping teams to clean guest rooms was a task of great proportion as it was a major change in how work was done (see Figures 11.5 and 11.6). The biggest obstacle was the human response to change or the reengineering of a process. As noted, involving the people impacted by process change was a vital part of the study's overall success. Using a total team approach and scientific tools also markedly increased the acceptability and buy-in of the whole change.

Large-scale change also took place in the laundry department as it is housekeeping's major supplier. Shift changes to accommodate terry and linen productivity, priority of wash loads, and modified handling of sorted, soiled pieces, all contributed to

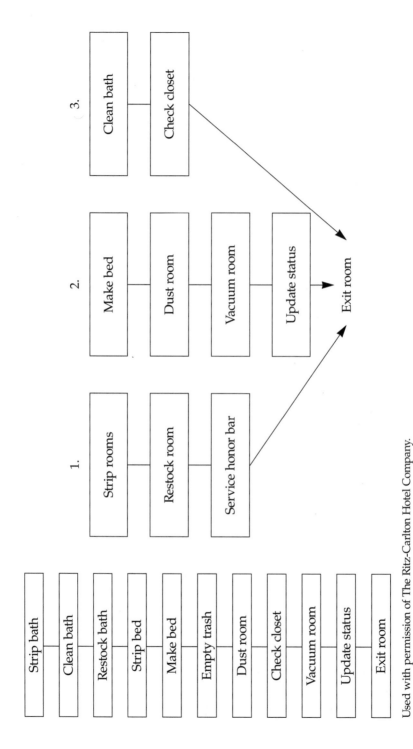

Used with permission of The Ritz-Carlton Hotel Company.

Figure 11.5. Consecutive versus simultaneous work flowchart.

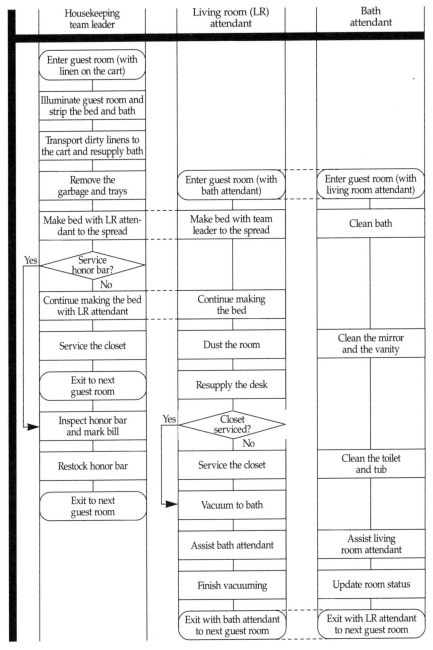

Housekeeping team leader	Living room (LR) attendant	Bath attendant
Enter guest room (with linen on the cart)		
Illuminate guest room and strip the bed and bath		
Transport dirty linens to the cart and resupply bath		
Remove the garbage and trays	Enter guest room (with bath attendant)	Enter guest room (with living room attendant)
Make bed with LR attendant to the spread	Make bed with team leader to the spread	Clean bath
Yes — Service honor bar? — No		
Continue making the bed with LR attendant	Continue making the bed	
Service the closet	Dust the room	Clean the mirror and the vanity
Exit to next guest room	Resupply the desk	
Inspect honor bar and mark bill	Yes — Closet serviced? — No	
Restock honor bar	Service the closet	Clean the toilet and tub
Exit to next guest room	Vacuum to bath	
	Assist bath attendant	Assist living room attendant
	Finish vacuuming	Update room status
	Exit with bath attendant to next guest room	Exit with LR attendant to next guest room

Figure 11.6. Housekeeping process flowchart.

increase productivity to return cleaned supplies to customers. The room attendants contributed to these handling changes by separating linen and terry on the guest room floors. It was discovered that the room attendants were the only ones who combined terry and linen items throughout the entire soiled-to-clean process. Keeping the items separated throughout the cycle saved time-consuming sorting and reduced the possibility of injury in the laundry chute room.

Planned Changes/Next Steps

The final frontiers to tackle for total process reliability in producing a clean, fresh, fully stocked guest room include the following:

1. Linen distribution system

2. Honor bar servicing system

3. Continuous training process for the housekeeping staff

4. Even use of guest rooms through rotation selling

5. Scheduling of housekeeping teams to meet identified customer requirements for room cleaning

Both internal and external customers are affected by these processes. Their involvement in producing reliability will be tested and measured for 100 percent satisfaction.

Customer-supplier relationships are crucial to the reliability of the housekeeping system. Error proofing these processes will ensure that the guests are served right the first time and that they are served on time. Clearly, the original goal of a 50 percent reduction in cycle time has been achieved and exceeded. For the future, the housekeeping system will continue to improve in cycle time and reliability with the participation of the ladies and gentlemen of The Ritz-Carlton, Dearborn.

Summary

- The Ritz-Carlton Hotel Company operates 30 business and resort hotels throughout the world. It has 13 international sales offices and employs 13,500 people.

- The Ritz-Carlton in Dearborn, Michigan, houses 308 guest rooms and features several dining options, over 20,000 square feet of meeting space, and a fitness center.

- The Ritz-Carlton Hotel Company identified several processes that customers judged with highly important, but low satisfaction, ratings.

- The company set forth the following tasks: identify what was important to customers and how they rated those features; complete a gap analysis; identify the primary processes and if the company had existing work areas or processes that were aligned to meet those needs.

- The Ritz-Carlton in Dearborn, Michigan, investigated the housekeeping system. Its goal was to create an error-proof, reliable process that could be standardized within the company.

- The process team's goal was to identify and reduce waste through analysis by simplifying, eliminating, and combining steps within the housekeeping system. This was done to meet the company's quality goals of six sigma; 50 percent cycle time reduction; and 100 percent customer retention.

- The team consisted of those individuals active in the housekeeping system and impacted by any changes to it. This included housekeeping and laundry department representatives and engineering and TQM personnel.

- Team-building exercises were discussed and practiced at weekly meetings. The team used consensus decision making and shared leadership.

- Ten characteristics of a clean, fresh, fully stocked guest room were identified as internal and external customer requirements.

- Consecutive, task-by-task work by one room attendant was the current method of room cleaning.

- The team explored the concept of simultaneous work done by a number of room attendants.

- Team cleaning, as brainstormed, was observed at a competitor's facility and piloted at The Ritz-Carlton, Dearborn.

- Seven key measures were used to check the reliability of both the current and new housekeeping processes.

- As the housekeeping department's primary supplier, the laundry department examined and changed its daily processes to better meet its customer's needs.

- At least seven tangible and eight intangible benefits resulted from the team-cleaning concept.

- A strong contributor to the success of the team-cleaning concept was involving people directly impacted by the housekeeping system and using their expertise to drive change.

- Using a total team approach and scientific tools markedly increased the acceptability of all the housekeeping changes implemented.

- Five additional planned changes have been identified to further increase the reliability of the housekeeping system.

CHAPTER 12

Coolant Management at Texas Instruments

Prepared with the cooperation of Chris R. Richardson, P.E., TQM manager, Texas Instruments, Sherman, Texas

The flavors are only five in number, but their blends are so various that one cannot taste them all.

- Background
- Customer Requirements
- Organizations or Industries Benchmarked
- Best Practices Found
- Actions Taken
- Summary

Background

Metal fabrication requiring milling, drilling, turning, tapping, and grinding of metal parts uses a variety of lubricating fluids. These carry chips away and cool the cutting tools. The fluids include oil, water, and chemicals that are specially formulated for an operation. Many of the fluids are disposed of after use. Some are recyclable and could be reused if a cost-effective process could be found. A typical cutting tool operation is shown in Figure 12.1.

Winner of the 1992 Malcolm Baldrige National Quality Award for manufacturing, the metal fabrication organization at the Texas Instruments (TI) plant in Sherman, Texas, manufactures defense products. Operations include milling, drilling, turning, tapping, and grinding of aluminum and stainless steel parts on numeric-controlled (NC) machines, manual mills and

Used with permission of Texas Instruments.

Figure 12.1. Typical cutting tool operation.

lathes, and special, custom-built machines. Almost all parts are less than 18 inches on each side. The product types are as follows:

- Prismatic parts represent 60 percent of the total load, and round parts represent 40 percent of the load.

- The materials used to manufacture the prismatic parts are 60 percent raw stock-based and 40 percent castings. There are no forgings.

In addition to the general machining operations, the plant also has screw machine, sheet metal, and chemical- and paint-finishing operations.

The Sherman plant employs about 200–250 touch labor staff, which includes machinists, chemical and paint finishers, and hardware subassembly and assembly personnel. It utilizes 92 NC machines, 25 screw machines, 75 conventional machines, and 45 special machines. Production volume includes a 5000 active parts base and 490,000 manufacturing hours per year on three shifts.

Objectives/Purpose

The metal fabricating organization of the Sherman, Texas, plant proposed to undertake a benchmarking study to identify industry best practices for utilizing and maintaining metalworking fluids. This investigation was chosen because it offered a significant opportunity for both cost reduction and improved employee morale.

There were several problems in the metal fabricating organization. The main problem was that many employees complained of rancid fluid odors. This severely impacted worker morale.

The objectives of the benchmarking team were to

- Maximize fluid sump life. This would eliminate odors because the longer the fluid was in the sump, the worse the odors were.

- Ensure a safe working environment.
- Minimize the costs of new fluid cleaner and defoamer.
- Minimize the amount of disposal waste generated.
- Minimize the amount of support labor for the coolant processes.
- Maximize fluid effectivity. This was measured in the quality of fluid, which drives many of the other listed indicators. Thus, the team had to ask: How was the quality of the fluid to be measured?

Focus/Topic (Work Process Selected)

The work process selected was defined as *metalworking fluids management*. It was agreed that the process would not include the operation of the wastewater treatment facility. The study would primarily concentrate on reducing the feed to that facility. The inbound and outbound logistics of purchasing the fluids were also excluded from the study.

The metalworking fluids management process was fully defined through the benchmarking team's deliberations. The process begins with the purchase of the cutting fluids. Between three and four barrels are used each week at TI's Sherman site. Each barrel contains 55 gallons of fluid and costs about $600. The process ends with the disposal of process outflow to the wastewater treatment facility. The complete process is mapped in Figure 12.2.

Team Operation

A benchmarking team was assembled and officially established in October of 1990. It conducted its investigations over the course of one year and established the new process in September of 1991. Implementation followed during the next three months.

Coolant management process map

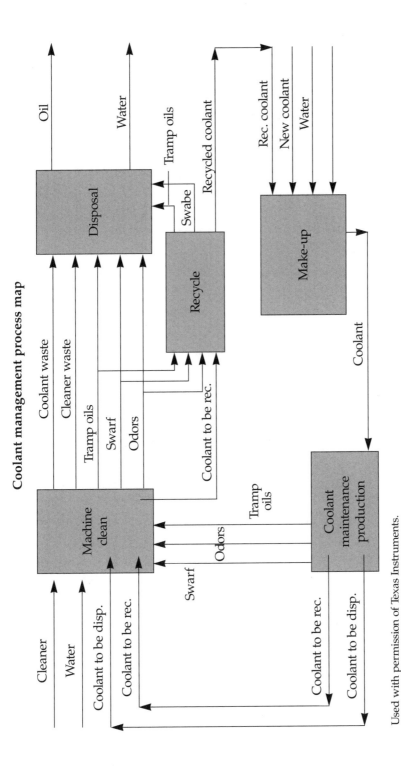

Used with permission of Texas Instruments.

Figure 12.2. Current process: Metalworking fluids management.

The overall conduct of the study involved collecting data on the current process and analyzing it to establish a baseline of current performance and research on the process. The research involved examining assumptions of coolant failure and maintenance methodologies.

The team had to determine what was important to measure in the quality of the coolant. This involved 6–12 months of testing. The team performed several internal tests to determine the importance of the following factors.

1. Bacteria growth in the fluid

2. pH control of the fluid

3. Coolant concentration control

4. Way lube miscibility causing the addition of sulfurized fat through way lube contamination

5. Metal fine removal and metal ion buildup

The benchmarking team determined that bacteria growth and pH control of the fluids were the most important parameters to measure. The team felt it was important to control the bacteria level; the removal of metal fines; the coolant concentration; and the tramp oil content, or miscibility, since the more miscible the way lube, the more tramp oil will result.

The team attended benchmarking training conducted by The Quality Network. The training involved engineers, managers, process owners, tooling technicians, and machinists—the customers and users of the process.

The benchmarking team was quite large. It had 23 individuals including 17 machinists—one from each self-directed work team—and one representative from each of the following functions: engineering; process owners; technicians; methods and tooling; repair and maintenance; and safety/industrial hygiene. A second, small team—a subset of the large team—consisted of six individuals: four machinists and one representative each from engineering and process owners. These six individuals attended benchmarking training.

As a direct outcome of the training, the entire benchmarking team documented its processes through flowcharting and determined the critical in-process performance measures. The team researched and assembled a candidate set of benchmarking partners and, later, finalized the list.

In order to assemble the candidate list of partners, the team conducted a literature search and discussed its metalworking processes with potential fluid suppliers. The literature search did not reveal much useful information; however, the discussions with potential suppliers proved more fruitful. They were most willing to share information. For instance, the suppliers were able to tell the TI team who recycles significant amounts of fluid and who does not need to buy much coolant.

These discussions resulted in a list of 16 potential benchmarking partners. The team then conducted telephone interviews with each candidate using the survey shown in Figure 12.3.

The process-to-process comparisons were made with selected partners. That analysis led to the establishment of a new process, which was presented to the management QIT for review and approval. The QIT's approval was unanimous, and implementation started shortly thereafter.

It should be noted that the QIT represents the functional management level at Texas Instruments. The team's function is to review projects and provide necessary resources to complete the tasks involved in those projects. The QIT is an ongoing team. It consists of 12 managers from various functions such as quality assurance, methods and tooling, and shop management.

Customer Requirements

The machinists were the primary customers of the benchmarking study. The primary requirement was the timely delivery of quality

Benchmarking partners
Prescreening data

Company name _____
Contact _____
Size (gallons of coolant) _____ Machines _____

Materials	Coolant type	Concentration	Central/sump	Average sump life

Operations _____

Recycling system

Type	Features		Type	Features

Way lubes: _____

Process description: _____
_____
_____
_____
_____

Responsibilities:

Additives: _____   _____
          _____   _____

Coolant volumes

   Disposal gallons per month _____
   Purchased gallons per month _____
   Turnover percentage per month _____
   Recycled gallonage _____

Notes: _____
_____
_____

Used with permission of Texas Instruments.

Figure 12.3. Telephone survey of potential benchmarking candidates.

coolant. It needed to have a stable pH, low bacterial count, and no odor. Additional requirements included availability of machine changeover equipment including tools, refractometers, and sump suckers.

Need/Reason for Improvement

The initial reason for this project came from the many complaints from the metalworking shop. These complaints related to the odors and rancid smells from the process. These were major employee dissatisfiers and formed an important reason to try and correct the situation.

Subsequent analysis of the problem areas revealed the following concerns.

1. There was minimal recycling of fluids despite the existence of recycling equipment.

2. The costs for fluids, cleaners, and defoaming agents were high.

3. There were frequent, unpleasant odor emissions.

4. High volumes of spent fluid were thrown away.

5. Frequent machine cleaning and changeover took a substantial amount of time, resulting in the operation having a high labor content.

6. There were frequent complaints about the availability of coolant, cleaners, sump suckers, wastewater treatment equipment, and refractometers.

7. There were isolated cases of employee dermatitis.

The biggest problem was the first one listed. Fluid was not recycled because most machinists felt that recycled coolant was inferior to new coolant. Their perceptions were correct based on current process; however, there were still some attitudinal concerns that had to be overcome.

The benchmarking team believed that, based on the research and analysis conducted to this stage, there were many improvements that could be made to the metalworking fluids process. One of the initial findings that led the team to this conclusion was the fact that some companies operated one to two years without ever disposing of any metalworking fluid. It was believed that this could also be accomplished at the Sherman facility.

Organizations or Industries Benchmarked

Current Process

The coolant solution is mixed in a XYBEX coolant recovery system with a ratio of 10 parts water to one part coolant concentrate. Distribution of the fluid to the machine tools is through a piping system. In some instances, the required amount of fluid is manually carried to the workstation. The XYBEX system for recycling coolant is shown in Figure 12.4.

Fluid is monitored at the machine station by using a refractometer to maintain the proper concentrate-water mix and by using skimmers on the fluid tanks to remove undesirable tramp oils. Routine machine maintenance is performed to keep sumps free of swarf, metal chips, fungus, and other undesirable impurities.

The used fluid is then transported from the machine to the disposal unit using a sump sucker, which suctions fluid and chips from the machine sumps and discharges them in the disposal or recycling equipment. This disposal unit pumps the fluid into the wastewater treatment facility, while the recycling equipment returns recycled fluid to the machines on the shop floor.

Key Measures and Other Facts

Several critical measures of fluid maintenance effectiveness were determined and documented. A total of seven measures of

XYBEX® System 100 for recycling coolants, manufactured by Master Chemical Corporation's Systems Equipment Division, Perrysburg, Ohio. XYBEX® is a registered trademark of Master Chemical Corporation.

Figure 12.4. The XYBEX system for recycling coolant.

process performance were identified. These included measures of the following:

1. Fluid turnover
2. Gallons disposed

3. Gallons recycled

4. Sump life

5. Gallons of cleaner used

6. Labor hours

7. Other ancillary items used in the process as a function of sump capacity, such as filters and biocides

The data were then categorized. The first four items were the primary basis of benchmarking comparison. Items 5 and 6 were appropriate measures of internal improvement. Item 7 was initially thought to be an indicator of efficient coolant management. Later, it was determined that significant data could not be collected, and this measure was eliminated.

Process-to-Process Analysis

The detailed coolant management process map, shown in Figure 12.2, identifies all the relevant fluid inputs, flow paths, and outputs of the process. Inputs were water, new coolant, and cleaner. Outputs were water and oil. All intermediate flows between the equipment and holding tanks and the coolant maintenance process were also mapped. The latter operation involved skimming tramp oils and maintaining proper fluid levels and concentrations.

With the process mapped and the key measurements determined, the team identified benchmarking partners it had judged to be exemplar and worthy of comparison. Four categories of comparisons were considered: (1) to internal operations; (2) to competitive operations; (3) to functional leaders; and (4) to generic processes. Of these, it was decided to focus on comparisons to internal operations and to functional leaders. This process uncovered best practices.

The internal operations comparison revealed a similar process at a Texas Instrument sister facility called Lemmon

Avenue. The comparison of the Sherman and Lemmon Avenue operations is shown in Figure 12.5.

Both facilities were throwing away large amounts of coolant. The Sherman facility was using a higher concentration of coolant than Lemmon Avenue. The facilities used different brands of coolant, and the one used at Lemmon Avenue may have been better for recycling. This fact, however, was not discovered until later in the benchmarking study.

The functional leader comparisons provided the most significant input to the identification of best practices and process improvements. These comparisons were to other operations of metal fabrication in which coolants were used and aluminum and stainless steel products were produced. These are the types of metal products produced at the TI Sherman facility. The 16 companies identified as benchmarking partners included manufacturers of aircraft, construction machinery, auto and auto parts, oil field tools, and other high-tech tubes.

One company had superior practices. These were adopted by TI. The other companies' best practices were modified and adapted to further improve TI's process.

Best Practices Found

Key Findings

The best practices findings for the proposed coolant management process resulted in the following 10 changes.

1. All coolant in all machines should be changed according to a predetermined schedule.

2. The machine coolant change process should be simplified.

3. Key responsibilities should be assigned to key, identified individuals on all shifts for the following tasks: oil and water separation; XYBEX recycling; sump sucker maintenance;

	Sherman	Lemmon	Estimated industry average	Estimated industry leader
1. Average fluid turnover per month (gallons) Purchased coolant to sump capacity	9680 5500 1.76	7700 6400 1.20	0.33	0.15
2. Average gallons of disposed fluid per month Pump per sump capacity (gallons)	6400 5500 1.16	6325 6400 0.988	0.10	0.02
3. Average gallons of recycled fluid per month per sump capacity	0	0	0.55	0.80
4. Average machine sump life (weeks)	4	4	4	2
5. Average gallons of cleaner used per month per sump capacity	110 5500	0	0	0
6. Average machine cleaning labor per month per sump capacity (hours)	0.045			0.040
7. Average usage of ancillary items, such as filters and biocides ($ per month per sump capacity)				

Used with permission of Texas Instruments.

Figure 12.5. Internal operations comparison (key measures).

coolant concentration maintenance; and machine operation and maintenance.

4. Coolant concentrations and levels should be monitored and controlled daily.

5. The sump sucker filters, solids, and main tank should be maintained daily.

6. Recycled fluid quality should be checked and maintained. Records to track trend data and process capability should cover the following: pH, bacteria, concentrations, conductivity, tramp oil concentrations, stabilizer, and dirt load of the coolant.

7. A survey should be used to gather data and analyze customer satisfaction.

8. Additional practices that are key to process improvement include the following: sump sucker filter capability; improved oil skimmer recycling equipment; improved recycling equipment filtering capacity; installation of flowmeters to track process capability; installation of filters on specific deburr equipment to reduce dirt load on the recycling equipment; and added sump sucker capacity. Note that these practices were not directly identified through benchmarking but became requirements based on new knowledge of the recycling process. This is a typical occurrence in original benchmarking investigations. These practices were implemented with the best practices found through benchmarking.

9. A comprehensive recycling and maintenance operation training program should be developed and instituted.

10. Benchmarking measurements, to be monitored monthly, should be established.

Internal Versus External Practices

The effect of implementing the best practices is evidenced in the new coolant maintenance process flowchart shown in Figure 12.6. This process has 11 decision points compared to the original 18. The new process has 17 steps compared to 25 in the old process. In addition, the data collection points are clearly defined for benchmark data, process capability, and customer satisfaction. The new, overall process also clearly delineates between machine maintenance, machine cleaning, and coolant make-up and recycling. This simplified process detail allows for quick inspection at any time.

Potential Opportunities for Improvement

One opportunity for improvement included one-time costs as well as ongoing savings. The one-time costs included the cost of conducting the benchmarking study and the conversion to a new process. These consisted of labor charges, training, and capital, and totaled $54,000. The operational savings consisted of reduced costs for disposal, labor, new coolant, filters, and stabilizers. These savings amounted to about $12,000 per month.

A second opportunity for improvement was the elimination of odors. This reduced the number of employee complaints and significantly improved employee morale.

A third opportunity for improvement involved machine maintenance. The TI benchmarking team had to determine who was responsible for the coolant changeout process. Some companies hire a maintenance company for this task. This usually becomes problematic because maintenance must be scheduled during production hours. The complete solutions to these three problems are further discussed in the next section.

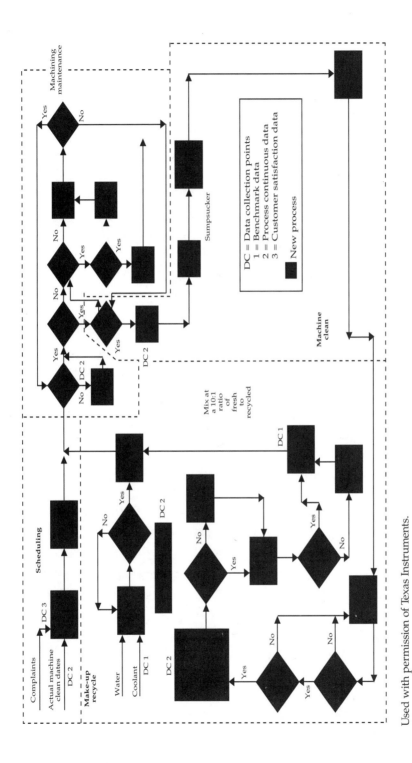

Used with permission of Texas Instruments.

Figure 12.6. Coolant maintenance process flow (new process).

Conclusions

The payback from the benchmarking study was significant. By saving $12,000 a month in operational expenses, the TI Sherman facility recouped its $54,000 labor, training, and capital investment in four and one-half months. Also, the reduced monthly operational expenses represent an ongoing annual savings of $144,000. Thus, the revised best practice process was well justified.

Since the new process has been implemented, there have been no employee complaints about coolant odors. Employee dermatitis, a relatively minor problem, has also been eliminated. In fact, employees have made complimentary comments about the new process.

The TI benchmarking team also found a unique solution to its machine maintenance problems. At the beginning of every month, a maintenance schedule is set up. Then, each self-directed work team is given a 24-hour period to do its own machine maintenance. This minimizes production-maintenance conflicts and empowers employees in the process. This maintenance program is significantly different than that of other companies with metal fabrication operations. It is something that no one else has done.

Two other important components stand out from this study. First, from a benchmarking standpoint, despite what a team learns about other companies' best practices, they can be adapted to the subject company's unique culture and situation. This adaptation may, in fact, result in a better process. The TI Sherman facility learned this through its benchmarking experience.

Second, the TI Sherman benchmarking team realized it had 260 people who were both in control, and customers of, the metalworking process. Thus, they had to be involved, or they had to at least feel like they were involved. That was why the benchmarking team was so large—23 members. The TI benchmarking team leaders tried to get representatives from each self-directed work team so that members of the benchmarking team could act as intermediaries between the team and the employees. These intermediaries brought study information back to employees, and solicited and brought forward their ideas to the benchmarking team. This representation demonstrated that employees' input was used to make decisions.

Actions Taken

Implementation

The benchmarking team met in September 1991 to review the status of the implementation for the coolant metalworking fluids management benchmarking study. The team compared the new process map to the old one. The team reviewed the data collection for the system, which was determined by the benchmark data points, process control data, and customer satisfaction data. The team also reviewed the specific responsibilities for each of the identified new process practices. The team also developed a schedule for plan implementation. TI implemented the new process during a three-month period, from October to December. This period gave everyone a chance to adjust to the new process.

Planned Changes/Next Steps

While the cost savings and waste reductions have demonstrated dramatic improvement, the TI Sherman team still sees opportunity for improvement in labor costs. The team continues to evaluate process practices and alternative fluids that offer opportunity for increased machine sump life and reduced frequency of fluid recycling.

The corrective action team (CAT), a fallout from the benchmarking study, now functions as a process improvement team, although its name has not yet changed. The CAT meets monthly to discuss ways to continually improve the process.

Summary

• Metal fabrication uses oil, water, and chemical fluids to lubricate various operations, carry chips away, and cool the cutting tools.

• The fluids are frequently disposed of after use. Some are recyclable and could be reused if a cost-effective process could be found.

• In order to reduce costs and improve employee morale, the metal fabricating organization of the TI Sherman, Texas, facility needed to identify industry-best practices for utilizing and maintaining metalworking fluids.

• A large benchmarking team, consisting of both process owners and customers, was assembled.

• The team's objectives were the following: (1) maximize fluid sump life; (2) ensure a safe working environment; (3) minimize the costs of new fluid cleaner and defoamer; (4) minimize the amount of disposal waste generated; (5) minimize the amount of support labor; and (6) maximize fluid effectivity.

• The team conducted many internal tests to determine the importance of five factors of the metal fabrication process.

• The team interviewed 16 potential benchmarking partners to find best practices to adopt and adapt.

• The team's customer requirements were as follows: (1) increase the amount of fluids for recycling; (2) reduce the costs for fluids, cleaners, and defoaming agents; (3) eliminate the frequent, unpleasant odors; (4) reduce the amount of spent fluid that was thrown away; (5) reduce the amount of time and labor for machine cleaning and changeover; (6) increase the availability of coolant, cleaners, and equipment; and (7) eliminate the isolated cases of employee dermatitis.

• Key measurements of the metalworking process were as follows: (1) fluid turnover; (2) gallons disposed; (3) gallons recycled; (4) sump life; (5) gallons of cleaner used; and (6) labor hours.

• The TI Sherman team benchmarked its process with a sister facility.

• Comparisons to functional leaders were most useful.

• Key findings included the following: (1) all coolant in all machines should be changed according to a schedule; (2) the machine coolant change process should be simplified; (3) key responsibilities should be assigned to key, identified individuals on all shifts; (4) coolant concentrations and levels should be monitored and controlled daily; (5) sump sucker filters, solids, and the main tank should be maintained daily; (6) recycled fluid quality should be checked and maintained; (7) a survey should be used to gather data and analyze customer satisfaction; (8) additional key practices should be improved; (9) a comprehensive recycling and maintenance operation training program should be instituted; and (10) benchmarking measurements should be established.

• The new, streamlined process has fewer steps and decisions points than the original metalworking process.

• Three significant improvement opportunities were satisfied: (1) ongoing cost savings of $12,000 per month; (2) improved employee morale; and (3) a unique machine maintenance program.

• Ongoing evaluation to continually improve the process is conducted by a corrective action team that meets monthly.

CHAPTER 13

Supply Chain Management at Xerox Corporation

Prepared with the cooperation of John A. Clendenin, manager, Supply Chain & Asset Management, Xerox Corporation, Rochester, New York

> *I do not repeat my tactics but rearrange them to circumstances in an infinite variety of ways.*

- Background
- Customers and Requirements
- Organizations or Industries Benchmarked
- Best Practices Found
- Actions Taken
- Summary
- References

Background

Xerox Corporation is a multibillion dollar international manufacturer that is using the application of business process management to support long-term efforts to achieve a world-class, integrated supply chain. At Xerox, this is considered a key enabler to accomplishing the Xerox 2000 intent.

Winner of the 1989 Malcolm Baldrige National Quality Award, Xerox's document-processing products range from the smallest desktop and briefcase-size device to the 28-foot-long DocuTech. This system can handle, in one pass, document creation, storage, and reproduction into a final bound book.

Around the globe Xerox manufactures over 250 products that are supported by service, software, supplies, and accessories. These products are marketed through four geographic-based organizations—the United States, Americas Operations, Europe, and Asia/Pacific. These organizations are responsible for sales, service, and business operations with customers in 130 countries. Products are marketed through a direct sales force and a network of dealers, distributors, agents, and third-party affiliates.

To get product from the multitude of sources to this wide array of geographic customer sales outlets, Xerox manages a supply chain that controls the movement of Xerox products, service parts, materials, components, software, and supplies. The logistics network for delivering product from the source to customers is a substantial global operation. This supply chain links Xerox suppliers, production sites, service engineers, distributors, and customers.

Objectives/Purpose

The primary objective of the Xerox logistics activity is to provide processes that will never fail to meet end-user requirements that satisfy customers. The secondary objective is to do this with the minimum of working capital devoted to inventory assets—a

balance sheet statement item, and minimum logistics expense—
a cost item appearing on the profit-and-loss statement. The combination of reduced cost and, therefore, increased profits and
optimized asset and service-level achievement, contributes the
three-level leverage on Xerox's primary business performance
goal—return on assets—while achieving 100 percent customer
satisfaction (see Figure 13.1).

As in most functionally structured organizations, there were
major divisions of responsibility for Xerox's supply chain operation among the traditional organizations of product development,
manufacturing, service, and marketing. In addition, there were
logistical product lines that had different networks for configured equipment, repair parts, consumables, and software. With

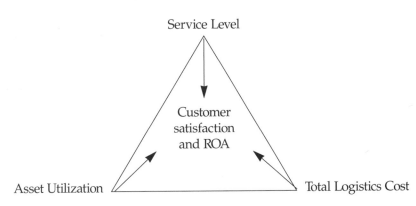

Service Level

Customer
satisfaction
and ROA

Asset Utilization   Total Logistics Cost

Results measurements

Level of service	=	% fill rate against customer-specified conditions
Asset utilization	=	% total inventory to revenue
Total logistics cost	=	% total logistics cost to revenue

Process measurements

Recycle utilization	=	% of cost of production
Response time	=	T.B.D.

Used with permission of Xerox Corporation.

Figure 13.1. ISC prioritization process.

this logistics fragmentation, and each organization attempting to efficiently manage its individual operations, it became clear that the whole supply chain was not being integrated to effectively and optimally utilize the corporation's substantial total inventory assets to successfully serve customers. With the number-one corporate goal of customer satisfaction, it became clear that accomplishing that goal through a more effective supply chain focusing on asset management would require a cross-functional approach.

The mission of the supply chain management improvement team was not to be the best in logistics service, asset utilization, or logistics cost. The team's mission was to be the best in all and the world-class best. Xerox expected to be the best in all three categories and to be a showcase world leader. The relationship of these three performance measurements is shown in Figure 13.2. It includes the improvement expected from the current state to the desired state.

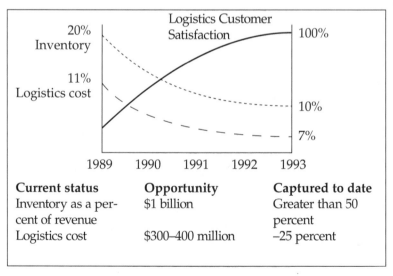

Used with permission of Xerox Corporation.

Figure 13.2. Performance improvement.

Therefore, any proposed logistics process practice improvements intended to improve asset utilization and logistics cost should also improve the logistics level of service. To accomplish this the process owners had to clearly understand how their processes supported customer requirements. They next had to document the process and determine its key performance measurements. The supply chain benchmarking then focused on improving those processes.

Focus/Topic (Work Process Selected)

At Xerox all work is defined in terms of processes. A process means a documented sequence of work steps that deliver outputs that satisfy either an internal or external customer. The classification scheme and relationship of the processes to customers is shown in Figure 13.3. Xerox classifies all its processes into 14 major, high-level, helicopter-view processes. These, in turn, decompose into many subprocesses. It is the systematic comparison of process to process that identifies the best practices that need to be improved to achieve higher levels of performance. Oftentimes the work processes are cross-functional. Therefore, improvement efforts involve several organizations.

Team Operation

As part of the quality improvement efforts launched in 1984 the Xerox CEO commissioned an assessment of all operations. The initial competitive benchmarking that was conducted indicated that Xerox was at a significant disadvantage compared to other companies on several key financial ratios, including return on assets. In response, a task force was established that examined how leading companies managed their assets and, in particular, their inventories. The task force concluded that Xerox was far too inefficient and fragmented in the management of this important corporate resource. The study showed that each organization

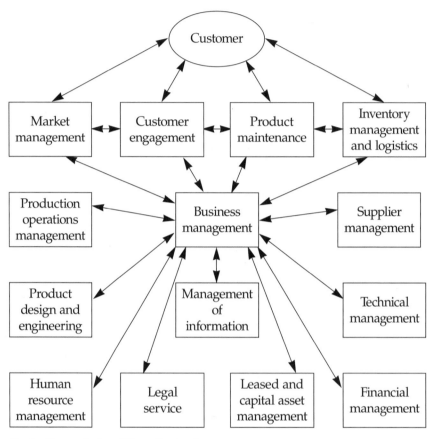

Used with permission of Xerox Corporation.

Figure 13.3. Xerox enterprise processes.

was holding its own inventory, hedging its own needs against possible sales, and not balancing surpluses in one organization with needs in another. The overall level of inefficiency is shown in Figure 13.4. Here, Xerox is compared to other exemplar organizations on inventory as a percent of sales. Xerox was substantially off the benchmark. To improve, Xerox would have to coordinate the worldwide use of its inventory assets to achieve

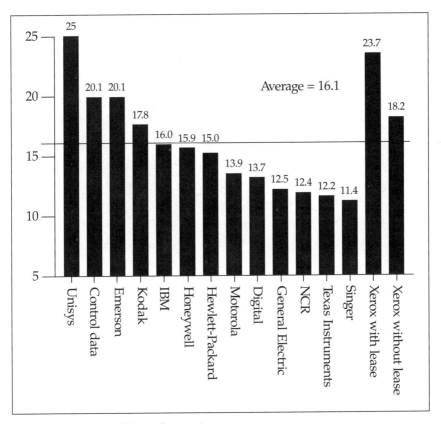

Used with permission of Xerox Corporation.

Figure 13.4. Inventory percent of sales for benchmark companies.

global inventory control and sharing of this important resource. Such coordination would require radical changes in operating practices and corporate culture.

This initiative, to critically examine the effective use of inventory assets, became the responsibility of the Central Logistics and Asset Management (CLAM) organization. It was a high-level group of change agents who were responsible for (1) examination, improvement, and implementation of the basic work processes that resulted in the more effective utilization of inventories; and (2) the development of a worldwide integrated supply chain.

The CLAM team was handpicked. It was composed of 12 individuals from development and manufacturing, the supply side of Xerox; 12 individuals from the field sales force and technical service organizations, the demand side of Xerox; and 12 individuals from other affected organizations, both internal and external. These experts became the process architects who focused on short- and long-term, cross-functional business process improvements. They were colocated in a suburban offsite facility not attached to the main Xerox offices in Rochester, New York.

Customers and Requirements

CLAM's customers were Xerox CEO Paul A. Allaire and selected senior executives whose organizations were directly affected by the process change. These organizations included manufacturing, U.S. Customer Operations, and Rank Xerox (Europe) Customer Operations.

Need/Reason for Improvement

The team developed a set of requirements that eventually became the vision for its existence. These included the following:

1. A continual and primary focus on customer satisfaction

2. A supply chain driven by demand, which meant building products and customizing them to order

3. Meeting the competitive time to physically deliver and making the order information time lag responsive

4. Developing and ensuring a common nomenclature for products, components, and materials

5. Managing internal Xerox complexity through high performance work processes insulated and invisible to customers

6. Recycling all assets to meet environmental standards

Organizations or Industries Benchmarked

Using benchmarking, Xerox examined its practices and established benchmarks for key product performance attributes, work processes, and their output performance measurements. This involved collaborative studies focused on domestic as well as international organizations, with those in the same industry as well as exemplar organizations outside the industry. These studies helped establish unbiased targets based on the performance levels of world-class organizations.

Current Process

The current logistics process operation, in principal, was really quite simple. Xerox was responding to customers by buying parts, assembling them into machines, inserting some software, delivering the devices to customers on time, and supporting the installation with service. The findings of the CLAM team, however, indicated that this was far too complex a process. An indication of the level of complexity is shown in Figure 13.5. It illustrates the sequence of operations that a new Xerox product goes through to arrive at a customer site and later be removed for disposal. It was taking too long; there were too many people involved in making the process work; there were more process steps than necessary; there were too many handoffs to those next in line and between organizations; there were too many decision makers at all levels; and there was far too many unique stand-alone information systems passing information among themselves. There was a commanding need to make major changes and make the entire process straightforward. There was a need

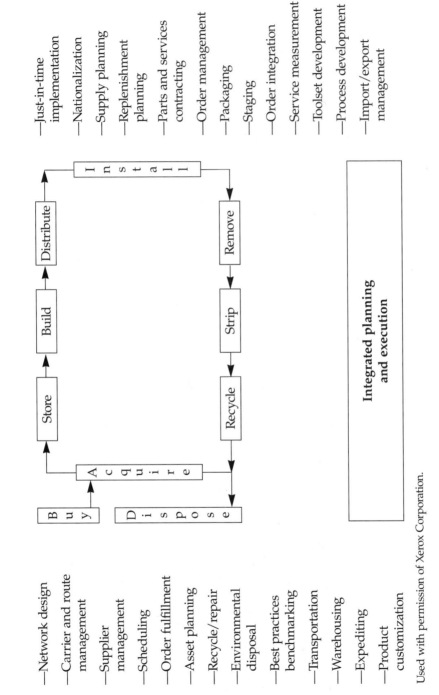

—Network design
—Carrier and route management
—Supplier management
—Scheduling
—Order fulfillment
—Asset planning
—Recycle/repair
—Environmental disposal
—Best practices benchmarking
—Transportation
—Warehousing
—Expediting
—Product customization

—Just-in-time implementation
—Nationalization
—Supply planning
—Replenishment planning
—Parts and services contracting
—Order management
—Packaging
—Staging
—Order integration
—Service measurement
—Toolset development
—Process development
—Import/export management

Buy

Acquire

Distribute

Build

Store

Install

Dispose

Remove

Strip

Recycle

Integrated planning and execution

Used with permission of Xerox Corporation.

Figure 13.5. Xerox supply chain.

to vigorously attack the business processes through reengineering and benchmarking.

Key Measures and Other Facts

Detailed numerical comparisons of the key financial performance measurements were developed for each benchmarking partner. These, in turn, were accompanied by logistics process analyses and site visits to confirm the data and information. The sum of the best practices found from the process analyses provided an endpoint view of the future supply chain and kept the cross-functional nature of the logistics operations process focused as well as results-oriented. None of the process comparisons made or best practices found could be readily adopted by Xerox. They could, however, be adapted. The end result was a set of subprocesses that were unique to Xerox but that incorporated the adapted exemplar practices of others. This, in turn, provided a competitive advantage.

Process-to-Process Analysis

An example of the process comparisons that were made and that lead to improvement was the internal differences in approaches within Xerox for managing service or repair parts. This form of internal benchmarking, and understanding Xerox best practices, were key contributors to the early success of the team. In the early 1980s, the European operations implemented a service parts replenishment and stocking process that dramatically improved service levels and reduced inventories. It was a best practice, which when implemented in the United States, Canada, and elsewhere in the Xerox world, resulted in immediate savings. This added credibility allowed the team to tackle even more substantial changes.

In the United States there had been a practice of having each service engineer decide what inventory items to carry in his or her immediate vehicle or trunk inventory. While decisions of what to carry were made on the basis of information provided in the form of a usage and stocking model, the ultimate decision was left to the discretion of the service engineer. Invariably, this resulted in many decisions being subjective, especially where there had been a rare instance of not having a part and not wanting to experience the event again. So based on the machines supported by the engineer, parts were kept for eventualities that were not going to occur for a long time. With individual service engineers squirreling away inventory, total inventory levels grew. Another effect was that once the part was issued to the service engineer it was assumed to have been used and therefore charged to the cost of service. In actuality, the parts accumulated in the service engineer's personal inventory. Since records of actual usage were not kept, the decision to stock an item became each engineer's decision and there was no way of matching actual usage to parts issued.

In Europe the process was quite different. A new information system recorded actual usage for the day and what remained in the engineer's trunk inventory at the end of each day. Data were gathered on actual usage of each part by major operation—such as the city or a suburb of London—by service engineer or by product. With the actual usage, the service engineers could now make more informed decisions about what to carry. In addition, decisions could now be made about selected service engineers carrying key parts but having the information known to the others in the area for possible exchange or loan. For example, this meant that not all engineers carried the same expensive circuit board, duplicating the inventory many times, but could call on a fellow engineer who did.

Therefore, each service engineer became an inventory location available to others, thus minimizing the total investment. Inventory decisions were also made on the basis of actual usage.

This permitted charging the service expense for items actually used on a machine. This was a matter of significantly changing the process, which in turn allowed major reductions in inventory, as well as the sharing of inventory across service engineer teams. It also permitted the stocking of some limited number of high-priced items in the service engineer's personal inventory since its use would now be accessible to several engineers. This prevented broken calls in which an engineer would have to leave a partially complete repair to go and get the needed part. It also prevented a return to the branch parts location some distance away or having to order from a central location. A broken call was identified as a major aggravation by customers, and the ability to prevent more of them became a significant contributor to customer satisfaction.

With the new process, the service teams no longer had idle parts in branch parts drops or with teams or with individual service engineers. In the United States the new process saved tens of millions of dollars and had a payback of less that two years. The overall results were reflected in the customer satisfaction measurement system, which periodically polled customers not only about their satisfaction with service but also with overall satisfaction with Xerox. There were significant increases to capstone questions like "How satisfied are you with Xerox products and services?" "Will you continue to do business with Xerox?" and "Would you recommend Xerox products to others?"

Benchmarking Partners

Xerox was and continues to be a long-time proponent of benchmarking against other leading exemplar companies that are in the same industry, that are competitors, and that are noncompetitors. Benchmarking was not only used for determining the size of the potential opportunity to improve, that is, the cost of quality, but also to identify those best practices, which when implemented in logistics processes, would markedly improve the outputs in order to satisfy customers.

The team prioritized its efforts by first identifying those processes that would improve the three major objectives; namely, increased inventory turns, increased service levels, and decreased logistics costs. The team benchmarked companies that were structured similarly to Xerox in their integrated worldwide operations. Those exemplar companies in the office products industry were also targeted. The benchmarking focused on what these best companies did differently in their work processes, namely what were the best practices that permitted them to achieve superior results.

Surprisingly, many of the other companies in the office products industry, such as Canon, Minolta, and Ricoh, were not identified as the best and hence were not selected as benchmarking candidates. Other companies were identified as the leaders in integrated supply chain management. These companies included Apple, Digital Equipment Corporation, DuPont, Hewlett-Packard, IBM, NCR, Siemens, and SUN Microsystems, as well as selected exemplar retailers, dealers, auto and airframe manufacturers, and major organizations in the service industries.

Best Practices Found

Key Findings

It became apparent that the basic approach to supply chain management had to change from a push system to one based on a pull replenishment system. In the push system, inventory was force-fed through the network and stocked in warehouses based on a forecast of demand. In a pull system, instead of shipping according to a forecast, manufacturing would ship equipment to a real customer order. Equipment would not leave the central warehouse for the marketplace until it had a customer's name, address, and installation date attached to it.

The supply chain replenishment approach would also be different for different types of products. There would not be a single Xerox supply chain with the same network and flow pattern for all products. Instead, the supply chain would vary for different types of products to allow Xerox to best meet customer requirements for delivery and installation as well as asset utilization and logistics cost. The significant supply chain structures are shown in Figure 13.6 for spare parts, commodity products, ship-to-order products, and configure- or build-to-order products. The processes for nonphysical products, such as software, could be downloaded and transmitted through local and other electronic networks for customer installation.

These different structures for the different product types were a direct reflection of the supply chain capability. The structures, found through benchmarking, needed to satisfy different customer requirements. The six product types are as follows:

1. Commodity products

2. Ship-to-order products

3. Build- or configure-to-order products

4. Spare parts

5. Consumables

6. Paper

Two of these product types will be described in detail to contrast the current operations with the best practice, benchmark processes that were eventually implemented.

This approach provides the flexibility, shown in Figure 13.7, for each product type. Each product or service may use any or all of the supply chain capabilities based on the following business needs.

• Channel selection and support

• Geographic market customization

• Recycle and disposal strategies

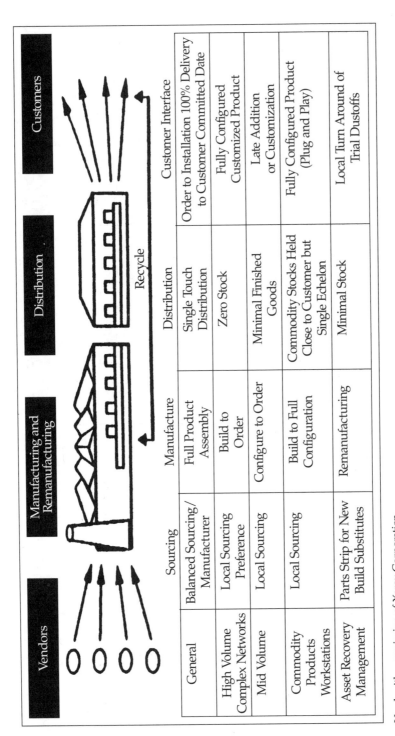

	Sourcing	Manufacture	Distribution	Customer Interface
General	Balanced Sourcing/ Manufacturer	Full Product Assembly	Single Touch Distribution	Order to Installation 100% Delivery to Customer Committed Date
High Volume Complex Networks	Local Sourcing Preference	Build to Order	Zero Stock	Fully Configured Customized Product
Mid Volume	Local Sourcing	Configure to Order	Minimal Finished Goods	Late Addition or Customization
Commodity Products Workstations	Local Sourcing	Build to Full Configuration	Commodity Stocks Held Close to Customer but Single Echelon	Fully Configured Product (Plug and Play)
Asset Recovery Management	Parts Strip for New Build Substitutes	Remanufacturing	Minimal Stock	Local Turn Around of Trial Dustoffs

Vendors — Manufacturing and Remanufacturing — Distribution — Customers

Recycle

Used with permission of Xerox Corporation.

Figure 13.6. Logistics and vision.

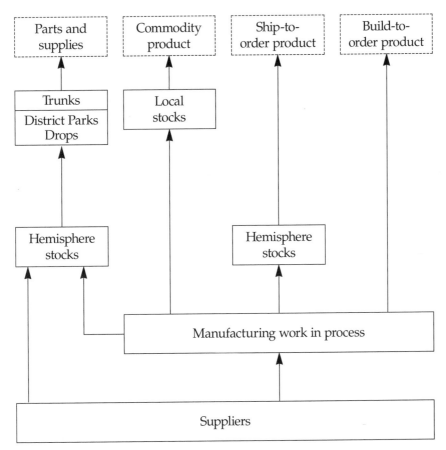

Used with permission of Xerox Corporation.

Figure 13.7. Supply chain process flexibility.

- Common products and parts
- Tactical competitive response

Internal Versus External Practices

Spare parts The spare parts stocking structure prior to the supply chain benchmarking was a multiechelon structure of storing and handling parts, at a minimum of four locations, on their route to the customer site for repair of a Xerox device. Parts were stocked at a country central location, usually adjacent to a manufacturing site; they were stocked in a regional location, usually a major city; they were stocked in a branch or suburban location, which was the territory of the service engineer; and lastly, parts were stocked with the service engineers in their personal inventory, often in the trunk of a vehicle. This multilayered structure required many handling and storage operations that were expensive and time-consuming. The system was heavily dependent on the transportation services available. There was also little sharing of common inventory in a geographically contiguous area. Information on availability was reduced to the sole knowledge of what the individual service engineers had in their personal inventory. Even that inventory was questionable because in many cases most records were kept manually.

The best practices revealed from supply chain benchmarking were to hold spare parts inventories in essentially two places— the service engineer's trunk and the hemisphere logistics center. This would mean, for example, that in the United States, the service engineer's inventory would be replenished daily from the hemisphere logistics center through a network of 65 convenient parts drops in each marketing district. The parts drops coincided with the marketing district's territory and were only pickup points for replenishment. These were not stocking locations for holding inventory. To accomplish the overnight replenishment there had to be information on parts usage that would be gathered daily and transmitted to the hemisphere location overnight. This scheme required substantially upgraded systems capability, electronic transmission, and the ability of the hemisphere logistics center to fill the order in time for overnight or next-day shipment. Wherever possible, the hemisphere logistics center would, in turn, be resupplied directly from a supplier or manufacturing site.

Build- and configure-to-order parts The largest document-creation device that Xerox sells is a 28-foot, $300,000 DocuTech production publisher. This is a top-of-the-line device that produces 120 copies per minute and competes directly with the offset press normally associated with printing thousands of copies per run. The DocuTech has a substantial amount of memory capacity, rivaling that of many PCs. The software options for controlling every aspect of producing a finished, bound book are extensive and just the font types and sizes alone number over 300 in the electronic publishing version of the DocuTech. Prior to supply chain benchmarking it was common practice to ship all the components to assemble a device to the customer site, often from different sources, arriving on different dates. Then the components were mated, and the software was installed on the customer's premises. It would take a service engineer several days to physically install the machine; join the options the customer wanted for input and output devices, such as stackers and binders; load the operating and other application software from floppy discs; and get the unit adjusted and running. It was a justifiably frustrating experience for customers to have this frantic activity occur at their site with a machine in which they had a substantial financial commitment and that often was critical to their operation. This was especially true if the device was the single output at the end of a computer center operation or the single multifunction device of a commercial printer. And this was particularly true when the installation meant downtime for customers when their old system had to be removed to make room for the new one.

The best practice developed from supply chain benchmarking was to completely assemble the unique combination of physical machine components, load the tailored software selected for the customer application, and run and adjust the entire system at the manufacturing site or possibly the hemisphere logistics center. In this setting technical help was readily nearby as was a complete set of adjustment and repair tools. Software could be loaded with high-speed buses in minutes, and the entire unit could then be completely adjusted and tested for its specification to customer requirements. After the unit was completely checked against the customer order, the major component units could be disengaged and sent to the customer site. The shipment would take only a matter of days, even if it was going across country. Dedicated moving vans, such as those used to transport household goods, were used. These have cushion underframes and air ride shock absorber suspension systems to prevent the units from getting out of adjustment from vibration. The installation then involved only the mating of the units in the customer's location and a nominal amount of startup systems checkout. Ideally, the hemisphere logistics centers would be able to provide a configuring capability of some defined technical level to handle last-minute changes in options.

Potential Opportunity for Improvement

The potential for improvement was substantial. It was based on cycle time reduction potential, reflected in inventory of $1 billion and logistics cost reductions opportunities of between $300 million and $400 million per year. The ISC progress at Xerox has been substantial, along with a simultaneous improvement in service level to satisfy customers. The business process management improvements have enabled significant future opportunities, as shown in Figure 13.8.

Conclusions

The best practices for the design of an integrated supply chain resulted in significant improvements in cycle time, reduction of inventory, and more cost-effective logistics. To ensure these results, however, and to continue to satisfy customers with their unique needs required that the supply chain operate with near

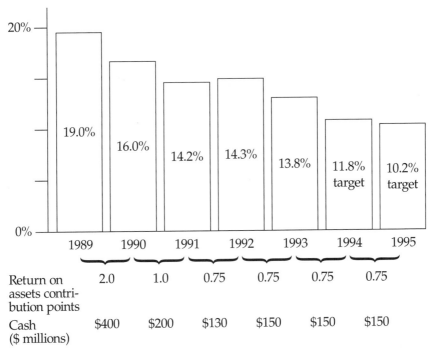

Used with permission of Xerox Corporation.

Figure 13.8. ISC progress.

perfection. With less inventory to buffer changes in demand, and with the time-sensitive assembly of system components that must come together for a successful assembly, there was little margin for error. All elements had to come together—the right material in the right configuration in the right condition at the right place at the right time. This type of success meant that the business processes on which the supply chain was based had to reach near perfection. Therefore, it was the concentration on the supply chain processes that had to be improved once the basic operating strategy had been determined. These processes can be identified and improved though benchmarking. A partial list of identified processes included the following:

- Customized installation and service
- Damage-free transportation
- Logistics quality expressed in terms of reliability and accuracy
- Ship-to-order configuration

Once these processes were determined, they would be documented and their key output and in-process measures would be determined. Then the processes would be benchmarked to other exemplar organizations to ensure that the new processes incorporated best practices and would, therefore, remain world-class. The end result of the benchmarking was a highly structured and rational design for the major logistical product lines (see Figure 13.9).

Actions Taken

Implementation

One of the team's key learnings that substantially improved the success of implementation was not to try and radically change old processes with the attendant disruption. It was found much more practical to introduce the new, improved process as new products were introduced. Thus, as new products came on-line, they were candidates for the new process. Similarly, as old products were replaced, the old processes naturally faded out of existence. In this fashion the processes, and therefore the operation, were gradually transformed using a very structured approach. There became a natural evolution of replacement and attrition.

While immediate process structural change was an imperative, there were side effects that also changed the assumptions and culture of the operations. Up until this time the primary

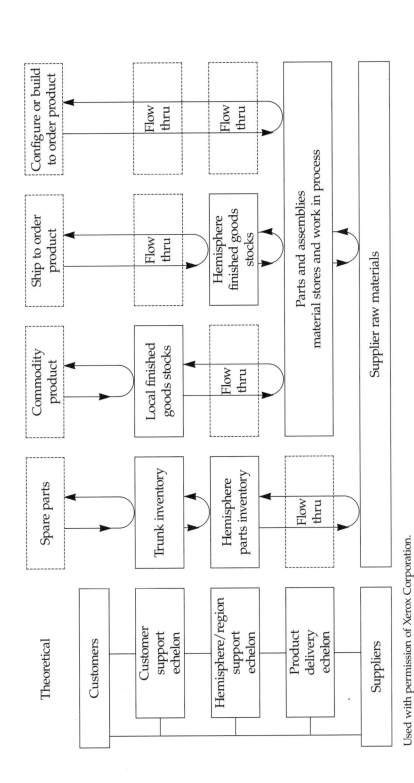

Used with permission of Xerox Corporation.

Figure 13.9. Pull replenishment supply chain logistics.

focus had been on reducing logistics costs. The change of emphasis to a demand-driven, ISC meant that Xerox had to be increasingly concerned with using time as a major focus to reduce inventories. So cycle time became a major focus of attention. It was then looked on as a significant competitive advantage. This required some subtle changes; for example, establishing a common item description and terminology so that parts, components, and whole designs had only one meaning and could be commonly communicated across the supply chain around the world. The focus on cycle time reduction also required major process changes and operating practices. This meant that a different protocol and behavior between organizations became the basis for how Xerox would be seen by its customers; that is, as an organization that was easy to do business with.

An example of a significant change was in the product planning process shown in Figure 13.10. This changed to a team meeting process to enable empowered supply chain discussions. The team's outputs included the following:

- Production plan updates
- Signals to execute a new production plan

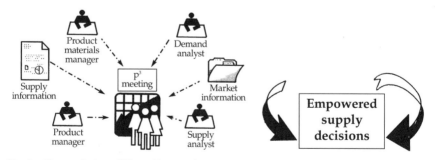

Used with permission of Xerox Corporation.

Figure 13.10. Production planning process (P3).

- Finished goods availability outlook
- Feedback to customer operations and business divisions
- Financial and performance measurements updates

Planned Changes

The changes were directed to take 70 percent out of the traditional cycle time. This was the time from buying parts for assembly from suppliers to having a machine with those parts installed in at customer's site. That, in turn, was calculated to reduce the worldwide supply chain inventory assets by $1 billion. That result, in turn, would reduce the asset-carrying charges—the expenses that support inventory, such as interest, facilities, and storage costs. These charges totaled about $200 million. Customer satisfaction was also targeted to rise from 70 to 90 percent toward a target of 100 percent. Thus, the higher customer satisfaction would encourage customers to do more business with Xerox and further increase revenues.

Impact on Priorities

Aside from a direct impact on the business priorities, why else should a logistics organization turn to benchmarking? There are several fundamental reasons.

1. Benchmarking heightens the sense of urgency when there is a need for improvement, whether from an external threat or from the need to strive for world-class excellence.

2. Benchmarking is a powerful way to obtain commitment and buy-in and to take the decision out of the realm of organization politics, since the objective facts of who is best are undeniably identified through the benchmarking study.

3. The facts—the identified best practices—form unbiased input to prioritizing those steps toward improvement.

4. Benchmarking speeds up the process for reaching agreement, since the facts of who is best are undeniable.

Finally, it should be noted that the supply chain case study described here was essentially a process reengineering project. While process reengineering, that is, the radical redesign of business processes, may or may not be necessary, benchmarking is essential. (The other option is to gradually evolve to a desired state.) Benchmarking is essential to understanding those practices that will lead to world-class status. Benchmarking is essential to determining what world-class means and then determining how to reach that goal.

Summary

- Xerox's document-processing products range from the smallest desktop device to the 28-foot-long DocuTech.

- Xerox manufactures over 250 products marketed worldwide through four geographic-based organizations.

- Xerox manages a global supply chain that controls the movement of products, service parts, materials, components, software, and supplies. This supply chain links Xerox suppliers, production sites, service engineers, distributors, and customers.

- The primary objective of the Xerox logistics activity is to provide processes that never fail to meet customer requirements. The secondary objective is to do this with minimum working capital devoted to inventory assets.

- The former logistics function was fragmented and inefficient. The whole supply chain was not optimally utilizing Xerox's total inventory assets to successfully serve customers.

- Xerox's mission was to develop a world-class supply chain management system. That meant being the best in logistics service, asset utilization, and logistics cost.

• CLAM was a high-level group of change agents who were responsible for (1) examination, improvement, and implementation of the basic work processes that resulted in the more effective utilization of inventories; and (2) the development of a worldwide integrated supply chain. The team became a change management organization when momentum was focused on specifications (see Figure 13.11).

• The 36-member, handpicked team represented development and manufacturing, the supply side of Xerox; field sales and technical service, the demand side of Xerox; and other affected internal and external organizations.

• The team identified six requirements that justified the reason for its existence. These included the following: (1) a focus on customer satisfaction; (2) a supply chain driven by demand; (3) meeting the competitive time to physically deliver and making

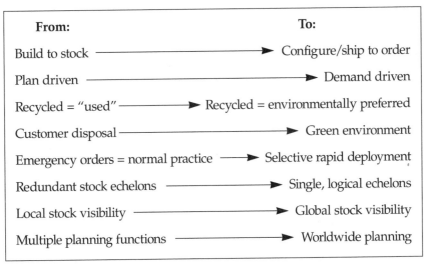

From:	To:
Build to stock	Configure/ship to order
Plan driven	Demand driven
Recycled = "used"	Recycled = environmentally preferred
Customer disposal	Green environment
Emergency orders = normal practice	Selective rapid deployment
Redundant stock echelons	Single, logical echelons
Local stock visibility	Global stock visibility
Multiple planning functions	Worldwide planning

Used with permission of Xerox Corporation.

Figure 13.11. ISCO as a change management organization.

the order information time lag responsive; (4) developing and ensuring a common nomenclature for products, components, and materials; (5) managing internal Xerox complexity through high-performance work processes; and (6) recycling all assets to meet environmental standards.

• The former process was complex. It involved too many people and more process steps than were necessary.

• The former process inventoried parts based on forecasts and service engineers' usage and requests. The parts were distributed from various locations.

• An internal benchmark to Xerox's European operation revealed a service replenishment and stocking process that dramatically improved service levels and reduced inventories.

• The new process inventoried parts based on actual usage. The parts were distributed from one hemisphere headquarters. Parts were also shared or loaned among closely located service engineers.

• Benchmarking with exemplar organizations both within and outside of the office products industry revealed best practices that could be adapted to Xerox's processes, thus providing a competitive advantage.

• Benchmarking partners were selected from a pool of candidates that included Apple, Digital Equipment Corporation, DuPont, Hewlett-Packard, IBM, NCR, Siemens, and SUN Microsystems, as well as selected exemplar retailers, dealers, auto, and airframe manufacturers.

• The team prioritized its efforts by identifying those processes that would improve three major objectives: (1) increased inventory turns; (2) increased service levels; and (3) decreased logistics costs.

- The basic approach to supply chain management had to change from a push system to one based on a pull replenishment system.

- The new supply chain varies for different types of products to allow Xerox to best meet customer requirements for delivery and installation as well as asset utilization and logistics cost.

- One best practice developed from supply chain benchmarking revealed that inventories should be stored in two locations—the service engineer's vehicle and the hemisphere logistics center. The engineer's inventory would then be replenished daily from the center through a network of drop points.

- The new scheme required substantially upgraded systems capability, electronic transmission, and the ability of the hemisphere logistics center to fill the order in time for overnight or next-day shipment.

- Another best practice developed from supply chain benchmarking was to assemble and test the unique components of the DocuTech at a manufacturing site or hemisphere logistics center. Then the nearly completed unit could be shipped directly to the customer.

- The potential for improvement of the supply chain process was substantial. It was based on cycle time reduction potential, reflected in inventory of $1 billion and logistics cost reductions opportunities of between $300 million and $400 million per year.

- The business processes on which the supply chain was based had to reach near perfection. Thus, it was the concentration on the supply chain processes that had to be improved once the basic operating strategy had been determined.

- Some of the identified processes included the following: customized installation and service; damage-free transportation;

logistics quality expressed in terms of reliability and accuracy; and ship-to-order configuration.

• It was practical to introduce the new, improved process as new products were introduced. Thus, the processes and operations were gradually transformed using a structured approach. There became a natural evolution of replacement and attrition.

• The changes were directed to take 70 percent out of the traditional cycle time—from buying parts from suppliers to having a machine with those parts installed in at customer's site. That, in turn, was calculated to reduce the worldwide supply chain inventory assets by $1 billion. That result would reduce the asset-carrying charges—about $200 million. Customer satisfaction was also targeted to rise to at least 90 percent.

• One side effect of the structural changes was the change in emphasis to a demand-driven, integrated supply chain. Thus, reduction of cycle time became a focus.

References

Bounds, Gregory. 1994. Xerox: Establishing and realizing the vision. Parts I and II of *Beyond total quality management*. New York: McGraw-Hill.

Eisenstat, Russell A. 1990. Managing Xerox's multinational development center. Harvard Business School Case, No. N9-490-029. Revised February 14, 1990.

Guske, Susanne. 1993. Supply chain performance reporting. In *Annual conference proceedings, Council of Logistics Management*. Oak Brook, Ill.: Council of Logistics Management.

Hewitt, Frederic. 1991. Benchmarking's contribution to becoming world-class in logistics and asset management. In *Annual conference proceedings, Council of Logistics Management*. Oak Brook, Ill.: Council of Logistics Management.

————. 1992. Supply chain integration myths and realities. In *Annual conference proceedings, Council of Logistics Management.* Oak Brook, Ill.: Council of Logistics Management.

Muller, E. J. 1990. Supply chain management. *Distribution* (September): 33–40.

Murphy, Jean V. 1992. Xerox corporation cutting shipping costs by focusing on return on assets. *Traffic World* (October): 21.

Presser, John H. 1993. Logistics processes a key to corporate engineering. *Traffic World* (October): 34–37.

CHAPTER 14

Employee Recognition Programs at Westinghouse Savannah River Company

Prepared with the cooperation of Stephen A. Kuhl, total quality manager, Reactor Division, Westinghouse Savannah River Company, Savannah River, South Carolina

Make the devious route the most direct and turn misfortune to advantage.

- Background
- Customer Requirements
- External Benchmarking Process
- Former Awards Program
- Key Findings
- Results of the Benchmark Study
- Implementation—Changing Concepts to Reality
- Summary

Background

Westinghouse Savannah River Company (WSRC) is a division of Westinghouse Electric Corporation headquartered in Pittsburgh, Pennsylvania. The Westinghouse Nuclear Fuels Division won the Malcolm Baldrige National Quality Award for manufacturing in 1988.

The Savannah River Site (SRS) is a U.S. government facility located near Aiken, South Carolina. It has been operated by WSRC for the U.S. Department of Energy since April 1989. Located in West Central South Carolina, the SRS encompasses 310 square miles and has 143 miles of primary road, 1200 miles of secondary road, and 64 miles of railroad. There are over 1000 buildings on the site with 6.3 million square feet of floor area. Although work sites are spread throughout the site, all of this accounts for only 5 percent of the land use. The remaining land is 22 percent wetland and 73 percent upland forest.

Besides being geographically separated, the site is functionally diverse and is staffed by approximately 17,000 people. There are 18 organizations at the site performing production, production support, service, research and development, and waste management activities. These organizations are referred to as divisions, and range in size from 35 to nearly 6000 people.

The two factors of geographical and functional diversity contribute significantly to the difficulty inherent in developing employee programs that meet the needs of all employees in all locations. In March of 1993 the total quality (TQ) managers of the various divisions began discussing the issue of employee recognition programs. They had been hearing comments that led them to believe that the then-current programs were not meeting employees' needs. Additionally, the level of participation and the quality of the achievements were increasingly coming into question. Subsequently, the TQ managers chartered, and the company executive vice president sponsored, a recognition team to research this issue. The team consisted of 13 individuals representing various WSRC divisions.

The team chose to focus on the Total Quality Achievement Award (TQAA) process because it was both the core and most widely used program. The TQAA program was a formal recognition where management presented the awards to recipients at a banquet. The TQAA program, which was administered by the site and implemented at both division and site levels, initially started as an informal recognition. Over time it was transformed into a formal recognition. Unfortunately, this transformation was not controlled and resulted in a formal program that lacked judging criteria. This introduced subjectivity, which consequently produced dissatisfaction with the program.

The recognition team first met in April 1993 to assess the TQAA program and to determine what the purpose of employee recognition was. This analysis was performed in a forum called the Westinghouse Technology to Improve Processes, or WesTIP. This is a four-day meeting held at an off-site location. In the WesTIP process, the team uses four days to

- Analyze the current program or process.
- Develop a step-by-step process map describing the process or program.
- Identify problems and issues associated with the current process.
- Perform root cause analysis of the identified issues.
- Develop a redesigned process or program that incorporates solutions to the identified issues.
- Brief the management sponsor on the findings and recommendations of the team.

In the case of employee recognition, it was decided to combine the benchmarking process with the WesTIP process. While these processes are independent and stand-alone, they also are complementary. Using them in conjunction produces substantial improvements to the program under review. For employee recognition, four days were spent entirely on analysis of the then-current program, followed by a full, six-week benchmark cycle. (Both internal and external benchmarks were conducted.) This was followed with completion of the WesTIP cycle by dedicating four days to the redesign of the new program. Figure 14.1 displays

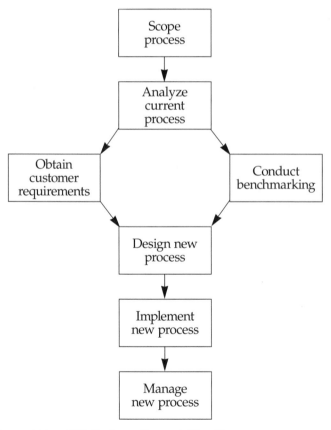

Used with permission of Westinghouse Savannah River Company.

Figure 14.1. Project approach.

the process followed. Twelve of the 18 WSRC divisions were represented in this effort.

During the analysis phase of the WesTIP it was determined that employee recognition should occur for two reasons: (1) To motivate employees to repeat the behavior that the company wants to have repeated; and (2) to demonstrate the company's value for employees and their contributions. After completing the analysis phase, the team was split into two groups: the customer requirements group, which performed the internal benchmark, and the benchmarking group, which performed the external benchmark.

Customer Requirements

Purpose

One aspect of the analysis process in WesTIP is the determination of customer values associated with the process that is being assessed. This dovetailed with performing an internal benchmark where the employees' (that is, customers') needs regarding recognition were determined. It is at this point where the team broke away from the standard WesTIP analysis process and entered benchmarking.

The expectation held for determining customer requirements was that employees would provide direct, honest communication of their needs and give the recognition team a basis for redesign of the program. It was also thought that this would provide the data to either confirm or deny the negative "rumblings" that were heard about the recognition program.

Process

The process followed to assess employee values was straightforward. The steps were as follows:

1. Identify the key customers. Seven worker categories that were key to the program were identified. These categories

were managers, professionals, weekly, craft, nominators, awardees, and nonawardees.

2. Develop employee survey and focus group questions.

3. Conduct the employee survey and the focus group meetings.

4. Consolidate and analyze the data.

5. Determine the customers' key values.

6. Feed the key values into the benchmarking interview question development process.

This last step was key. To get the most out of benchmarking, the recognition team had to ensure that the answers to the questions it asked contained information pertinent to meet customers' values. This was accomplished by finalizing the benchmarking questions after the customers' key requirements were determined. This was one part of the preparation process that had to be done in series. If the team was very clear on its customer values requirements, then the benchmarking questions could have been developed in parallel.

Two methods were used to assess the employees' values—a random survey of 2000 employees and the conduct of seven focus group meetings. Here, approximately 30 representatives from each key customer group met. One focus group was held for a specific key customer; that is, worker types were not mixed in the meetings.

This dual approach was taken for a basic reason: Conducting focus groups was a very good way to obtain information. The benchmarking team built credibility and obtained honest opinions with face-to-face interactions. In some circumstances, however, employees would not say everything they had on their minds while in the group setting. Hence the survey, which was strictly anonymous, was conducted. No names were requested, only classification of employee and division. This information was used to provide various overall data groupings, as well as division-specific results.

Employee Survey

The employee survey consisted of 12 questions, many of which were multipart, and a section for comments. The survey was sent to 10 percent of the site population, which was, at the time, 2000 people. It was requested that the survey be completed and returned within seven days. The response was tremendous, and it gave the recognition team a sense of the interest associated with this topic. Within the week, 976 surveys were returned, for a response rate of 48.8 percent.

The survey queried employees as to their knowledge of, and value for, the recognition programs that were in place. It included questions that asked employees to rate and give their personal value for different types of recognition, award items, and ceremonies. The survey also asked employees administrative questions, such as their opinion regarding the level of communication associated with each program. Employees were also asked about their participation or experience with the recognition programs, and a one-half page section was provided for their comments. This section was the most popular, and provided some very candid insight into the employees' frame of reference. Some representative survey items included the following:

- For each program listed, give your personal value (low, medium, high, unknown).

- Do you believe the distinctions between each recognition program have been adequately communicated?

- Rate (from strongly disagree to strongly agree) several reasons for which formal recognition should occur; for example, doing my job, a single outstanding occurrence, and so on.

- Rate the value placed on several types of informal, personal recognition, such as a pat-on-the-back.
- Rate different types of award items and events.

The data gathered by the survey were then rolled up and analyzed to determine trends and consensus. Reports were generated that graphically portrayed the employees' input. Basic bar and pie charts were used to display the data. The recognition team used this data, in conjunction with the focus group information, to identify weak areas in the recognition programs.

Focus Groups

The focus groups were more direct than the employee survey, in that the groups did not ask employees to engage in detailed analysis, but the questions were broader. Specifically, the following six questions were asked of the focus groups.

- What achievements deserve recognition?
- What motivates you to do a good job?
- What role should recognition play in motivation?
- How do our recognition programs fill that role?
- How can we get more people involved in recognition?
- What would be the ideal recognition program for SRS?

The employee value structure data obtained from the focus groups identified three areas where primary opportunities for improvement clearly existed: (1) the fairness of the recognition awards; (2) consistent recognition of appropriate achievements; and (3) management involvement and support (see Figure 14.2). Secondary opportunities for improvement identified were the value of the awards to the employees; the timeliness of the awards; and the level of participation. These trends were then compared to the survey input.

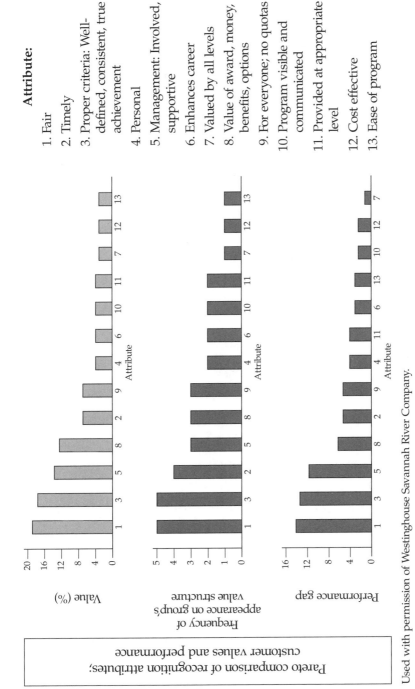

Figure 14.2. Employee value structure data.

Results

Key specific recommendations obtained from the employees included the following:

- Recognition must have peer involvement.
- Recognition must involve the immediate supervisor.
- Formal recognition, rather than informal recognition, must acknowledge continual demonstration of exemplary quality performance by the employee.
- Formal recognition must acknowledge performance above and beyond normal job expectations.
- Informal recognition should occur within four weeks of the accomplishment; formal recognition should occur within three months.
- Awards must be appropriate to the accomplishment.
- Recognition programs must be flexible to meet the needs of different customers.
- Management must be educated on the importance of good recognition practices.
- Recognition programs must be fair, simple, and understandable.
- Programs must include effective communication of requirements and achievements.

The analysis of the seven focus groups' input and the survey data also allowed the team to identify the following important, overall, employee perceptions concerning recognition.

- Employees feel that recognition is necessary in order for the company to demonstrate its value for employees and their contributions to the company.
- Being valued motivates employees to greater performance.

- Employee perceptions of the then-current programs were negative, in that employees felt that the programs were not fair, credible, valued, timely, personal, for everyone, supported by management, or appropriate to achievement.

These identified perceptions were not wholly unexpected, but the level of emotion and the strength of feeling regarding recognition were underestimated. These results also gave impetus to the external benchmarking team to do a thoroughly detailed job.

External Benchmarking Process

After examining what employees wanted in a recognition program, the team proceeded to gather information, through benchmarking, from outside companies. The intent was to identify and compare best practices or key enablers used by others to make their employee recognition programs successful. The WSRC team expected to be able to identify common threads associated with a majority of the programs. Additionally, the team strove to choose partners with company structures similar to that of WSRC. This would include the diversity of functions. The team also wanted to obtain outside perspectives. Ultimately, seven of the nine benchmarks were performed with partners outside of WSRC's industry.

This effort required a substantial commitment of time from a core group of people. It was performed in three stages: preparation, conduct, and analysis of the information obtained. The overall process included the steps shown in the next section.

Preparation

Preparation included development of a benchmarking partner survey and the selection of partners. The survey development was fairly straightforward, in that after obtaining the customer requirements, survey questions were generated that would address each requirement. In addition to the usual care which must be taken to ensure that the questions would be understood, and would provoke the desired responses, the WSRC team performed one special preparation: It answered each question based upon its programs.

This was done so that the recognition team would be prepared to answer any questions the partners might pose about the WSRC program. In some instances, the questions were turned back to the team, so this preparation was useful. It should be noted that all members of the recognition team answered the questions, and that, together, consensus answers were developed. This was done because each division implemented the program in a slightly different manner. The partner survey contained 10 multipart questions and addressed the following areas.

- The goals of the partner recognition programs
- The partner's program structure and administration
- How (or if) the partner validated achievements
- How the partner communicated its programs to its employees
- How the partner measured the effectiveness of its programs
- Content and gist of employee feedback regarding the program
- The partner's keys to success
- Aspects of the partner's program that it would change, including a single greatest improvement
- Cost of process or program administration

Obtaining responses to these questions is discussed in the conduct section, and the analysis of the data is discussed in the analysis section. The other aspect of preparation, that is, the selection of WSRC's benchmarking partners, was more involved and consisted of the following steps.

1. **Brainstorm a list of potential benchmarking partners.** The team had to start somewhere, so it began with its members' impressions. What companies did the team think had good employee programs?

2. **Develop selection criteria to identify the companies with the highest potential for having information useful to WSRC.** This was the most critical and difficult aspect of the preparation. The criteria used to evaluate the potential partners had to be appropriate to ensure that the partners obtained were able to help the team. Development of the criteria required careful thought and analysis. With a soft subject such as employee recognition, the criteria become even more important and more difficult.

The team had to define both the criteria with which to evaluate the partners, and the measures with which to assess how well the criteria were met. Ultimately, the team developed four criteria, each with three categories of performance measures. Figure 14.3 is the matrix of the team's selection criteria, and the associated measures and weighting factors that were used to define the relative importance of each factor.

For example, the first criterion was "world-class for recognition programs." This criterion had a weighting factor of 0.5, which meant that it was viewed as being important enough to be allocated half the possible points. A company that evaluated well in this category would score well overall because the category was weighted so heavily. This criterion then had three performance or measurement categories: high, medium, and low, worth 5 points, 3 points, and 1 point, respectively.

The three performance categories had increasing levels of performance factors. For example, a high rating could be earned

Benchmarking partner selection criteria matrix

Criteria	Measures		
	High = 5	Medium = 3	Low = 1
World-class for recognition programs (Weighting factor = 0.5)	• Program has received public acknowledgment from more than one source or has won awards. • Recognition program is known and understood by all employees. • Employees talks freely and positively about the program.	• Program is less visible, and recognition is mentioned only in passing. Only one source has publicly acknowledgment the program. • There are pockets of knowledge and understanding by employees. • Answers are vague, and questions are referred to the company expert.	• Program has received no public acknowledgment. • There is no recognition program. • There is no known subject matter expert or contact.
Good reputation in the marketplace (Weighting factor = 0.3)	• More than five years in the business • Fortune 100 or equivalent • Quality award winner • Strong personal recommendation	• One–five years in business • Fortune 500 or equivalent • Quality award nominee or runner-up • Noncommittal personal recommendation	• Less than one year in business • No ranking • Not a quality award nominee • Negative or no personal recommendation from a knowledgeable source
Number of employees (Weighting factor = 0.05)	• More than 2000	• 500–2000	• Less than 500
Organizational structure and diversity (Weighting factor = 0.15)	• Diverse products and services—both internal and external • Flat organization, five tiers or less	• Few/similar (three–five) products and services • Six to eight tiers	• Singular product or service • More than eight tiers

Used with permission of Westinghouse Savannah River Company.

Figure 14.3. Selection criteria matrix.

if the company's recognition program had received positive public acknowledgment from more than one source, or if its programs had won awards. A medium performance would involve a less-visible program, perhaps mentioned in passing, or noted only by one source. A low score would be earned if the company's program had no positive public acknowledgment.

The remaining criteria, "good reputation in the marketplace," "number of employees," and "organizational structure and diversity" also had increasing levels of performance defined. These three criteria were mainly used to align potential partners with WSRC's structural and functional diversity. The team recognized the importance of taking its time and properly developing the selection criteria. This cannot be overemphasized. It was the foundation upon which the success of the benchmark was built.

3. **Conduct research on prospective partners to better define their potential.** A difficulty encountered in this benchmark was obtaining information dealing specifically with other companies' recognition programs. Unlike manufacturing processes, which are more readily described, the soft subject area of employee recognition was more elusive. In rare instances the WSRC team found information directly addressing a specific company program, but generally, the team had to infer and extrapolate information.

The team conducted a database literature search. Team members were asked about their personal experiences with the potential partner companies. The team reviewed company literature and publications, as well as job-hunting guides. Finally, word of mouth was employed; that is, the common knowledge or experiences of coworkers. Based on this information the potential partners were evaluated for appropriateness.

4. **Rank the companies and identify the ones with the greatest potential.** Screening these high-potential companies for interest and willingness to be a benchmarking partner then followed.

Matrix scores were calculated by summing the products obtained when the performance measure score was multiplied by the criterion's weighting factor. For example, if a company was rated as a high performer for the "world-class for recognition" criterion, then it scored 2.5 points for this evaluation item [(5.0, for the high rating) × (0.5, the weighting factor for the criteria) = 2.5]. This process was repeated for the remaining criteria, and the total score was the sum of these products. The maximum score possible was 5.0 points. The evaluation scores were calculated and companies in the top two groups (5.0 and 4.7 points) became candidates for benchmarking.

These two groups encompassed 12 companies, 7 of which agreed to become benchmarking partners: Texaco (petroleum), 3M-Corporate (manufacturing), 3M-Traffic Control Material Division (manufacturing), Milliken (textiles), Lyondell (petrochemicals), Xerox (office automation equipment), Ritz-Carlton (hotels), and Westinghouse-Columbia Nuclear Fuels.

As shown, 3M graciously agreed to benchmark on two levels, corporate and division. A ninth benchmark performed was with Westinghouse Idaho Nuclear Company, one of WSRC's sister business units. It was benchmarked because of its remarkable similarity to WSRC, and because it had a very good understanding of WSRC's frame of reference.

Two points must be highlighted regarding this list of partners: (1) Five of the companies are Malcolm Baldrige National Quality Award winners; and (2) The types of industries from which the partners were chosen are quite diverse.

5. Obtain completed confidentiality agreements from each company that agreed to be a benchmarking partner. This was the final preparatory step.

It is important to note that, in this preparation stage, it was very easy to go overboard analyzing just who would be the absolute best partner. The WSRC team found that it could have "analysis paralysis" trying to get everything just right. In the end, the team members had to use common sense and their judgment to regain momentum and get on with the task at hand.

Conduct

Conduct merely consisted of submitting the team's questions to the partners and documenting their responses. In the case of this benchmarking study, there was no need to travel to the partner's location—there was little value in seeing recognition in action—so the questions were sent to the partners via facsimile.

The WSRC team gave the partners between three and seven working days to assess their programs and document their responses. The team then contacted them via a conference call, and discussed their answers in a one and one-half to two-hour conversation. In some instances the partners sent back the completed questionnaires prior to the telephone conversation.

During the course of this conversation team members performed various functions. First, the interviewer discussed the topics and avoided turning the benchmarking study into a stilted, journalistic, "here-is-the-question-what-is-your-answer" type of interview, or even worse, an inquisition. The team found that a natural conversational style generated a greater flow of information.

In addition to the interviewer, two or three people acted as recorders. They documented the partner's responses and wrote down impressions and questions. The interviewer was available to write notes, but the burden of capturing the information was on the recorders.

Finally, one person acted as an administrative controller of the session. This person would note any commitments made by either parties, would pass questions to the interviewer, and would fill in gaps as needed.

It was realized at the beginning of the benchmarking interviews that to maintain continuity between interviews, one, or better yet, two people should be dedicated to be present at every interview. Two people were chosen by the WSRC team, and that served the team well. These two people heard similar information on subsequent interviews and were able to ask more detailed follow-up questions as they became more experienced in the process.

The final phase of the conduct of the benchmarking study was transferring each individual's written notes to one cohesive group of responses. Because everyone hears differently, each individual's notes would be slightly different. Immediately upon completion of the interview—usually within 30 minutes—the interview team would discuss each of the partner's responses and a consensus of the partner's answers was developed. If the team had waited any longer to obtain the consensus, it was felt that pertinent, unrecorded information would be lost from the individual's memory.

Analysis

Analysis of the partners' information was the final stage of the benchmarking study. The analysis was started by coming to consensus on the responses. The next step was identifying key enablers of the partners' programs that would be applicable to meeting WSRC employees' needs, and then incorporating them into the team's redesign. Additionally, the team wanted to identify innovative ideas and the concepts or program characteristics that were common to the partners. After these key enablers, innovations, and commonalities were identified, they were categorized as either administrative or ideological; that is, philosophical perspectives and beliefs that enabled the program to be successful. The specific items identified are discussed in a later section.

The tool developed and used to perform this analysis was a matrix that correlated each partner's response to each question. Figure 14.4 shows a portion of the matrix. The rows of the matrix identified the partner, and the columns reflected the questions. For example, each company was asked if it felt recognition to be a factor in employee job satisfaction (question 1a). Each partner's response was recorded, and the benchmarking team developed a consensus answer for this question. As can be seen in Figure 14.4, except for one unknown response, each partner answered yes to this question, and so it is very clear what the consensus was.

In many instances the consensus was not arrived at as easily. Responses to question 1d, regarding the impact recognition has on saving money, were split with five yes answers, three no answers, and one unknown answer. In these situations where it could go one way or the other, the team used its judgment based upon the context in which the answers were given. For example, was it an emphatic "YES!" or perhaps a less-heartfelt "no, not really"?

Many of the questions—and consequently the answers— were subjective; they were not as clear-cut as the yes-or-no type questions. In these instances it took substantial discussion by the team to develop the consensus answer. It should be remembered that the point of this benchmarking study was to identify common threads between the programs and to find applicable

Company	1a Job satisfaction Y is positive N is negative ? = ? * = other	1b > Productivity Y is positive N is negative ? = ? * = other	1c > Sales Y is positive N is negative ? = ? * = other	1d $ Save Y is positive N is negative ? = ? * = other	Barriers	Comments
A	Y	Y	N	Y	Management not taking time to nominate; employees perceptions of fairness	
B	Y	Y	Y	Y	Management buy-in, good trys recognized; recognition meaningful and objective	
C	Y	Y	Y	Y	Maintaining focus on low cost (paramount business objective)	
D	Y	Y	N	N	Management buy-in, criteria, perceived fairness; actual item	
E	Y	Unknown; hard to measure	N	N	Workload—people don't take the time to participate	
F	Y	Y	N	Y	Fair method of evaluation; all-manager selection committees	
G	Y	Y	N	Y	Time and resources	
H	Unknown	Unknown	Unknown	Unknown	Didn't know what customer valued	
I	Y	N	N	N	Rush to judgment; focus on negative; not taking time to coach	
Consensus	Y	Y	N	Y	1. Lack of management buy-in 2. Perceived fairness 3. Time to participate	

Used with permission of Westinghouse Savannah River Company.

Figure 14.4. Sample of benchmarking information analysis matrix.

innovations and key enablers (best practices). Because of this, some subjectivity was allowable. At this point it is appropriate to further discuss the topic of subjectivity.

Subjectivity This discussion is qualified in that it is felt that while subjectivity has little, if any, place in the benchmark of a production or manufacturing process (can it ever be totally eliminated?), some is certainly allowable when a team is dealing with a soft subject area such as employee recognition.

What are the sources of subjectivity? One is that benchmarks of soft subjects generally do not contain hard numbers or facts. They usually have inferential data and information. A second source is the origin of the data. The basis of the WSRC team's questions was its customers' input—those who have a stake in the outcome of the analysis process. The source of the answers to these questions was the partners, most of whom are also the process owners.

When reviewing the questions and answers, it is wise to ask whether the information given might be biased. Was a rosy picture painted? Was there a hidden agenda? This is not saying that a team should disbelieve what it has been told. Rather, it is saying that the team should be discriminating in how it interprets the information, because subjectivity is inherent. The team should simply want to make the best analysis possible and should be aware of the potential for subjectivity. These characteristics are essential to success.

After the WSRC team acknowledged that subjectivity in its benchmarking study would exist, it had to decide if the subjectivity would be acceptable. That is, could the team live with it? The team decided that it could, and there was a logical basis for that decision.

- The team knew what the then-current program did not do because the employees said so, and because the recognition team members were process experts.

- The employees also told the team their values and what they wanted a recognition program to do.
- Finally, through benchmarking, the team determined the best practices of its partners.

Based on these three facts, the team matched up the customers' needs with the partners' best practices and innovations to successfully redesign the employee recognition program. This analysis allowed the team to arrive at the decision that the inherent subjectivity was acceptable. This approach also was the foundation upon which the team built its program. An illustration of how this approach was applied may be helpful.

- **What was missing.** The then-current program did not have an informal, immediate, supervisor-controlled recognition.

- **What customers wanted.** Customer feedback indicated that the employees valued the following:
  —Immediate supervisor recognition
  —Timely recognition
  —Recognition appropriate to the achievement
  —Fairness
  —A credible program
  —Peer participation

Each of these attributes can be directly related to the immediate supervisor. They are within the immediate supervisor's control.

It should be noted that the phrase immediate supervisor does not imply one specific level of management. All employees, be they hourly or salaried workers or managers, have an immediate supervisor.

- **What the partners do.** Through benchmarking, the team found that its partners had immediate, supervisor-controlled programs.

The WSRC team developed an informal recognition program that was controlled by immediate supervisors. It is fast; that is, timely. It is at a level of recognition that never existed before. Thus, it is appropriate. The program is applied by the immediate supervisor, which promotes fairness and credibility. Finally, anyone can nominate anyone else, thereby promoting peer partic- ipation and credibility. As this example shows, even with subjec- tive information, positive changes can be made that better meet customers' needs.

The final step of the analysis was identifying which of the many, identified innovations and enablers would be applicable to WSRC. This was accomplished by gathering the whole bench- marking team to review the findings and then choosing the items that were deemed both applicable and feasible to implement. Once these items were agreed upon, the next step was to start the redesign.

Because of the large amount of information that was pre- sented, consensus on where to start the redesign was difficult to obtain. Ultimately, a team member who had been involved in each aspect of the project developed and presented to the team a model of a new program. It was suggested that the model be used as the basis of the redesign. The model was reviewed and adopted by the team as the starting point for the new program. The actual redesign process will not be discussed in this case study, other than to say that the WesTIP process was again used to conduct the development of the new recognition program.

Former Awards Program

At this point, and prior to discussing the specific findings of the benchmarking study, it is appropriate to detail how the former recognition program was structured. The TQAA process was the main form of recognition used at the SRS. As previously indicated, this program was initially started as an informal recognition program, but with use it was transformed into a formal program. Criteria, however, which would normally be associated with a formal program, were not developed because the transformation was not structured or controlled.

The TQAA program was applied on both divisional and site levels. Administratively, the division-level competition was structured as follows: Nominators developed written nominations, obtained mid-manager approval, and then submitted them to a review and selection committee. This committee evaluated the nominations and selected winners. Note that each division had its own selection process with unique characteristics, but conceptually this is how the program worked.

The best of the division winners were then forwarded by the divisions to the site, where they automatically became site-level winners. A review process did not exist for the site level—whomever the divisions submitted automatically became the site winners. The number of people allowed to be submitted as site winners was limited to 10 percent of the division nominees. For example, if a division had 50 winners, it could submit five people as site winners.

Upon being selected, division winners received a certificate and their choice of award items. These items were of nominal value ($20 or less) and were things such as travel alarm clocks, stone pyramid desk clocks, coasters, pen stands, and paperweights. Each item was emblazoned with the terms SRS and total *quality.* As the program became mature, the number and types of award items were reduced, based upon customer feedback.

The division-level honorees also attended an awards breakfast at a local country club or hotel. This awards ceremony, which occurred during normal business hours, was a gathering of the division's senior management, the honorees, and the nominators.

Each individual or group achievement was discussed, and then the award items were presented to the winners.

On the site level, this same basic structure was used; however, it was the site's senior staff—the company president, executive vice president, and the division vice presidents—who were present at an evening awards banquet. The award item for winning at the site level was a wristwatch worth approximately $125.

These award ceremonies, at each level, were conducted three times a year. Although employee participation in this program looked, on the surface, to be adequate, further inspection showed that it was basically the same people winning again and again. There were whole departments who had lost faith in the program and declined to participate. Employees increasingly perceived the program negatively, and consequently the number of complaints began to increase. This was the driving force for evaluating the program.

Key Findings

The benchmarking team evaluated the information received from the partners and categorized the best practices and innovations as either administrative or ideological. Prior to detailing the significant innovations, it should be pointed out that some big-picture items were identified. Simply put, it became obvious that the following three factors contributed greatly to the success of the partners' programs: (1) flexibility; (2) an informal recognition program; and (3) customer (employee) orientation. WSRC's programs were lacking in these three areas. They were inflexible; an informal recognition program did not exist; and there was no focus on employee needs. Once these three things became obvious, it was time to focus on what specific items could be incorporated into a new recognition program so that it would better meet employees' values.

Key Administrative Enablers

The following key administrative enablers were identified.

- Flexibility, which included a defined program framework, but with allowances so that each organization could tailor its program to best fit its specific needs

- Peer involvement

- Recognition based upon the company's business objectives, which meant that achievements must be directed toward meeting the organization's business objectives

- Minimal criteria, which can be a real "paradigm-buster" for some teams

- A supervisor-controlled, informal program

- A program that generates and publicizes employees' best practices, which reinforces positive behavior and highlights better ways to get work done

- A self-correcting program that uses publicity and management

The WSRC team discussed this last issue when it discovered that some companies give fairly large sums of money to their award winners, yet their programs do not have classic counterbalances to ensure that abuse did not occur. When the partners were queried as to how they prevented a possible "lining of pockets," they indicated that by publicizing who gave and received awards, and what was accomplished, it would become very obvious when an award was undeserved. This created both peer pressure, to ensure parity of the program, and visibility for management, who would take any required corrective action.

Key Ideological Enablers

While most successful organizations are quite adept at developing and implementing administrative change, the same is not true of ideological change. Hence these enablers were harder to ingrain to the culture of the workplace, yet they were fundamental to the success of the recognition program.

• The act of recognition is more important that the dollar value of the award. Too many times the emphasis was placed on how much the award item cost the company, and not on the fact that the company is demonstrating value for the employees' contribution. Thus, the focus should be on the act of recognition.

• Do not recognize the correction of a self-imposed error. This is a very subtle point. When recognition is given for the correction of a self-imposed error, it can act as a negative reinforcement; that is, errors create opportunities for recognition. This obviously is not a message any company wants to send. The only way to avoid sending it is to not recognize this type of "achievement."

• The program must have total management support. Support is one of those nebulous words with many different levels and interpretations. In this case it means that management empowers employees to develop the programs and make them work, as well as having management participation in the program, both as a giver and a receiver of recognition.

• Recognition can not be delegated. Everyone must participate. This simply says that proper recognition requires the time of everyone. Managers should not tell an employee to "write yourself up, and I'll sign the form." This does not show the proper ownership and belief in the program, and it also sends a negative message to the employee; that is, "your accomplishment is not worth my time to write up." On the other hand, employees must be willing to nominate their peers; they can not simply leave it to management to create all of the nominations.

• Recognize "good tries" to reinforce creativity and innovation. This is one tool to support attaining a goal of being cost effective. Employees should be dared to challenge themselves and to strive for and achieve stretch goals.

• Flexibility creates empowerment and ownership. This is perhaps a recurrent theme, but with a slight twist. Employees more readily accept recognition programs that they helped develop. Basically, they are responsible for making it meet their needs. Complaints from employees must be answered by themselves. This allows improvements to focus on critical areas, because it negates idle complaints.

• Awards should not be given for the sake of giving awards. Awards must be earned for meeting business objectives.

Results of the Benchmark Study

Application of the information gained in the benchmarking study resulted in the creation of two new, informal recognition programs—Informal-Personal and Informal-Tangible. The formal recognition program was also refocused on company business objectives. The newly designed programs were implemented on January 1, 1994, and were very well received by both management and employees.

Program Improvements

Figures 14.5, 14.6, and 14.7 provide comparisons between the old and new programs. Many of the key enablers identified by the benchmarking study were incorporated into the new programs. Particular attention should be given to Figure 14.7, which is a matrix comparing the new program attributes with customer values previously identified; that is, items that the employees said the then-current program should have, but did not have. This matrix shows how the new program attributes overlap and

WSRC recognition WesTIP and benchmark		
	Old	New
Division	No structure, dependent on manager's own initiative	Personal and tangible
Site	No structure, dependent on manager's own initiative	Oversight of informal process by Total Quality Process department.

Personal = Focus on what we are doing right in our routine work.

Tangible = Focus on what we are doing that exceeds normal job expectations.

Used with permission of Westinghouse Savannah River Company.

Figure 14.5. Informal program comparison.

WSRC recognition WesTIP and benchmark		
	Old	New
Division	• Site controlled • Inflexible • Not focused on business objectives and loosely tied • Catch-all/only source of recognition	• Division controlled • Flexible • Focused on business objectives and supported by 12 TQ conditions of excellence • Prestigious/selective
Site	• Quota based • Three ceremonies • Best of divisions • No parity for job category • Not focused on business objectives • Routine award	• Merit based • One celebration • Best of site • Peer competition only • Focused on business objectives • Prestigious, all may not be granted

Used with permission of Westinghouse Savannah River Company.

Figure 14.6. Formal program comparison.

WSRC recognition WesTIP and benchmark Meeting and Customer Values

New program attributes / Customer values	Fairness	Credibility	Management involvement	Program value	Appropriate awards	Appropriate level	Timely	Personal	Flexible	Simple	Nonexempt participation*	Nonexempt recognition*
Peer nomination	X	X		X							X	X
Compete within worker category	X	X		X								X
Compete within topic category	X	X		X								
Controlled by immediate supervisor	X	X	X	X	X	X	X	X	X	X	X	X
Public recognition	X	X	X	X		X	X			X	X	X
Publicized results	X	X		X	X						X	
Variety—organizations choose awards			X	X	X	X	X	X	X		X	
Immediate informal awards		X	X	X	X	X	X	X	X	X	X	X
Tools for immediate recognition			X	X	X	X	X	X	X	X		X
Simple nominating process			X	X		X				X	X	
Based on business objectives		X	X	X							X	
Self-correcting	X	X	X	X		X					X	
Education	X	X	X	X	X	X	X	X	X	X	X	
Minimal approvals				X			X			X	X	
Programs adjustable per feedback	X	X		X	X	X		X	X	X	X	
Nominee and immediate supervisor endorsements	X	X	X	X		X		X	X			
Budget driven to the division level, not the site level			X	X		X			X			
Award sponsors involved		X	X	X		X						

*Note: Nonexempt refers to hourly wage employees.

Used with permission of Westinghouse Savannah River Company.

Figure 14.7. Meeting customer values matrix.

support meeting employee values. For example, credibility of the program is enhanced by 13 attributes, including structuring the competition such that employees compete within the same worker categories; publicizing the recognition; having immediate recognition; and having the nominees endorse their nominations.

For reference, the Informal-Personal program consists simply of focusing on what employees are doing right in their everyday job performance, and giving them a personal thanks for their efforts. The Informal-Tangible program is so named because a tangible item, a token of appreciation, is given to employees for accomplishments slightly above their job expectations. The formal program is conducted on two levels—division, with the Vice President's Award, and site, with the President's Award. This program focuses on significant and exemplary accomplishments performed while achieving business objectives.

Lessons Learned

Previously, performing the benchmark study was divided into three phases: preparation, conduct, and analysis of the information. Correspondingly, there are lessons learned in each of these phases. Although there were numerous lessons learned, this discussion will only concentrate on the major ones.

Preparation In this phase of the project there were four major lessons learned. The most important lesson was also a "paradigm-buster." The program or process redesign should not be biased by developing measures of the new program before completing the benchmarking study. Traditionally, measures are developed that will be used to evaluate the benchmarking data in light of the intended redesign structure. This should not be done, because existing paradigms are then inserted into the new program before it even exists. The team artificially restricts itself by saying, "These are our measures, so the program has to do this."

Instead, the team should start with a clean slate, and take the benchmarking data on its own merit.

The second lesson is that it is imperative that the customers' values are identified prior to the development of the benchmarking interview questions. This is necessary to ensure that the questions address the customers' values.

The third lesson is that in order to minimize any potential "analysis paralysis," goals, objectives, and deliverables should be clearly identified and scheduled due dates should be agreed upon. Specific people should be assigned to each task, and completion of the task should be made their responsibility.

The fourth lesson is to allow sufficient time between the benchmarking interviews and the redesign. This allows the team to pursue any follow-up with its partners.

Conduct When actually performing the benchmark, these lessons should be kept in mind.

• Everyone hears differently, so when conducting an interview, the recorder should try to capture the words exactly as they are spoken. This will go a long way to minimizing misunderstanding.

• Each aspect of the team's effort should have a core group of at least two people who are involved in all facets of the aspect.

• In order to identify and analyze internal benchmarks and customer requirements, the team should conduct focus groups, but it should also use a survey or some other vehicle that will allow for anonymous input.

• The team should not be too tied to its questions. The team should be able to have a meaningful conversation around them. Many times more information results from side conversations. The team should not be afraid to indulge in these, but should be scrupulously aware that its partner's time is very valuable.

Analysis When rolling the benchmarking information up, these were the major lessons that the WSRC learned.

- The team should wrap up and gain consensus of the partner information *immediately* after the interview has been completed. The team must do it right, take it the one last step, and properly close the interview by coming to consensus about what it just heard.

- The partner's interview responses should be grouped by the customers' key values.

- Statistical expertise and dedicated clerical support are needed.

- When a benchmarking study is conducted without site visits, it becomes more difficult to discern opinion from fact. Teams should be aware of the rosy-picture syndrome.

- The worker categories should be tracked. If all the interviewees were of the same category, this may affect how the team evaluates the information. If, for example, all the information came from managers, then cognizance of this allows the team to realize that the managers are also the process owners, or that they are toeing the corporate line, or whatever their particular bias might be.
While having the same category does provide a common base from which the information comes, it also blinds the team to other perspectives. The team may wonder, after hearing process owners talk about their process, what a worker having to live the process would say. That is the essence of this lesson.

- The team must be aware that it will have a large amount of data to assimilate in a very short period of time.

- This last lesson relates back to the subjectivity issue. After a while, teams get a feel for what will or will not work. This feel is based upon the team's new knowledge, as well as its previous experience and reasoning abilities. The team should take advantage of this to improve its awareness of subjectivity and to make better decisions.

Supporting Mechanisms

To make the effort of the benchmark pay off, the following items are needed.

- Total management support for the new program
- An effective communication process, which will explain the new program and the reasons why and how it was developed (that is, it was not just thrown together and developed for the sake of change)
- Employee participation in the new program
- Follow-up and mechanisms for obtaining of customer feedback (Do they perceive that they are now getting what they previously lacked?)
- A willingness to make adjustments if the feedback does not meet the team's expectations

Implementation—Changing Concepts to Reality

To convert its concepts and ideas into reality, the WSRC recognition team needed a project management approach. The team identified seven areas in which extensive effort would have to be performed to develop the administrative mechanisms necessary to support implementation of the new program. A project manager (one of the team members) was agreed upon. The team identified specific tasks and deliverables within each area. The tasks were then delegated to team members for completion.

The seven areas within which supporting work was performed were as follows:

1. **Administrative project management** This includes administration of the overall project, as well as the development of budget, funding sources, and resources for the new program. This management sector is also responsible for keeping senior staff apprised of the project, and to obtain its concurrence or direction as required.

2. **Communications strategy and feedback mechanism** This is the plan for telling employees about the new program and for hearing what they had to say about it.

3. **Site celebration structure** Several smaller (300 people), boring, tedious, cyclic award banquets were combined into one large (1000 people) annual site celebration.

4. **Recognition tools and award logistics** This really is two efforts. The recognition tools effort is the development of items that help employees engage in effective recognition, such as fact sheets, helpful hints, program information, lists of assisting personnel, and so on. The award logistics effort deals with identifying and procuring the actual award items, as well as controlling them once purchased.

5. **Formal selection criteria and nomination form** The WSRC's informal recognition programs do not have criteria, only guidelines, such as lists of categories to which informal recognition should be focused. Actual approval of the award lies solely with the supervisors; it is at their discretion.

The new formal program does have criteria to ensure parity of the competition. The criteria, referred to as judging guidelines, consist of 37 points of performance against which a nomination is evaluated. The judging guidelines are standardized across the site. They are used by all divisions. The site development of the judging guidelines was a balance between having minimal criteria and obtaining parity in the evaluation process.

6. **Process guidelines** This is a binder developed as a training aid and a desktop reference. This book compiled all the information developed by the subteams, such as forms, the judging guidelines, "How to Recognize," and "What to Recognize" fact sheets, and many other items. These books were then issued to 105 people who were trained as recognition coordinators. These books are revised as necessary, and are located throughout the SRS, so they are readily available.

7. **Recognition coordinator training** A two-day training module was developed and conducted to train the 105 newly named recognition coordinators.

Once these seven tasks and their specific deliverables were identified, the site's senior staff (president, executive vice president, and division vice presidents) were briefed on the new program. At this point their approval for implementation of the new program was gained, and work on the seven projects began.

Implementation of the new program was scheduled to occur after completion of these projects. Additionally, two other award programs were to be integrated with the new program. These two other programs were allowed to complete their natural cycles and then were integrated. Overall, the complete project ran nine months—from conception of the idea that employee recognition needed evaluation to the implementation of the new program. The full benchmark and complete WesTIP took three months to set up and perform, while the seven projects that developed the supporting administrative mechanisms took six months to complete.

Roadblocks to Implementation

Several roadblocks to implementation were identified during the course of the benchmark, and a brief discussion has merit. Again, for the purpose of this case study, only the major items will be discussed. These roadblocks are not insurmountable. They have been included in this case study simply to assist the reader by identifying potential difficulties.

The first issue was time limitation. It was a very tight schedule in which to perform the benchmark. Particular periods of concern were between customer value assessment and the benchmark, and redesign and implementation. Overall, nine months was still tight.

The second issue was that there was a distinct difference in team dynamics between redesign and implementation. Historically, team members are selected because of their process knowledge and their ability to contribute to the process redesign. They are not selected for their ability to implement, and this can be a problem. The WSRC team found that in addition to having the usual team development stages of forming, storming, norming, and performing, the transition from redesign to implementation produced four more behaviors.

1. **Beating—as in beating around the bush.** Redesign is easy; it is easy to say what is wrong and what one thinks should be done. It is another thing entirely to actually do something different. Getting started was sometimes slow because of this.

2. **Defeating—as in hidden agendas.** People who did not completely agree during the redesign now tried to use the implementation as leverage to reintroduce their ideas. This caused the team to back up and rediscuss previously completed issues, with all the associated second-guessing and gnashing of teeth.

3. **Repeating.** Some people seemed to be less driven to conscientiously attend meetings where they were expected to perform. This caused them to miss important information, and also required discussions of old information just to bring them back up to speed when they did attend.

4. **Retreating.** This was the most obvious form of noncommitment to implementation. In this behavior, team members who were present for the redesign tended to disappear when it came time for implementation. They physically distanced themselves from the implementation phase.

The basic difference between redesign and implementation is that they have different focuses, and implementation is much more difficult. These two factors produce the new behaviors. And these behaviors had to be considered when first defining the team.

The third roadblock encountered was conceptualization skills. Redesign was very detail-oriented, where the focus was on a logical sequence of events. Implementation was more global, and required team members to be able to see the big picture. They had to be able to visualize the relationships between tasks and deliverables, as well as the impacts that resulted from changing things around (cause and effect). The necessary conceptualization skills for implementation may not be present on the team, which will slow down the project.

The fourth roadblock to implementation was culture. While it is human nature to resist any change, it appears that ideological change is the most strongly resisted type of change. For implementation to occur, especially implementation of a new program such as recognition—where everyone is an expert and everyone has opinions on what is right and wrong—required ideological change and acceptance. This could have been a major problem. If it was not overcome, it would have negated any chance of successfully putting the new programs in place.

Finally, benchmarking is a collateral duty. Generally the people performing the benchmark had their "real" job to do, and were not always willing to give the benchmarking study the effort it needed.

Benchmark Again?

Given everything the WSRC team knows and has learned about benchmarking, the question has to arise: Would the team do it again? The answer is an emphatic yes! The team would also recommend benchmarking to its friends and colleagues.

Here's why. Benchmarking required an intensive analysis of current programs. Benchmarking caused the team to perform extensive research on how the best companies conduct their programs. Benchmarking forced the team to refocus on its customers. (This customer reorientation by itself was worth all the work.) Finally, by conducting the benchmark, the team gained the credibility necessary to obtain approval to implement the new program. All of these are extremely worthwhile results. But this is not all!

The benchmarkers were not the only ones who benefited from the study. The partners (the "benchmarkees") also gained. The team provided them with an opportunity to examine their programs. Additionally, in return for the candor and initiative that they provided, the team developed and issued to them an extensive report that pulled all the information together—all the best practices, all the common threads, everything. Essentially, for providing the team with company-specific information, the partners earned a synthesized report to use in strengthening their programs—if they so chose. It was a fair trade, and one, which based upon feedback from a partner, is being used for just such a purpose. So what is the bottom line? Would the team benchmark again? Of course!

Summary

• The WSRC is geographically separated and functionally diverse. It is staffed by 17,000 people in 18 organizations performing production, production support, research and development, and waste management activities.

• In March of 1993, it was clear to TQ managers that employees were dissatisfied with their recognition program and awards.

• The WesTIP and the benchmarking processes were used to analyze the current program; to develop a process map; to identify problems and issues; to perform root cause analysis; to develop a redesigned program; and to brief management of the study's findings and recommendations.

• As the customers of the process, the WSRC employees' values and requirements were assessed through a survey and seven focus groups, each representing a category of workers.

• The employee survey consisted of 12 multipart questions and a section for comments. Ten percent of the site population was surveyed (2000 people). The response rate was 48.8 percent or 976 surveys returned.

• The seven focus groups concentrated on assessing employees' values using six questions.

• The results of the survey and focus groups yielded 13 specific recommendations to improve the employee recognition program. These became the internal benchmark.

• External benchmarking partners were also sought. A detailed survey and selection process, including a criteria matrix, were utilized to screen benchmarking candidates. Eight partners were eventually selected to participate in the study.

• The conduct of the external benchmarking survey involved questionnaires and conference calls. No site visits were conducted. During these conversations, three roles were fulfilled: (1) interviewer; (2) recorder; and (3) administrative controller.

• Analysis of the benchmarking partners' questionnaire and interview data included coming to a consensus on the partners' responses. Then key enablers, applicable to the WSRC program, were identified. Finally, innovative ideas and concepts common to the benchmarking partners were identified, discussed, and categorized.

• The benchmarking partners' data were analyzed using a matrix that correlated each partner's response to each item on the questionnaire.

• Subjectivity of the questions and answers had to be considered in this study since it benchmarked a soft subject area—employee recognition. Sources of subjectivity were identified, and the possibility of biased information was evaluated.

• The employee recognition program was redesigned based on the benchmarking partners' best practices and innovations that were applicable to the WSRC program. A model of a new program was developed and implemented.

• In January 1994, two new informal programs were initiated, and the formal employee recognition program was refocused on company business objectives.

• The hallmarks of the new program are (1) flexibility; (2) an informal recognition program; and (3) customer (employee) orientation.

• Seven key administrative enablers and seven key idealogical enablers were identified.

• Additionally, seven mechanisms critical to support the new programs were implemented. These included (1) administrative project management; (2) communication strategy and feedback mechanism; (3) site celebration structure; (4) recognition tools and awards logistics; (5) formal selection criteria and nomination form; (6) process guidelines; and (7) recognition coordinator training.

- The roadblocks to implementation included the following: (1) time limitations; (2) recognizing the difference in team dynamics between redesign and implementation; (3) lack of conceptualization skills; and (4) culture—it is human nature to resist change.

- The benchmarking team learned several lessons during its three phases of the study—preparation, conduct, and analysis.

- Several supporting mechanisms that helped the benchmarking study pay off were also identified.

CHAPTER 15

Benchmarking the Customer Satisfaction Management Process at IBM-Rochester

Prepared with the cooperation of Steven H. Hoisington, manager of customer satisfaction, and Dr. Gerald J. Balm, senior quality consultant, IBM Corporation, Rochester, Minnesota

In peace prepare for war, in war prepare for peace.

- Background
- Customers and Requirements
- Organizations or Industries Benchmarked
- Best Practices Found
- Actions Taken
- Planned Changes
- Conclusions
- Summary

Background

International Business Machines (IBM) has been a leading company in the information technology and office equipment industries for over 70 years. It is organized into 13 manufacturing and development divisions, a worldwide marketing and service force divided into four major geographies, and several other operating units. Its corporate headquarters are in Armonk, New York. The electronic computer was synonymous with the name IBM in its early years, however, now it is a centerpiece within a very competitive industry.

This chapter describes a customer satisfaction management (CSM) process at IBM-Rochester, Minnesota. Rochester is the mainstay of the AS/400 Division being responsible for much of the design and manufacture of IBM's midrange business computer systems. The AS/400, this division's major computer family, is the world's most popular multiuser midrange computer. It has won numerous industry awards and accolades since its 1988 introduction. IBM's smaller magnetic disk storage devices are also designed at the Rochester site. IBM-Rochester won the Malcolm Baldrige National Quality Award in 1990.

At IBM-Rochester, a strong sense of quality and customer focus is ingrained in the culture. The IBM AS/400 is still very successful due to the early and direct involvement of customers in all phases of the design process. That success is also based, in part, on an effective CSM process capable of ensuring that customers' requirements and expectations are continually met or exceeded.

One of the noteworthy strengths identified by Malcolm Baldrige National Quality Award examiners in 1990 was a strong CSM process that is the backbone of high customer satisfaction results and world-class levels. As a Baldrige award recipient, Rochester was, and continues to be, inundated with requests for information about its CSM process. In addition, numerous requests to benchmark the process are received.

IBM-Rochester has learned that satisfied customers mean loyal customers that will continue to purchase products and services from IBM. Rochester has determined that a one-point improvement in customer satisfaction will result in increased revenue of $257 million over five years. Therefore, an effective CSM process, predicated on listening to and acting upon customer concerns, is paramount to the future success of both IBM-Rochester and its customers.

Objective/Purpose

The objectives of IBM-Rochester's CSM process are

1. To establish a structured strategy to handle all customer requests, concerns, and recommendations
2. To continually improve customer satisfaction levels
3. To develop and create partnerships between IBM and its customers that contribute to the success of each
4. To improve customer relationships

The mission of the CSM process team is to support IBM-Rochester's goal to be the undisputed leader in customer satisfaction by

- Administering customer feedback programs that monitor product and service satisfaction
- Identifying and clarifying customer issues that will enhance and improve customer satisfaction
- Advocating changes that will improve customer satisfaction results worldwide

Focus/Topic (Work Process Selected)

The CSM process is administered by a small team of customer satisfaction specialists who report to the director of quality. Customer satisfaction data from a variety of sources, including surveys, complaints, and customer visits, are solicited, collected, and aggregated by the customer satisfaction department. Pervasive issues are identified through data analysis and then assigned ownership in areas that have direct responsibility for invoking action. The issues owners conduct further root cause analysis using a formal, six-step process approach. Specific actions are identified and progress is reviewed monthly by IBM senior managers. Individual customer complaints identified through surveys or complaint channels are resolved, and results are communicated directly back to customers. The whole process is predicated on the accuracy, timeliness, and actionability of the customer satisfaction data that are initially collected by the customer satisfaction department. The process is detailed in Figure 15.1.

Team Operation

The company developed a formal benchmarking checklist in 1991 to help it select benchmark partners and to help identify companies and organizations with whom to share information. The checklist is shown in Figure 15.2. At the same time, the company integrated into the benchmarking strategy the analysis of world-class leaders in customer satisfaction management from outside the computer industry.

The CSM process benchmarking team was composed of customer satisfaction specialists from the IBM-Rochester customer satisfaction department as well as key issue owners from functional areas across the Rochester site. A total of seven members analyzed the existing CSM process and associated subprocesses to arrive at the benchmarking checklist.

This list is comprised of a series of comparable questions that are associated with measurements of efficiency and effectiveness of each element of the IBM-Rochester CSM process and associated subprocesses. For each item on the checklist, an associated

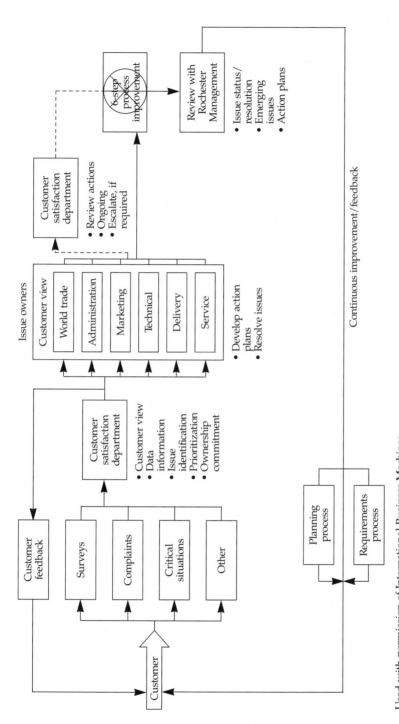

Used with permission of International Business Machines.

Figure 15.1. IBM-Rochester customer satisfaction management process flow diagram.

1. What is your customer satisfaction management (CSM) process? Please provide a copy of your CSM process flow diagram.
   - How are issues identified?
   - How frequently do you reassess issues?
   - How is issue ownership assigned?
   - Are your products/services shipped to a non-U.S. location or subsidiary? If so, what is your process that assures worldwide issues are represented?
   - How are improvements made?
   - What status is reviewed? How? By whom? How often?
   - Are data collected and consolidated in one place?
   - How many people directly support the CSM process?
   - What are your current satisfaction levels and trends?
   - What is the CSM department reporting structure (e.g., marketing, quality, etc.)?
   - Have you benchmarked your CSM process with others? If yes, identify your partners.
   - How is customer feedback distributed?

2. How are the needs and expectations of customers defined?

3. Are customer satisfaction surveys conducted?
   - If so, are they conducted by you or an external provider. Please identify the provider.
   - If surveys are conducted by your company, who conducts them (i.e., staff of trained telemarketers, engineers, managers, etc.)?
   - What is the sample size?
   - How frequently is the survey conducted?
   - What is the cost per survey?
   - What head count is required to conduct the survey?
   - What head count is required to analyze the survey?
   - What type of survey is used (e.g., mail or telephone)?
   - What is the return rate?
   - What computer-assisted interviewing (CAI) system platform is used?
   - What CAI software package is used?
   - What data analysis system platform is used?
   - What data analysis software package is used?
   - What report generation tools and software are used?
   - What report generation format is used? Please provide a copy of the report.
   - Describe the contact control process (survey fatigue).
   - Describe the closed loop process to customer.
   - How are identified dissatisfied customers handled?

Used with permission of International Business Machines.

Figure 15.2. Benchmarking checklist.

- If customers are still dissatisfied after final focus, what is the process to satisfy them?
- How many questions are asked?
- How much time does it take to conduct a survey?
- What functional organization does the survey department report to (e.g., marketing, quality, etc.)?
- Who funds the survey?
- Can your survey handle comments? If so, how are they analyzed?
- Who is surveyed (e.g, decision makers, influencers, etc.)?
- How soon are customers contacted after the initial purchase?
- Are surveys conducted worldwide?
- How is the survey script structured? (Measure the customer view.) Who writes the survey script? Please provide a copy of a sample survey script.
- Is *importance* addressed as one of the attributes measured?

4. Do you have an ongoing training program to assure your survey staff is technically competent?
   - Do you use survey caller training?
   - Do you use data analyzer training?
   - Are survey callers trained on how to handle dissatisfied customers?

5. What tools do you use to obtain customer feedback?
   - Are external data sources (i.e., Datapro, Reliability Ratings) analyzed?
   - What methods do you apply in analyzing qualitative research data?
   - What customer feedback is distributed? To whom? How often? In what format? How do you know the feedback is getting to and being used by the right audience?

6. How do you know if your programs are effective?
   - What are the measurements of effectiveness of your CSM process? Please provide a copy if possible.
   - How do you know if your organization is adding value?
   - Do you survey internal customers?
   - Have you quantified the value of customer satisfaction to your company?
   - Do your CSM programs and processes complement one another?
   - Are any of your subsidiaries conducting similar research? If so, is it coordinated?
   - What are the specific benefits of each of the programs?

7. Does your company use indirect sales channels (i.e., business partners and dealers)?
   - Do you include intermediaries in your survey?
   - What effect does indirect versus direct sales channels have on overall customer satisfaction?

Figure 15.2. *(continued)*

measurement or subprocess description for IBM-Rochester's CSM process was developed. Therefore, when a formal benchmark was conducted, results could be compared, and best practices could be adopted.

Customers and Requirements

There are two primary customers groups of the CSM process. The first group consists of external customers or final users and consumers of IBM-Rochester's products and services. The second group is composed of the internal issue owners who must use the external customer information to invoke changes.

The CSM team is at the heart of Rochester's CSM process. Information concerning customer satisfaction and dissatisfaction is generated and collected by this team, analyzed for issues and root causes, and then disseminated to line areas responsible for corrective actions. These line areas, responsible for converting the information into actions, want additional assistance to help justify cost and returns in implementing these actions. They also need assurance that actions taken address the needs of the entire worldwide customer base, including issues unique to a particular geographical area. Ultimately, both internal and external customers of the CSM process want the assurance that when customer satisfaction data are collected, it is done so in the most expedient and efficient manner, with minimal disruption to all affected parties. All external customers want the assurance that the information they provide is being used to drive improvements. They also want easy access to complaint or comment channels.

Needs/Reasons for Improvement

The CSM team's quest through benchmarking is to

1. Continually improve the CSM process for better efficiency and effectiveness.

2. Find breakthrough concepts and approaches to keep IBM-Rochester in a leadership position.

3. Remain ahead of competitors as they examine and adopt IBM-Rochester's world-class processes and techniques.

Organizations or Industries Benchmarked

Current Process

The current process employed by IBM-Rochester is depicted in Figure 15.1. This process consists of a series of subprocesses including survey design and structure, complaint management, data aggregation, conversion of data into information to invoke action, issue management and review, and customer feedback. One of the existing subprocesses, that of converting customer satisfaction data into action, is shown in Figure 15.3.

Customer dissatisfaction data are received from complaints or from surveys. The specific reason for dissatisfaction is determined and expediently resolved. The actions taken are then communicated to the customer; however, the root cause or causes that resulted in the original complaint must then be identified and resolved to prevent similar occurrences. For instance, it may be determined that a customer did not receive all the components that were ordered. Replacement parts would be shipped immediately to resolve the customer's concern. Root cause analysis, however, must be conducted to ensure that this problem does not happen again.

Key Measures and Other Facts

The key measurements and parameters used to conduct a process-to-process comparison are identified in Figure 15.2. The comprehensive checklist contains all the parameters of the IBM-Rochester's CSM process and associated subprocesses.

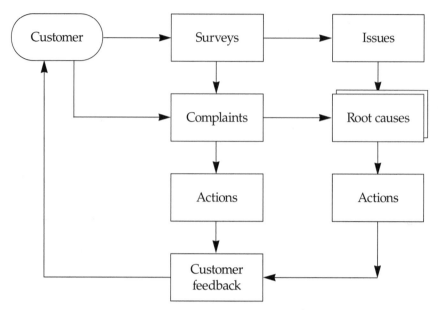

Figure 15.3. Issue management process.

Process-to-Process Analysis

Analysis was used to select benchmarking partners who were recognized world-class leaders in customer satisfaction management, particularly those outside the computer industry. If IBM-Rochester focused its attention primarily within its industry, it could only expect to maintain par with the best competitors. Selection criteria included companies or organizations

- With a formal CSM process that includes the administration of surveys and complaint aggregation

- Who are recognized as world-class leaders in customer satisfaction management

- With international sales and that manage customer satisfaction on a worldwide basis

- With similar marketing channels, including direct sales and sales through intermediaries such as dealers

- Who track customer satisfaction to the end-user customer, regardless of whether sales are made through direct or intermediary channels

- Who monitor and track customer satisfaction of large accounts, as well as individual consumers

- Who are outside the computer industry, in an attempt to discover breakthrough concepts and approaches

Methods used to identify and select benchmarking partners included

- Researching companies and industries using library resources

- Accessing the International Benchmarking Clearinghouse database

- Researching international conferences on customer satisfaction including the International Quality and Productivity Center (IQPC), the American Society for Quality Control (ASQC), the Quality and Productivity Management Association (QPMA), and the Conference Board

As a result of inquiries about IBM-Rochester's process, the team established a significant network with others involved in the CSM process. This included other Baldrige award winners and applicants, as well as independent consultants of customer satisfaction. This network provided the opportunity to gather data to help in the selection of benchmarking partners. Further, it allowed the formation of an informal consortium with several companies to continually share information on best practices and processes. Research shows that IBM-Rochester has one of the best CSM processes in the IBM Corporation, and that many units have adapted this process as their own.

Benchmarking Partners

Although numerous benchmarks were done from 1991 to 1993, the IBM-Rochester team focused its attention on two major ones that it initiated. Using the selection criteria, the list was narrowed to four potential partners. Company A is a large company in the same industry and one of IBM's competitors. Company B is a large company in the automotive industry. Company C is a major division within a large company that specializes in consumer credit and financial transactions. Company D is a large company that specializes in the distribution of packaged goods. Companies A and B were selected to provide the most opportunities for identifying best practices and breakthrough approaches. Companies C and D were both in the process of modifying or developing their CSM processes and were not yet considered world-class leaders. Therefore, they were not selected as benchmarking partners. Figure 15.4 illustrates the selection criteria and process used.

Best Practices Found

IBM-Rochester's CSM process is among the best, and its partner companies were as enthusiastic about the benchmarking study as was the Rochester team. The process flow diagram of Rochester's customer satisfaction process was very similar to the process flow diagram of Company B, although each evolved independently of one another. The IBM-Rochester team learned that its customer satisfaction survey costs were equal to or lower than any of the other companies with whom it benchmarked. The participation or return rate of IBM-Rochester's customer satisfaction surveys is significantly better than the best.

Even though IBM-Rochester has been able to develop a formula for quantifying the impact of customer satisfaction on revenue (one-point improvement in overall customer satisfaction has a net impact on revenue of $257 million over five years), it is very

	Company A	Company B	Company C	Company D
Formal customer satisfaction management process	X	X	Emerging	Emerging
Conduct/administer customer satisfaction surveys	X	X	X	X
Formal complaint handling, management, and aggregation process	X	X	X	X
Recognized as a world-class leader in customer satisfaction	X	X	Emerging	Emerging
International sales	X			X
Track customer satisfaction worldwide	X			X
Direct sales	X		X	X
Sales through intermediaries	X	X		
Track customer satisfaction to the end user consumer	X	X	X	X
Consumers include large accounts as well as individuals	X	X		X
Dissimilar industry		X	X	X

Used with permission of International Business Machines.

Figure 15.4. Benchmarking partner selection process.

complex and not easy to update. The formula used to determine a similar impact for Company B was simpler and allowed for continual updating due to its tracking of loyalty and recommendation factors on all surveys.

Company A had devised a method of comparing worldwide customer satisfaction results into meaningful measurements. These measurements allow Company A to derive issues unique by geography. Both Companies A and B incorporate importance ratings into their survey process to assist in setting priorities. Company B incorporates and tracks customer satisfaction results by dealer, and thus identifies its top dealers using this method. Company B also focuses on buying behaviors and issues unique to geographical areas.

Both Companies A and B have fewer toll-free telephone numbers to allow customers easy access to customer service specialists. Company B has just one toll-free number, which is highly publicized and allows customers one point of contact for any inquiries, comments, or complaints.

Company A conducts a consistent customer satisfaction survey on a worldwide basis. Company B forwards customer complaints and customer satisfaction results directly to dealers without going through any intermediary channels.

Company A provides feedback on pervasive issues to its entire customer base on an annual basis. Although individual complaints are addressed immediately with the customer who raised the issue, overall progress on processes and practices that are improved as a result of conducting root cause analysis, and that impact the customer base as a whole, are communicated to all customers through a newsletter. This feedback cycle demonstrates to its customers Company A's commitment to improve its relationship with them and to take actions based on information customers provide.

Although Companies A and B and IBM-Rochester have established measurements of efficiency and effectiveness, all three benchmarking partners learned new techniques. Numerous similarities were noted between CSM processes of IBM-Rochester and Companies A and B.

For instance, IBM-Rochester and Companies A and B all have dedicated CSM teams that solicit, gather, and analyze satisfaction data from a variety of sources and then convert these data into pervasive issues. All the companies use internal and external sources to gather customer satisfaction data, including comparisons to competitors. All the companies measure and track overall satisfaction as a key indicator. All surveys and data analyses are based on a determination of elements defined as important by customers, as opposed to elements defined as important by the respective companies.

Actions Taken

As a result of the benchmarks conducted, IBM-Rochester has incorporated the following actions into its CSM process.

- Track customer satisfaction results by dealer to identify those needing assistance.
- Track results by geographical area to identify unique issues.
- Incorporate questions on loyalty and recommendation into all surveys, and track the relationship of these factors to overall satisfaction to determine revenue opportunities.

Internal customer satisfaction has improved nine points since these changes were made. External customer satisfaction levels have continued to climb, partially because of improved data accuracy and the availability of actionable data for use in corrective actions.

The formal benchmarks noted were conducted in late 1992. Most actions were in place by mid-1993. Changes were made directly by the CSM team.

Implementation

Most of the changes that have been implemented, along with some of the changes yet to be implemented, have required enhancements to software used to collect and analyze data. The time required and the availability of programming resources to make the software changes have been the only barriers to implementation. These were overcome by subcontracting for additional programming sources and by scheduling additional time for software changes.

Planned Changes

The following additional changes are planned as a result of the benchmarks conducted.

• Reduce the quantity of toll-free numbers to allow customers a single point of contact for inquiries, comments, and complaints.

• Devise one consistent customer satisfaction survey and administer it worldwide.

• Distribute complaints and customer satisfaction results directly to dealers.

• Determine and implement additional measurements of effectiveness and efficiency commensurate with actions taken and planned.

• Implement a feedback program similar to that of Company A, in which actions and improvements made to processes and practices that impact the entire customer base are annually communicated through a newsletter.

The barriers to implementation of planned changes are primarily driven by the fact that the changes affect many units within the IBM Corporation. Software and databases throughout the corporation worldwide need to be modified. This requires resources beyond that which IBM-Rochester has direct control.

Conclusions

IBM-Rochester has determined that benchmarking needs to be an ongoing process aimed at continual improvement and identification of breakthrough concepts. What was once considered a world-class CSM process quickly becomes status quo as others adapt portions of it and add their own improvements. Ongoing benchmarking is the catalyst to prevent complacency. Constant pressure to reduce costs, eliminate deficiencies, and reduce analysis and information transfer cycle times make the concept of benchmarking even more critical. Additionally, a benchmarking strategy, including a structured benchmarking checklist and selection process, is important to control costs associated with benchmarking and to ensure that all key concepts are used effectively.

Summary

• An effective CSM process is dependent on early and direct customer involvement.

• An effective CSM process is capable of continually meeting or exceeding customer requirements and expectations.

• IBM-Rochester's CSM process is one of the best.

• The objectives of IBM-Rochester's CSM process are (1) to establish a structured strategy to handle all customer requests, concerns, and recommendations; (2) to continually improve customer satisfaction levels; (3) to develop and create partnerships between IBM and its customers; and (4) to improve customer relationships.

• The mission of the CSM process team is to support IBM-Rochester's goal to be the undisputed leader in customer satisfaction.

• The CSM process is administered by a small team of specialists who solicit, collect, and aggregate customer data and information.

• A benchmarking checklist was developed that is comprised of a series of comparable questions that are associated with measurements of efficiency and effectiveness for each element in the CSM process.

• External customers of the CSM are final users and consumers of IBM-Rochester's products and services. Internal customers include the issue owners who must use the external customer information to invoke changes.

• The CSM team's mission is (1) to continually improve the CSM process for improved efficiency and effectiveness; (2) to find breakthrough concepts and approaches to keep IBM-Rochester in a leadership position; and (3) to remain ahead of competitors.

• Process-to-process analysis included comparisons to practices outside the computer industry.

• Two benchmarking partners were selected.

• Several similar practices were found among the benchmarking partners and IBM-Rochester.

• As a result of benchmarking, the CSM process now (1) tracks customer satisfaction results by dealer to identify those needing assistance; (2) tracks results by geographical area to identify unique issues; and (3) incorporates questions on loyalty and recommendations into all surveys, and tracks the relationship of these factors to overall satisfaction to determine revenue opportunities.

• Additional improvements to the already world-class CSM process at IBM-Rochester are also under way.

Appendix A

Benchmarking Bibliography

Books

Balm, Gerald J. 1992. *Benchmarking: A practitioner's guide for becoming and staying the best of the best.* Schaumburg, Ill.: QPMA Press.

Benchmarking for process improvement. 1994. Rochester, N.Y.: Xerox Quality Solutions.

Bosomworth, Charles E. 1993. *The executive benchmarking guidebook.* Boston: The Management Roundtable.

Brassard, Michael. 1989. *The Memory Jogger+.* Methuen, Mass.: GOAL/QPC.

Camp, Robert C. 1989. B*enchmarking: The search for industry best practices that lead to superior performance.* Milwaukee, Wis.: Quality Press and White Plains, N.Y.: Quality Resources.

————. 1990. Competitive benchmarking: Xerox's powerful quality tool. In *Making total quality happen,* edited by Frank Caropreso. Research Report No. 937. New York: The Conference Board.

————. 1991. *Benchmarking: Come Analizzare le Prassi Delle Aziende Migiori per Diventare i Primi* (Benchmarking: The search for industry best practices that lead to superior performance). Milan: Editoriale Itaca.

————. 1992. *Conversations for the 90s: The search for superior performance*. Chicago: Harris Bank.

————. 1992. *Le Benchmarking: Pour Atteindre L'Exellence et Depasser Vos Concurrents* (Benchmarking: The search for industry best practices that lead to superior performance). Paris: Les 'Editions D'Organisation.

————. 1993. *Benchmarking Baant de weg Naar Superiure Prestaties, de Praktihk Bevstigt het Verband Tussen Kwaliteit en Concurrentiekracht* (Benchmarking: The search for industry best practices that lead to superior performance). Antwerpen, Nederlandse: Kluwer Technische Boeken B.V.

————. 1993. *Benchmarking: La Busqueda de las Mejores Practicas de la Industria Que Conducen a un Desempeno Excelente* (Benchmarking: The search for industry best practices that lead to superior performance). Distrito Federal, Mexico: Panorama Editorial.

————. 1993. Benchmarking: The search for industry best practices that lead to superior performance. In *Handbook for Productivity Measurement and Improvement,* edited by William F. Christopher, and Carl G. Thor. Cambridge, Mass.: Productivity Press.

Codling, Sylvia. 1992. *Best practices benchmarking: The management guide to successful implementation*. Beds, U.K.: Industrial Newsletters.

Czarnecki, Mark T. 1993. *Benchmarking strategies in accounting and finance*. New York: American Institute of Certified Public Accountants.

Furey, Timothy R., Robert M. Fifer, Lawrence S. Pryor, and Jeffrey P. Rumberg. 1988. *Beating the competition: A practical guide to benchmarking.* Viena, Va.: Kaiser Associates.

Haim, Alexander, ed. 1992. *Closing the quality gap: Lessons learned from America's leading companies.* Englewood Cliffs, N.J.: Prentice Hall.

Hooper, John A. 1992. *Borrowing from the best: How to benchmark world-class people practices.* Beaverton, Ore.: HR Effectiveness.

Hou, Wee Chow, L. K. Sheang, and B. W. Hidajat. 1991. *Sun Tzu: War and management, application to strategic management and thinking.* Singapore: Addison-Wesley.

International Benchmarking Clearinghouse. 1992. *Planning, organizing, and managing benchmarking activities: A user's guide.* Houston: American Productivity and Quality Center and International Benchmarking Clearinghouse.

Jacobsen, Gary, and John Hilkirk. 1986. *Xerox: American samurai.* New York: Macmillan Publishing.

Karlof, Bengt, and Svante Ostblom. 1993. *Benchmarking: Vagvisare Till Masterkap i Productivetet Och Kvalitet* (Benchmarking: A guide to productivity and quality championship). Borga, Svenska: Svenska Dagbladet Förlags AB.

Kearns, David T., and David A. Nadler. 1992. *Prophets in the dark: How Xerox reinvented itself and beat back the Japanese.* New York: Harper Business.

Leibfried, Kathleen, and Carol J. McNair. 1992. *Benchmarking: A tool for continuous improvement.* New York: Harper Business.

Miller, Jeffrey, Arnoud DeMeyer, Jinichiro Nakane, and Kasra Ferdows. 1992. *Benchmarking global manufacturing.* Homewood, Ill.: Business One Irwin.

Palermo, Richard C., ed. 1993. *A world of quality: The timeless passport.* Rochester, N.Y.: Xerox Quality Solutions and Milwaukee: ASQC Quality Press.

Spendolini, Michael J. 1992. *The benchmarking book.* New York: AMACOM Press.

Sun Tzu. 1983. *The art of war.* Edited by James Clavel. New York: Delacorte Press.

The Verity Consulting Group. *Benchmarking.* 1991. Los Angeles: Verity Press.

Watson, Gregory H. 1992. *The benchmarking workbook.* Cambridge, Mass.: Productivity Press.

Articles Since 1989

- A -

Adriance, Nancy. 1991. Benchwarmers need not apply. *World* (Peat Marwick) 2, no. 2:36–37.

Ahlbom, Helen. 1993. Mastaren Mastrar Mattstockarna. *Veckans Affarer* (Sweden), 9 June, 31–32.

Allaire, Paul A. 1990. Quality improvement: A never-ending journey. *The Journal for Quality and Participation* (March): 68–72.

Alster, Judith. 1990. Competitive benchmarking paves the road to quality. *Human Resources Briefing* (The Conference Board, New York) 6, no. 4 (May): 1–4.

Altany, David. 1990. Copycats. *Industry Week* (November): 11–18.

———. 1991. The hottest new buzzword: Benchmarking. *World Executive's Digest* (May): 32–34.

———. 1991. Share and share alike: Benchmarkers are proving the wisdom of mother's reproach. *Industry Week,* 15 July, 12–16.

————. 1992. Benchmarkers unite: Clearinghouse provides needed networking opportunities. *Industry Week,* 3 February, 25.

Appelman, Hillary. 1990. How Xerox duplicates the success of other companies. *Philadelphia Inquirer,* 21 April, p. 5B.

Auguston, Karen. 1992. Warehousing/distribution: Compare yourself to the best . . . and Worst! *Modern Materials Handling* 47, no. 6 (May): 48–51.

- B -

Balm, Gerald J. 1992. Benchmarking—Nicety or necessity. *Tapping the Network Journal* 3, no. 1 (spring): 6–8.

Band, William. 1990. Benchmarking your performance for continuous improvement. *Sales & Marketing Management* (Canada) (May): 36–38.

Barry, Jack. 1988. Benchmarking: Aiming at the wrong targets? *Distribution Center Management* (Marketing Publications Newsletter) 23, no. 6 (June): 3–4.

Bean, Thomas J., and Jacques G. Gros. 1992. R & D benchmarking at AT&T. *Research-Technology Management* (July–August): 32–37.

Bemowski, Karen. 1991. The benchmarking bandwagon. *Quality Progress* 24, no. 1 (January): 19–24.

Benchmarking: A classic approach to using a valuable quality tool. 1993. *Quality Assurance Bulletin,* no. 1604 (February): 1–6.

Benchmarking: Up-front preparation and strategic perspective lead to benchmarking success. 1991. *Productivity* (September): 10–12.

Benchmarking: What you need to do to make it work. 1993. *Purchasing*, 14 January, 63–69.

Biesada, Alexandra. 1991. Benchmarking. *Financial World* 160, no. 19:28–54.

———. 1991. The second opinion. *Financial World* 160, no. 25:88, 90.

———. 1992. Strategic benchmarking. *Financial World* 161, no. 19:30–36.

Blumenstyk, Goldie. 1993. Colleges look to "benchmarking" to measure how efficient and productive they are. *The Chronicle of Higher Education* 40, no. 2 (September): A41–42.

Bowers, Fred. 1993. The future of benchmarking. *Continuous Journey* 2, no. 1 (October/November): 38–42.

Brown, Thomas L. 1993. Capitalizing on comparisons: Can benchmarking actually slow you down? *Industry Week*, 15 March, 46.

- C -

Camp, Robert C. 1989. Benchmarking: The search for best practices that lead to superior performance. Parts 1–5. *Quality Progress* 22, no. 1 (January): 61–68; no. 2 (February): 70–75; no. 3 (March): 76–82; no. 4 (April): 62–69; no. 5 (May): 66–68.

———. 1991. Being better than the best. *Compass* (The Magazine of Northern Telecom) no. 1 (autumn): 6–9.

———. 1992. Benchmarking: The search for industry best practices that lead to superior performance. *Creativity* (IBM East Fishkill edition) 11, no. 1 (March): 3–5.

———. 1992. Learning from the best leads to superior performance. *Journal of Business Strategy* 13, no. 3 (May/June): 3–6.

————. 1993. Benchmarking: Cautrea Celor Mai Eficiente Metode Care Sa Conduca La Performante Superoare. Business Tech International (Romania) 1, no. 8:29–31. Reprint of Quality Progress series.

————. 1993. Benchmarking: The search for best practices in industry. *Manufacturing Europe* (Sterling Publications, UK), 1993, 24-28.

————. 1993. A bible for benchmarking, by Xerox. *Financial Executive* (July/August): 23–27.

————. 1993. Xerox benchmarks the spot, the best in business. *Inside Guide* 7, no. 1 (February/March): 13–14, 23.

Capa, A. Arte. 1993. Do Benchmarking: Reinventar a Roda E Bobagem. *Exame* (Brazil) 25, no. 8, 14 April, 40–46.

Cecil, Robert, and Richard Ferraro. 1992. IEs fill facilitator role in benchmarking operations to improve performance. *Industrial Engineering* 24, no. 4 (April): 30–33.

Chvatal, Kris, W. 1990. Xerox benchmarking studies paying off: Costs have gone down, quality has improved. *Electronic Buyers' News*, 2 July, 27.

Companies profit from monitoring competitor's service practices. 1990. *The Service Edge* 3, no. 1 (January): 1–3.

- D -

Day, Charles R., Jr. 1992. Benchmarking's first law: Know thyself. *Industry Week*, 17 February, 70.

Davis, Herbert W. 1991. Benchmarking: It's more than just comparing operations. *Davis Database* 16, no. 1 (April): 1–4.

Deutsch, Claudia H. 1990. Emulating the best of the best. *New York Times*, 31 December, p. 23.

Doades, Ronald. 1993. Benchmarking opportunities/traps. *Boardroom*, 15 April, 9–10.

Donatelli, Ralph F. 1992. The quality of the bottom line. *Information Week*, 9 March, 78.

- E -

Enslow, Beth. 1992. The benchmarking bonanza. *Across the Board* (April): 16–22.

Ettorre, Barbara. 1993. Benchmarking: The next generation. *Management Review* (June): 10–16.

Eyrich, H. G. 1990. Benchmarking to become the best of breed. *Manufacturing Systems* (April): 40–47.

- F -

Fifer, Robert M. 1989. Cost benchmarking in the value chain. *Planning Review* 17, no. 3 (May/June): 18–27.

The fine print: Legal guidelines for the benchmarking process. 1992. *Continuous Journey* (October/November): 18–21.

First Find Your Bench. 1991. *The Economist*, 11 May, 72.

Flower, Joe. 1993. The source. *Healthcare Forum Journal* 36, no. 1 (January/February): 30–36.

Foster, Thomas A. 1992. Logistics benchmarking: Searching for the best. *Distribution* 91, no. 3 (March): 31–36.

Frasier-Sleyman, Ken. 1992. Benchmarking your way to forecasting excellence. *The Journal of Business Strategy* 11, no. 1 (spring): 6–10.

Freedman, David. 1992. Those who can teach. *CIO* (Chief Information Officer) 5, no. 17 (September): 46–51.

Fuld, Leonard. 1989. Taking the first steps on the way to benchmarking. *Marketing News* 11 September, 15, 20–21.

- G -

Gerber, Beverly. 1990. Benchmarking: Measuring yourself against the best. *Training* (November): 36–44.

Graham, Scott. 1991. Futurescape: Utilities turn to benchmarking. *Reddy News Sourcebook* 49, no. 3 (March): 18–22.

Grayson, C. Jackson, Jr. 1992. Taking on the world. *Total Quality Management* (June): 139–143.

———. 1992. Benchmarking: Learn or die. *Continuous Improvement* 1, no. 1 (October/November): 8–11.

- H -

Hakleroad, David H. 1992. Competitive intelligence: A new benchmarking tool. *Management Review* 81, no. 10 (October): 26–29.

Harmon, Marion. 1992. Benchmarking. *Quality Digest* (July): 20–31.

Heque, Marc. 1993. The limits of benchmarking. *Training* (February): 36–41.

Hitchcock, Nancy A. 1993. Benchmarking bolsters quality at Texas Instruments. *Modern Materials Handling* 48, no. 3 (March): 46–48.

Holberton, Simon. 1991. Benchmarking: How to help yourself to a competitor's best practices. *Financial Times,* 24 June, 12.

How Do You Measure Up? *Traffic Management* 32, no. 4 (April): 60–64.

- J -

Jaros, Elaine M. 1991. Benchmarking: How and why. *Apparel Industry* (February): 28–29.

Jennings, Kenneth, and Frederick Westfall. 1992. Benchmarking for strategic action. *Journal of Business Strategy* 13, no. 3 (May/June): 22–25.

Johnson, Kathryn E. 1993. Benchmarking: Learning from the best. *Healthcare Forum Journal* 36, no. 1:14–57.

Johnson, Phyllis. 1991. Benchmarking catching on in U.S. *Johnson City Press* (Tennessee), 21 April.

Johnson, Randall. 1992. Benchmarking: Tips help to ensure your time, dollar investment pay off. *Service Edge* 5, no. 6 (June): 1–3.

Johnson, Samuel E. 1992. Benchmarking facility management practices. *Modern Office Technology* 37, no. 6 (June): 64–66.

- K -

Kanicki, David P. 1991. Benchmarking: Striving to be the best of the best. *Modern Castings* 81, no. 5 (May): 20–22.

Karch, Kenneth M. 1992–1993. Getting organizational buy-in for benchmarking: Environmental management at Weyerhaeuser. *National Productivity Review* (winter): 13–22.

Katsantonis, John. 1990. If it works, improve it. *TQC World* (publication of Texas Instruments) 2, no. 3 (October): 15.

Kearns, David T. 1989. Xerox: Satisfying customer needs with a new culture. *Forum* (February): 61–63.

Kemmerer, Barbara E., and V. Aline Arnold. 1993. The growing use of benchmarking in managing cultural diversity. *Business Forum* (winter/spring): 38–40.

Kempmer. Daphne E., and Barbara S. Shafer. 1993. The growth of the NACUBO benchmarking project. *NACUBO Business Officer* (National Association of College and University Business Officers) 27, no. 6:22–31.

Kendrick, John J. 1992. Benchmarking survey builds case for looking to others for TQM models. *Quality* (March): 13.

- L -

Lambertus, Todd. 1993. Benchmarking the inpatient admitting process. *Continuous Journey* (April/May): 32–35.

Landry, Pete. 1993. Benchmarking strategy. *Executive Excellence* (June): 8–9.

LaPlant, Alice. 1992. Job performance is often rated by how much money you save. *InfoWorld* 13, no. 28 (July): 54.

Larson, Peter. 1991. Setting operational targets: Xerox methods are copied. *Montreal Gazette,* 22 April.

- M -

Main, Jeremy. 1992. How to steal the best secrets around. *Fortune* 126, no. 8, 19 October, 102–106.

Markin, Alex. 1992. How to implement competitive-cost benchmarking. *The Journal of Business Strategy* 13, no. 3 (May–June): 14–20.

Marlow, Paula. 1992. Benchmarking: Emulating the best. *Exhibitor* 11, no. 8 (September): 18–19.

Martin, Patricia. 1991. Benchmarking: A leg up on the learning curve. *Manage* (May): 7, 22–23.

Maturi, Richard J. 1989. Benchmarking: Studying, evaluating others. *Investors Daily,* 28 April, p. 1.

———. 1990. Benchmarking: The search for quality. *Financial Manager* (March/April): 26–31.

McMorrow, Eileen. 1992. Proud as a peacock: NBC's Pedalino Facilities. *Design & Management* 11, no. 3 (March): 44–47.

Mittelstaedt, Robert E., Jr. 1992. Benchmarking: How to learn from best-in-class practices. *Executive Issues* (summer): 2, 6, 8.

Mortimer, John. 1993. Benchmarking in action: Measuring up to the mark. *The Engineer* 267:34.

- N -

Nevens, T. Michael, Gregory L. Summe, and Bro Uttal. 1990. Commercializing technology: What the best companies do. *Harvard Business Review,* no. 3 (May–June): 154–163.

- O -

O'Dell, Carla. 1992. Benchmarking: America looks to the customer and best practices. *Continuous Journey* 1, no. 1 (October/November): 6–7.

- P -

Pantalon, William, III. 1992. Quality: Xerox's savior. *Democrat & Chronicle,* 10 March.

Patrick, Michael S. 1992. Benchmarking—Targeting "best practices." *Healthcare Forum Journal* 35, no. 4 (July/August): 71–72.

Peters, Tom. 1989. Six ways to stave off a corporate heart attack. *Atlanta Business Chronicle,* 7 August, p. 27A.

Port, Otis, and Geoffrey Smith. 1992. Beg, borrow, and benchmark. *Business Week,* 30 November, 74–75.

Powers, Vicki J. 1993. Touring Texas for best-in-class: Benchmarking study mission focuses on customer service. *Continuous Journey* 1, no. 3 (February/March): 36–39.

Prairie, Patti. 1993. American Express/IBM consortium benchmarks information technology. *Planning Review* (January/February): 22–27.

Pryor, Lawrence S. 1989. Benchmarking: A self-improvement strategy. *Journal of Business Strategy* (November/December): 28–32.

- *R* -

Rakstis, Ted J. 1992. When benchmarks point to success. *Kiwanis* (April): 38–41.

Randall, Robert. 1993. Strategic benchmarking. *Planning Review* 21, no. 1 (January/February): 6–36.

Recovering the future at Xerox. 1990. *The Quality Executive* 2, no. 3 (July): 4–5, 7.

Richardson, Helen L. 1992. Improve quality through benchmarking. Part 2. *Transportation & Distribution* (October): 32–37.

The right way to benchmark: A multi-industry approach to try. 1993. *Distribution Center Management* 28, no. 6 (June): 1–3.

Russell, H. Bruce. 1992. The property puzzle. *Financial Executive* 8, no. 4 (July/August): 42–45.

- *S* -

Sharman, Paul. 1992. Benchmarking: Opportunity for accountants. *CMA Magazine* 66, no. 6 (July/August): 16–18.

Sheridan, John H. 1993. Where benchmarkers go wrong. *Industry Week,* 15 March, 28–34.

Sillyman, Steve. 1992. Guide to benchmarking resources. *Quality* (March): 17–18.

Sprow, Eugene E. 1993. Benchmarking: A tool for our time. *Manufacturing Engineering* 111, no. 3 (September): 56–69.

Swanson, Roger C. 1992. Benchmarking: Search for "best" practices. *Journal of Applied Manufacturing Systems* 5, no. 2 (winter): 37–43.

————. 1993. Quality benchmarking deployment. *Quality Progress* 26, no. 12 (December): 81–84.

- T -

Temes, Judy. 1993. Benchmarking: Toward a common language. *CFO* (Chief Financial Officer) 9, no. 3 (March): 13.

Terracciano, di Chiara. 1992. Stregati Dal Primo: Gestione D'Impresa. *Benchmarking Management* (Italy), no. 3 (March): 41–45.

Thompson, James. 1992. Benchmarking rules of thumb. *Transportation & Distribution* 33, no. 7 (July): 46–50.

Tonkin, Lea. 1991. Benchmarking bound? Don't "just do it." *Target* 7, no. 5 (winter): 13–16.

Tyndall, Gene. 1990. How you apply benchmarking makes all the difference. *Marketing News* 24, no. 23, 12 November, 18–19.

- U -

Ueland, Inger. 1994. Avoid the data trap. *Status* (Statoil Group Journal, Norway), 10 February, 10.

Ulrich, Dave, Wayne Brockbank, and Arthur Yeung. 1989. Beyond belief: A benchmark for human resources. *Human Resources Management* 28, no. 3 (fall): 311–335.

Up-front preparation and strategic perspective lead to benchmarking success. 1991. *Productivity* 12, no. 9 (September): 10–12.

- W -

Walleck, A. Steven. 1991. A backstage view of world-class performers. *Wall Street Journal*, 26 August.

Watson, Gregory. 1993. Deciding what to benchmark: A new method answers the "big question" in benchmarking. *Continuous Journey* (April/May): 46–49.

———. 1993. How process benchmarking supports corporate strategy. *Planning Review* (January/February): 12–15.

Weimer, George A. 1992. Benchmarking maps the route to quality. *Industry Week*, 20 July, 54.

Weisendanger, Betsy. 1993. Benchmarking by the numbers, best in business. *Inside Guide* 7, no. 1 (February/March): 9–12.

Whiting, Rick. 1991. Benchmarking: Lessons from the best-in-class. *Electronic Business*, 7 October, 129–134.

Willding, Liz. 1989. Use benchmarking methods to become "the best of the best." *TQC World* (publication of Texas Instruments) 1, no. 3 (September): 10–11.

World-class organizations: Xerox. 1990. *Industry Week*, 9 March, 14, 16.

- Y -

Yanes, William B. 1990. Benchmarking shows the way to become the best. *Investor's Daily*, 28 December.

- Z -

Zivan, Seymour M. 1990. Benchmarking: The effective manager's tool. *Boardroom Reports*, 15 November, 3–4.

Videotapes, Audiotapes, Software, and Networks

Benchmarking: Competing through quality with David Garvin and an interview of John Kelsch from Xerox. Boston: Nathan/Tyler, 1991. Harvard videotape series.

The Benchmarking Exchange: On-line Information and Communication for Search, Contact, and Share. The Benchmarking Exchange, Aptos, Calif.

Benchmarking manufacturing processes. Dearborn, Mich.: Society of Manufacturing Engineers, 1994. Videotape series.

The Benchmarking Network: On-Line Database of Key Performance Indicators. The Benchmarking Network. Houston, Tex.

Business conference analysis conference. New York: The Institute for International Research, 1993. Audiotape.

Getting started in the benchmarking process, effective benchmarking, and integrating benchmarking data into the strategic process. Chicago: Encyclopaedia Britannica Educational Corporation, 1992. Videotape series.

Harrington, H. James. Benchmarking: A Software Application. LearnerFirst, Birmingham, Ala.

In business: How to steal the best ideas in the world. Edited by Stephen Chilcott. 1993. London: BBC Radio 4, 22 September. Audiocassette.

Courseware and Training Materials

Benchmarking: Staying competitive in the 1990s. 1991. Rochester, N.Y.: The Quality Network.

The Best-of-the-Best Companies

This appendix is a sample of companies with outstanding practices demonstrated over the past few years. It is intended to show the diversity and international scope of companies that should be investigated when looking for best practices.

A company cannot be picked from these lists and be *the* candidate company to benchmark. To make its benchmarking effective, the team must research its area of interest and the prospective companies. Large companies are constantly being approached to benchmark. For them to consider a partner, they must perceive some value for themselves from the benchmarking relationship. The team must be clear on what it wants, what it can offer to a partner, and how it feels the candidate company can help the team's efforts. This all requires investigation by the team.

Best practices are not static. They are constantly being improved or being replaced with new practices. This is another reason to research. The companies in this appendix are a starting point for research, not the end of it.

Allied Signal
Health care management
American Express
Billing and collection
Apple Computer
Inventory control
Ben & Jerry's
Environment management
Canon
Product development
Cap Gemini
Quality systems, technology
transfer
Citibank
Technology management
Coors
Health care management
Corning
Manufacturing, technology
management
Dow Chemical
Environment management,
technology transfer
Edison
Health care management
Federal Express
Inventory control
Florida Power & Light
Quality systems
Ford
Training
Fujitsu
Technology transfer

General Electric
Robotics, training
Goldstar
Concurrent engineering
Helene Curtis
Marketing
Hershey Foods
Warehousing, distribution
Hewlett-Packard
Manufacturing
Honda Motor
Purchasing
IBM
Sales management
L. L. Bean
Customer service, warehous-
ing, distribution
MCI
Inventory control
Merck
Sales management
Microsoft
Marketing, software develop-
ment
Monsanto
Technology management
Motorola
Product development, quality
systems, manufacturing
NEC Corporation
Quality systems

NCR
Purchasing, concurrent engineering
Nordstrum
Customer service
Philip Morris
Manufacturing
Polaroid
Training
Procter & Gamble
Sales management, technology management
Sharp
Product Planning

Sony
Product development
Square D
Technology transfer
3M
Environment management, technology transfer, product development
Westinghouse
Inventory control
Xerox
Customer service, quality systems, purchasing

Subject	Company	Says who . . .
Benchmarking	AT&T, Digital Equipment Corporation, IBM, Motorola, Texas Instruments, Xerox	Port and Smith
Benchmarking	Digital Equipment Corporation, Florida Power & Light, Ford, IBM/Rochester, Motorola, Xerox	Altany
Billing/collection	American Express, Fidelity Investments, MCI	Port and Smith
Billing/collection	American Express, MCI	Altany
Customer focus	General Electric (plastics), Wallace Company, Westinghouse (furniture systems), Xerox	Altany
Customer satisfaction	Federal Express, General Electric (plastics), L. L. Bean, Xerox	Port and Smith
Customer service	American Express, L. L. Bean, The Limited, Marriott, Procter & Gamble	Foster
Design for manufacturing assembly	Digital Equipment Corporation, NCR	Altany
Distribution and logistics	L. L. Bean, Wal-Mart	Port and Smith

Figure B.1. The best of the best.

Subject	Company	Says who . . .
Employee empowerment	Corning, Dow Chemical, Millikin, Toledo Scale	Port and Smith
Empowerment	Honda of America, Millikin	Altany
Employee suggestions	Dow Chemical, Millikin, Toyota	Altany
Equipment maintenance	Disney	Port and Smith
Flexible manu-facturing	Allen-Bradley/Milwaukee, Baldor Electric, Motorola/Boynton Beach	Altany, and Port and Smith
Health care programs	Allied-Signal, Coors	Port and Smith
Inbound transportation	Digital Equipment Corporation, Dow Chemical, Motorola, 3M, Xerox	Foster
Industrial design	Black and Decker (household products), Braun, Herman Miller	Altany
Leadership	General Electric/Jack Welch, Hanover Insurance/ Bill O'Brien, Manco/Jack Kahl	Altany
Marketing	Procter & Gamble	Altany, and Port and Smith
Materials management	Dupont, General Electric, IBM, Motorola, Xerox	Foster
Outbound transportation	Digital Equipment Corporation, IBM, Johnson & Johnson, Procter & Gamble, 3M	Foster
Private fleet management	Frito Lay, Harley Davidson, Kimberly Clark, Wal-Mart, West Point Pepperill	Foster
Product develop-ment	Beckman Instruments, Calcomp, Cincinnati Milicron, Digital Equipment Corporation, Hewlett-Packard, 3M, Motorola, NCR	Port and Smith
Quality methods	AT&T, IBM, Motorola, Westinghouse, Xerox	Port and Smith
Quality process	Florida Power & Light, IBM/Rochester, Toyota, Wallace Company	Altany
Quick changeovers	Dana Corporation/Minneapolis, Johnson Controls/ Milwaukee, United Electric Controls	Altany
Quick shop floor changes	Dana Corporation, General Motors/Lansing, Johnson Controls/Milwaukee	Port and Smith
Research and development	AT&T, Hewlett-Packard, Shell Oil	Altany
Self-directed work teams	Corning, Physio Control, Toledo Scale	Altany

Figure B.1. (*continued*)

Subject	Company	Says who ...
Supplier management	Bose, Ford, Levi Strauss, 3M, Motorola, Xerox	Altany, and Port and Smith
Total productive maintenance	Tennessee Eastman	Altany
Training	Square D, Wallace Company	Altany
Warehousing	Hershey Foods, Kodak, L. L. Bean, Wal-Mart, Xerox	Foster
Waste minimization	Dow Chemical, 3M	Altany
Worker training	Disney, Federal Express, Ford, General Electric, Square D	Port and Smith

Altany, David. 1991. Share and share alike: Benchmarkers are providing the wisdom of mother's reproach. *Industry Week,* 15 July, 12–16.

Foster, Thomas. 1992. Logistics benchmarking: Searching for the best. *Distribution* 96 no. 3 (March):30–36

Port, Otis, and Geoffrey Smith. 1992. Beg, borrow, and benchmark. *Business Week,* 30 November, 74–75.

Figure B.1. *(continued)*

Benchmarking Case Histories

Balm, Gerald J. 1992. *Benchmarking: A practitioner's guide for becoming and staying best of the best.* Schaumburg, Ill.: QPMA Press. Includes a case history on use of AHP titled "An IBM/Rochester Gap Analysis Example."

Biesada, Alexandra. 1991. Benchmarking. *Financial World*, 17 September, 36–47. Contains 10 mini case studies citing best practices in asset management, facilities, supplier management, information systems, fleet management, accounting, sales management, natural resource management, technology management, advertising, employee training, health care management, flexible manufacturing, distribution, productivity, manufacturing excellence, new product development, billing, compensation and benefits, and customer retention.

Bounds, Greg. 1994. Part I: Establishing the vision; Part II: Realizing the vision; and Part III: Accomplishing behavioral change. In *Beyond total quality management.* New York: McGraw-Hill. Examines supply chain management.

Bourque, Daniel P. 1993. *The benchmarking process: An approach for improving quality, cost, and clinical performance (a guide).*

Irving, Tex.: Voluntary Hospitals of America. Includes two case studies citing Holmes Regional Medical Center benchmarking cardiovascular care and Robert Packer Hospital benchmarking the medical records process.

Camp, Robert C. 1989. *Benchmarking: The search for industry best practices that lead to superior performance.* Milwaukee, Wis.: Quality Press and White Plains, N.Y.: Quality Resources. Details the Xerox/L. L. Bean experience at the end of chapters 3–12 and contains "The Sale Order Process: A Practices Benchmarking Investigation," in the appendix.

Codling, Sylvia. 1992. *Best practices benchmarking: The management guide to successful implementation.* Dunstable, Beds, U.K.: Industrial Newsletters. Includes six case histories on Shell Chemicals U.K., Hawker Fusegear, Rover Body & Pressings, TNT Express (U.K.), Digital Equipment Corporation, and Hewlett-Packard.

Hopper, John A. 1992. *Borrowing from the best: How to benchmark world-class people practices.* Beaverton, Ore.: HR Effectiveness. Cites three case studies on the following: Weyerhaeuser's staffing compensation, training, and performance management processes; Bank of New Zealand's culture development, rewards and recognition, and employee communications; and Instromedix's performance management.

Johnson, Kathryn, ed. 1993. Benchmarking: Tales from the front, the search for what really works. *Healthcare Forum Journal* 36, no. 1 (January/February): 37–52. Contains 16 mini case studies.

Loeb, Jeff. 1993. Highly configured products benefit from expert order entry. *Manufacturing Systems* 11, no. 7 (July): 100–106. Describes a benchmarking study on the integrated supply chain conducted by Pittiglio, Rabin, Todd, and McGrath.

Pryor, Lawrence. 1993. How benchmarking goes wrong (and how to do it right). *Planning Review* (January/February): 6–11, 53. Is a case study of a producer of specialized industrial products suffering from slow growth. It benchmarked sales effectiveness against four competitors, a noncompetitor in the industry, and one of the best sales forces in the nation.

Randall, Robert, ed. 1993. Strategic benchmarking (5 cases studies). *Planning Review* 21, no. 1 (January/February): 6–49. Cites the benchmarking application to sales effectiveness, R & D productivity, information technology, and health care.

Roberts, Edward B. 1993. *Strategic management of technology: Global benchmarking.* Report 02-052-93. Cambridge, Mass.: MIT Industrial Liaison Program. Do U.S. firms manage technology differently than their European and Japanese competitors? Preliminary results of a recent survey of senior technology executives at some of the world's leading R & D firms show some telling differences.

The Verity Consulting Group. 1991. *A hands-on guide to benchmarking: The path to continuous quality and productivity improvement.* Los Angeles: Verity Press. Includes four case studies on product development, manufacturing cost, sales force, and in-house computer services.

Watson, Gregory H. 1993. *Strategic benchmarking: How to rate your company's performance against the world's best.* New York: John Wiley & Sons. Includes four case histories citing internal benchmarking of Hewlett-Packard's R&D function; competitive benchmarking of the Ford Taurus design; functional benchmarking of GM's quality practices; and generic benchmarking of L. L. Bean's shipping process.

Wilkerson, David, Andres I. Delgado, and Jefferson Kellogg. 1993. Experience with cultural benchmarking at Dunlop Tire. *Employment Relations Today* 20, no. 2 (Summer): 159–166. Describes the five-phase application of the benchmarking process to investigating best practices for cultural change.

Xerox Corporation. 1990. *Benchmarking: A practical application.* Booklet no. 700P91708, pp. 21–22. Includes the case study "How the Phoenix District Created a Business Plan: Case History."

How to Find Information*

*This appendix was adapted from the American Productivity and Quality Center's International Benchmarking Clearinghouse. These information sources are normally available at most business and technical libraries. This includes libraries found in private organizations, universities, and public places.

Categories of Information Sources

Association reports, conference proceedings, and journals Associations are a rich source of information on topics on which they may have commissioned research. Conference proceedings detail presentations and often include videotape or audiocassette media. These reflect the current industry issues and technical and environmental activities as the focus of the association.

Business periodicals These are an excellent source of articles on organizations, functions, or topics that are of current interest. The articles usually contain opinions or statements of pride, which could lead to the discovery of best practices. These articles also cover announcements, organizational changes, new product launches, strategies, and interindustry comparisons.

Databases and information networks These sources are constantly growing. Databases capture information on processes and practices of interest. These may be the repositories of key performance measures and trends in the industry or function. Networks provide bulletin board matching of common interests on a particular subject.

Government reports Detailed information on industry performance and trends relative to other countries is published by the U.S. Department of Commerce.

Public financial statements The annual report data and additional, detailed data required by the Securities Exchange Commission provide excellent summary statistics for comparisons within and among organizations in different industries.

Trade periodicals and technical journals These provide specific information about an industry and its products and services. They contain detailed information, including customer feedback, on product design, features, and services. Technical journals often provide articles on product engineering and design that lead to technological best practices.

Basic Information References

Business Periodicals Index Contains abstracts of articles that appear in important business periodicals.

Directories in Print Lists over 10,000 business and industrial directories. Almost every industry has a directory that provides a detailed overview of the industry and key performance ratios and statistics.

Directory of On-Line Databases Provides a descriptive listing of on-line databases and services for locating specific types of information.

Directory of Special Libraries Provides information about libraries at companies, research centers, associations, and other organizations.

Encyclopedia of Associations Lists information on all professional and trade associations including their size, location, chief operating officers, and publications.

Fortune business reports Assembles company profile information from several sources. Includes general information, company overviews, recent trends, business descriptions, and recent news.

International Businesses Lists the principal public and private companies in over 100 countries. Published by Dunn & Bradstreet. Also available on-line.

Moody's manuals Provide public financial information about specific organizations in and out of the United States. Includes information on corporate history and capital structure, financial statements, and a discussion and analysis of the firm.

Standard & Poors Provides basic information about corporations and business executives. Used to locate and understand a business.

Thomas Register Is the standard guide for buying and selling products in the United States. Also available electronically.

U.S. Industrial Outlook Is a Department of Commerce publication of the trends in U.S. business.

Value Line Is an investment advisory service for over 1500 stocks from nearly 100 countries. Also available on-line.

Wall Street Transcript Provides information about specific companies and industries from articles in the *Wall Street Journal*.

Databases of Information

Public Databases

DRI/McGraw-Hill This database provides on-line information on global, economic, and financial conditions and trends.

NEWSNET This database provides full-text articles from over 400 news services. It includes special subdatabases such as SEC Filings, Business Profiles, and News/Flash electronic clipping services.

NEXIS This Mead Data Central database provides financial information on companies, such as their 10K reports, and articles from more than 600 news, business, government, financial, trade, and technical sources.

World patents index This on-line service provides listings of patent documents from many countries. It should be used by someone who is knowledgeable of its structure.

Private Databases

International Benchmarking Clearinghouse IBC provides a wide variety of products and services for benchmarking including a database that is constantly growing. It includes case studies and best practices classified by key work processes.

Other clearinghouses There are a few other private databases that are accessible for a fee. These focus on documenting key performance measurements and practices. Some have interpreted the data to develop knowledge bases.

Private (internal) databases Individual companies and organizations have developed internal best practices libraries and databases of abstracts of completed benchmarking studies. These are primarily for internal organizational use to prevent duplication of studies and to maintain previously established contacts.

Process Classification Scheme

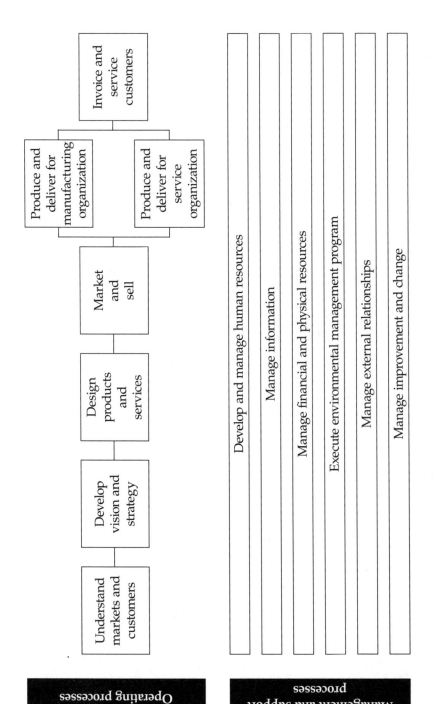

Figure E.1. Process classification scheme: Overview.

1. **Understand markets and customers.**
    1.1 Determine customer needs and wants.
        1.1.1 Conduct qualitative assessments.
            1.1.1.1 Conduct customer interviews.
            1.1.1.2 Conduct focus groups.
        1.1.2 Conduct quantitative assessments.
            1.1.2.1 Develop and implement surveys.
        1.1.3 Predict customer purchasing behavior.
    1.2 Measure customer satisfaction.
        1.2.1 Monitor satisfaction with products and services.
        1.2.2 Monitor satisfaction with compliant resolution.
        1.2.3 Monitor satisfaction with communication.
    1.3 Monitor changes in market or customer expectations.
        1.3.1 Determine weaknesses of product/service offerings.
        1.3.2 Identify new innovations that are meeting customer's needs.
        1.3.3 Determine customer reactions to competitive offerings.

2. **Develop vision and strategy.**
    2.1. Monitor the external environment.
        2.1.1 Analyze and understand competition.
        2.1.2 Identify economic trends.
        2.1.3 Identify political and regulatory issues.
        2.1.4 Assess new technology innovations.
        2.1.5 Understand demographics.
        2.1.6 Identify social and cultural changes.
        2.1.7 Understand ecological concerns.
    2.2 Define the business concept and organizational strategy.
        2.2.1 Select relevant markets.
        2.2.2 Develop long-term visions.
        2.2.3 Formulate business unit strategy.
        2.2.4 Develop overall mission strategy.
    2.3 Design the organizational structure and relationships between organizational units.
    2.4 Develop and set organizational goals.

3. **Design products and services.**
    3.1 Translate customer wants and needs into product and/or service requirements.
    3.2. Create product/service life cycle plan.

Figure E.2. Process classification scheme: Operating processes.

3.3 Develop product/service concept and plan.
    3.3.1 Develop quality, cost, and timing targets.
    3.3.2 Develop and integrate leading technology into product/service concept.
3.4 Design, build, and evaluate prototype products or services.
    3.4.1 Document design specifications.
    3.4.2 Develop engineering drawings.
    3.4.3 Apply for patents or copyrights.
3.5 Prepare for production.
    3.5.1 Develop and test prototype production process or service methodology.
    3.5.2 Design and order necessary material, tooling, and equipment.
    3.5.3 Install and verify process or methodology.
3.6 Monitor product/service performance and make refinements as needed.
    3.6.1 Add new products/services.
    3.6.2 Improve existing products/services.
    3.6.3 Eliminate quality/reliability problems.
    3.6.4 Eliminate outdated products/services.
3.7 Test effectiveness of new or revised products or services.
3.8 Implement new product engineering techniques.
    3.8.1 Conduct concurrent engineering.
    3.8.2 Develop detail product specifications.
    3.8.3 Implement value engineering.
    3.8.4 Use CAE/CAD/CAM and simulation techniques.
3.9 Manage the product/service development process.
    3.9.1 Plan and deploy quality targets.
    3.9.2 Plan and deploy cost targets.
    3.9.3 Manage product life cycle and development timing.
    3.9.4 Plan and deploy required resources.

4. Market and sell.
4.1 Market products or services to relevant customer segments.
    4.1.1 Develop advertising strategy.
    4.1.2 Develop market messages to communicate benefits.
    4.1.3 Estimate advertising resource and capital requirements.
    4.1.4 Identify specific target customers and their needs.
    4.1.5 Develop sales forecast.
    4.1.6 Sell products or services.

Figure E.2. *(continued)*

4.1.7 Respond to customer requests for quotations or proposals.
4.1.8 Negotiate terms.
4.2 Process customer orders.
    4.2.1 Accept orders from customers.
    4.2.2 Enter orders into production and delivery process.

5. Product and deliver for manufacturing-oriented organization.
5.1 Plan for and acquire necessary resources or inputs.
    5.1.1 Acquire capital goods.
    5.1.2 Hire employees.
    5.1.3 Obtain materials and supplies.
    5.1.4 Obtain appropriate technology.
5.2 Convert resources or inputs into products.
    5.2.1 Develop and adjust production process (for existing process).
    5.2.2 Schedule production.
    5.2.3 Move materials and resources.
    5.2.4 Make product.
    5.2.5 Package and store the product or service.
    5.2.6 Stage the product for delivery.
5.3 Make delivery.
    5.3.1 Schedule delivery with customer.
    5.3.2 Schedule delivery vehicle to be used.
    5.3.3 Develop and adjust routing conventions.
    5.3.4 Load, go, and unload.
    5.3.5 Install (if specified).
    5.3.6 Maintain documentation.
5.4 Manage the process.
    5.4.1 Document and monitor order status.
    5.4.2 Control and reconcile inventories.
    5.4.3 Assure quality and inspect.
    5.4.4 Schedule maintenance.
    5.4.5 Do maintenance.
    5.4.6 Monitor environmental constraints.
    5.4.7 Encourage improvement initiatives.
    5.4.8 Develop employee training.

6. Produce and deliver for service-oriented organization.
6.1 Plan for and acquire necessary resources.
    6.1.1 Hire employees.
    6.1.2 Obtain materials and supplies.

Figure E.2. *(continued)*

6.1.3 Obtain appropriate technology.
6.1.4 Acquire capital goods.
6.2 Develop human resources skills.
  6.2.1 Define skill requirements.
  6.2.2 Identify and implement training.
  6.2.3 Monitor and manage skill development.
6.3 Deliver service to the customer.
  6.3.1 Identify specific customer needs.
  6.3.2 Translate customer needs into service to be provided.
  6.3.3 Provide the service to specific customers.
6.4 Manage the process.
  6.4.1 Schedule actual delivery of the service.
  6.4.2 Provide quality assurance.
  6.4.3 Schedule human resources.

7. Invoice and service customers.
7.1 Bill the customer.
  7.1.1 Develop, deliver, and maintain customer billing.
  7.1.2 Invoice the customer.
  7.1.3 Provide information on usage, products, or bills.
7.2 Provide after-sales service.
  7.2.1 Provide in-the-field service.
  7.2.2 Handle warranties and claims.
  7.2.3 Provide follow-up service to customers.
7.3 Respond to customer inquiries.
  7.3.1 Respond to information requests.
  7.3.2 Manage customer complaints.

Figure E.2. *(continued)*

8. Develop and manage human resources.
  8.1   Create human resource strategy.
  8.2   Ensure employee involvement.
  8.3   Educate and train employees.
  8.4   Recognize and reward employee performance.
  8.5   Ensure employee well-being and morale.
  8.6   Manage relocation of personnel.
        8.6.1 Manage movement of international personnel.
        8.6.2 Manage movement of domestic personnel.

9. Manage information.
  9.1   Manage information systems.
  9.2   Evaluate and audit information quality.

10. Manage financial and physical resources.
  10.1   Manage financial resources.
        10.1.1 Develop budgets.
        10.1.2 Manage resource allocations.
        10.1.3 Design capital structure.
        10.1.4 Manage cash flow.
  10.2   Process finance and accounting transactions.
        10.2.1 Process accounts payable.
        10.2.2 Process payroll.
        10.2.3 Process accounts receivables, credit, and collections.
        10.2.4 Close the books.
  10.3   Report information.
        10.3.1 Provide external financial information.
        10.3.2 Provide internal financial information.
  10.4   Conduct internal audits.
  10.5   Manage the tax function.
        10.5.1 Ensure tax compliance.
        10.5.2 Plan tax strategy.
        10.5.3 Employ effective technology.
        10.5.4 Manage tax controversies.
        10.5.5 Communicate tax issues to management.
        10.5.6 Manage tax records.
  10.6   Manage physical resources.
        10.6.1 Manage facilities.
        10.6.2 Plan fixed asset additions.
        10.6.3 Manage risk.

Figure E.3. Process classification scheme: Operating processes.

11. Execute environmental management program.
11.1 Formulate environmental management strategy.
11.2 Ensure compliance with regulations.
11.3 Train and educate employees.
11.4 Implement pollution prevention program.
11.5 Manage remediation efforts.
11.6 Implement emergency response program.
11.7 Manage government, agency, and public relations.
11.8 Manage acquisition/divestiture environmental issues.
11.9 Develop and manage environmental information system.
11.10 Monitor environmental management program.

12. Manage external relationships.
12.1 Communicate with shareholders.
12.2 Manage government relationships.
12.3 Build lender relationships.
12.4 Develop public relations program.
12.5 Interface with board of directors.
12.6 Develop community relations.
12.7 Manage legal and ethical issues.

13. Manage improvement and change.
13.1 Measure overall organization performance.
13.2 Conduct quality assessment.
13.3 Benchmark performance.
13.4 Make process improvements.
13.5 Manage change.
13.6 Implement TQM.

Figure E.3. *(continued)*

Process Inspection Checklist

The materials in this appendix are excerpts from *Benchmarking: The Search for Industry Best Practices That Lead to Superior Performance.*

10-Step Benchmarking Process Inspection Checklist
Step 1: Identify benchmark output.

- Was the benchmarking study topic an outgrowth of the function's mission and deliverables?

- Was the subject selected critical to the success of the operation?

- Were practices benchmarked as well as performance measures?

- Were the subject and purpose of the benchmarking study reviewed with functional management and customers for their concurrence?

Step 2: Identify comparative companies.

- Were the comparative companies selected the best competitors or the functional industry leaders?

- Were all types of benchmarking considered in identifying functional, industry best leaders?

Step 3: Determine data collection methods.

- Was a questionnaire prepared prior to gathering the data?
- Were the questions pretested by answering them for the internal operation?
- Were internal sources researched for data and information?
- Were existing public data and information sources researched?
- Were original sources and investigations, including direct-site visits, considered?
- Were all research methods reviewed before the benchmarking investigations were conducted?
- Was the basis for information sharing reviewed before the research was conducted?

Step 4: Determine the correct competitive gap.

- Did the benchmark findings identify the differences in practices?
- Did the practices show for what reasons the differences resulted?
- Was a gap identified? Negative? Parity? Positive?

Step 5: Project future performance levels.

- Did the projection of the gap consider the best industry knowledge of trends?
- Was the gap understood in terms of tactical and strategic actions required?

Step 6: Establish functional goals.

- Were the findings communicated to the affected organizations?

- Were all methods for gaining acceptance considered?

- Was there concurrence and commitment to the findings from the affected organization(s) or customer(s)?

Step 7: Develop functional action plans.

- Were functional goals reviewed to incorporate benchmark findings?

- Were the benchmark practices clearly delineated to show how the industry best accomplished their results?

Step 8: Implement specific action steps.

- Did the action plans clearly show how the gap would be closed?

- Was the action plan implemented?

Step 9: Monitor and report progress.

- Were benchmarks incorporated with the management and financial processes?

- Was an action plan implemented?

Step 10: Recalibrate and determine maturity.

- Is there a plan for recalibration?

- Has benchmarking become institutionalized?

- Has a leadership position been attained?

Correlation to Benchmarking

The following is a list of quick reference guides from *Benchmarking: The Search for Industry Best Practices That Lead to Superior Performance.*

Roles and Responsibilities

This appendix deals with the roles and responsibilities of

- Customers of benchmarking, such as functional managers, vice presidents, and process owners
- Suppliers for benchmarking including the following:
  —Corporate benchmarking competency
  —Division benchmarking competency
  —Benchmarking networks
  —Functional benchmarking representatives

Customers

Principal responsibilities include the following:

- Determining the most significant areas of focus for benchmarking. This prioritization is a major responsibility of senior managers interested in obtaining the greatest return for the invested benchmarking resources.
- Ensuring that the benchmarking findings are implemented. This includes providing assistance as needed and removing any roadblocks, so that benchmarking best practices are converted to action.

- Ensuring that a vital few, high-level performance measures are maintained as benchmarks to serve as indicators of progress.
- Reviewing benchmarking progress at key milestone dates and steps of the process.

The Manager's Role
The following tasks are essential.

- Obtaining senior management agreement on the overall approach
- Relating benchmarking to the units' objectives
- Maintaining benchmarking competency in the organization
- Commissioning teams
- Implementing benchmarking results in business plans
- Promoting benchmarking throughout the organization
- Encouraging excellent benchmarking through recognition and reward

Suppliers

Corporate Benchmarking Competency
This benchmarking supplier operates at a company level. Roles and responsibilities include the following:

- Setting the direction for benchmarking
- Maintaining the benchmarking emphasis
- Assuring cross-unit information sharing to minimize duplication
- Ensuring that unit champions are identified and used to promote benchmarking

- Providing constant reminders that benchmarking must be considered when major decisions are made

Division Benchmarking Competency

Responsibilities include

- Expanding, intensifying, and ensuring that benchmarking efforts leverage business results across all functional units
- Scanning for information and maintaining contacts
- Ensuring that all legal, ethical, and protocol guidelines are followed in a code of conduct
- Maintaining wide outside contacts to assist the organization in its benchmarking efforts
- Maintaining a competency resource to assist teams and to set benchmarking expectations
- Summarizing the organization's progress in benchmarking through an annual progress report

Benchmarking Networks

The benchmarking network

- Shares ideas on how to best assist the organization that is conducting the benchmarking study
- Communicates, collaborates, and shares benchmarking experiences
- Coordinates activities with external organizations
- Ensures that benchmarks are maintained
- Ensures that activities are prioritized to improve business results
- Increases the promotion and communication of benchmarking successes

- Develops product support materials and services for benchmarking

Functional Benchmarking Representatives

Their responsibilities include

- Ensuring benchmarking process discipline and preparedness
- Evaluating incoming and outgoing benchmarking requests for appropriateness
- Training
- Assisting with visit coordination
- Ensuring that appropriate field personnel are advised of pending benchmarking activities

Index

Activity network diagram, 137
Affinity diagrams, 137
Alcoa, benchmarking process at, 8
Allied Signal, 424
American Express, 424
American Management Association
    (AMA), 183
American Productivity and Quality
    Center (APQC), 176, 183
        International Benchmarking
            Clearinghouse service
            of, 36, 129–30, 173,
            176, 191, 433, 436
Analysts, as information source, 112
Analytical hierarchic process (AHP),
    50, 170
Analytical hierarchic process (AHP)
    maturity index, 9, 137, 141
Apple Computer, 328, 424
Arrow diagraming, 58, 59, 60
Articles, as information sources,
    109–11
Association reports, 433
AT&T Network Systems, 183, 255–72
    actions taken at, 267–68

background at, 256–58
    focus/topic at, 257
    goal/objective of, 256–57
    team operation at, 257–58
benchmarking process at, 8, 24
best practices found at, 267
customers and requirements for,
    258, 260–61
    need/reason for improvement
        in, 260–61
implementation of, 268–69
organizations or industries bench-
    marked, 262–67
    current segmentation process
        at, 262–63
    key measures and facts at,
        263–66
    process-to-process analysis at,
        266–67
planned changes at, 269
*Process Quality Management and
    Improvement Guidelines* at,
    257
*Total Quality Management
    Guidebook* at, 258

453